Blockchain

The internet was envisaged as a decentralised global network, but in the past 25 years it has come to be controlled by a few, very powerful, centralised companies. Blockchain is a technological paradigm shift that allows secure, reliable, and direct information transfer across individuals, organisations, and things, so that we can manage, verify, and control the use of our own data.

Blockchain also offers a new opportunity for humanity to fix some major problems. It can authenticate data, manage its analysis, and automate its use. With better data comes better decision-making. In this way, Blockchain can contribute to solving climate change, reduce voting fraud, fix our identity systems, improve fair trade, and give the poor an opportunity to improve their lives by monetising their (digital) capital. A world built upon peer-to-peer transactions and smart contracts can empower individuals and communities.

This book offers a fresh perspective with which to consider this transformative technology. It describes how Blockchain can optimise the processes that run our society. It provides practical solutions to global problems and offers a roadmap to incorporate Blockchain in your business. It offers a blueprint for a better world. Filled with easy-to-understand examples, this book shows how Blockchain can take over where the internet has fallen short.

Mark van Rijmenam is Founder and CEO of Datafloq and Imagjn, author and speaker, The Netherlands.

Philippa Ryan is a Barrister and Lecturer in the Faculty of Law at the University of Technology Sydney, Australia.

"The authors tackle a timely and important new technology in an accessible and engaging way. This is a book that will reward you for the time you spend reading it, and we are already looking forward to reading it a second time. It is a worthy addition to the emerging collection of informative and helpful books on the world of blockchain."

Simon Cocking, Editor in Chief, Irish Tech News & CryptocoinNews

"The digital revolution's first era failed to solve pressing social, economic and environmental challenges. Blockchain offers a once-in-a-generation opportunity to get it right. *Blockchain* skillfully champions the opportunities offered by a new internet of value."

Don Tapscott, Executive Chairman, Blockchain Research Institute and Co-author of Blockchain Revolution: How the Technology Behind Bitcoin is Changing Money, Business, and the World

"So much more than JABB (Just Another Blockchain Book). Van Rijmenam and Ryan take you on a tour of the world's potential with the blockchain trust protocol and its ability to change our world. When you're done reading this book, you'll be sketching the art of the possible . . . not dreaming about it.

Trust is a competitive advantage. You earn it in droplets and lose it in buckets. Van Rijmenam and Ryan turn the typical boring blockchain book upside and create a journey on how trust can change our world. More so, the book makes you dream big – not just about the changes that are coming, but ones that you can participate in or imagine on your own. Never really had a 'Must Read 2018 Books' list . . . until now.

Blockchain will do for trust what the internet did for search. In a world of good and bad actors, where trust becomes a differentiator, Van Rijmenam and Ryan expand the blockchain aperture from the ubiquitous (and overwritten) cryptocurrency discussion, to a discussion how trust can change the world: business, social, equality, and more."

Paul Zikopoulos, IBM, VP Cognitive Systems, Big Data speaker and author

"This is a fine and important read, especially the Blockchain history. I thoroughly recommend you read, ponder and absorb for your token strategy planning."

Thomas Power, Board Member, 9Spokes PLC New Zealand

"Blockchain's potential is so much more than digital currency. *Blockchain: Transforming Your Business and Our World* is a step towards bringing that potential to life, exploring positive use cases and practical solutions to a diverse range of global social issues, from climate change and healthcare access to digital identity and poverty. For anyone interested in how we can build a better world with blockchain technology, this book provides an educational snapshot into what a more decentralized future could look like."

Vinny Lingham, CEO and Co-Founder of Civic Technologies, Inc.

Blockchain

Transforming Your Business and Our World

Mark van Rijmenam and
Philippa Ryan

Routledge
Taylor & Francis Group
LONDON AND NEW YORK

First published 2019
by Routledge
2 Park Square, Milton Park, Abingdon, Oxon OX14 4RN

and by Routledge
711 Third Avenue, New York, NY 10017

Routledge is an imprint of the Taylor & Francis Group, an informa business

British Library Cataloguing-in-Publication Data
A catalogue record for this book is available from the British Library

Library of Congress Cataloging-in-Publication Data
Names: Van Rijmenam, Mark, author. | Ryan, Philippa, author.
Title: Blockchain : transforming your business and our world / Mark van Rijmenam & Dr Philippa Ryan.
Description: 1 Edition. | New York : Routledge, 2019. | Includes bibliographical references and index.
Identifiers: LCCN 2018015347| ISBN 9781138313224 (hbk) | ISBN 9781138313248 (pbk) | ISBN 9780429457715 (ebk)
Subjects: LCSH: Blockchains (Databases)
Classification: LCC QA76.9.D32 V35 2019 | DDC 005.74—dc23
LC record available at https://lccn.loc.gov/2018015347

ISBN: 978-1-138-31322-4 (hbk)
ISBN: 978-1-138-31324-8 (pbk)
ISBN: 978-0-429-45771-5 (ebk)

Typeset in Bembo
by Swales & Willis Ltd, Exeter, Devon, UK

Contents

Foreword

A major cause of poverty and conflict is the failure to transform resources into capital without predation by intermediaries (e.g. government corruption, corporate mischief) in that process. As an economist and entrepreneur, I am passionate about Blockchain's potential to plug such structural leakages.

In September 2015, more than 150 world leaders gathered at the United Nations' headquarters in New York for the Sustainable Development Summit. That event was the launch pad for action by the international community and national governments to promote shared prosperity and well-being for all. The UN wants to end poverty by 2030. The question is *how*.

I first heard about *Blockchain: Transforming Your Business and Our World* during the Third Global Blockchain Summit held in Shanghai in September 2017. After delivering my keynote, I attended a lunch hosted by one of its sponsors. Seated next to me was one of the co-authors of this ambitious and inspirational book. We talked about ways that blockchain-based business solutions and philanthropy could address some of the world's 'Wicked Problems', as the authors call them. It is in this spirit that Van Rijmenam and Ryan have approached their book. Focusing on five of the UN's 17 Sustainable Development Goals, the authors suggest practical and commercially applicable blockchain-based solutions.

From the outset, this book makes explicit its intention: to identify ways that blockchain technology can solve some of the world's more complex problems. Drawing on the cultural and philosophical forces that combined make the blockchain's primordial soup, the authors have applied their democratic and optimistic vision of how sophisticated distributed ledger technology can be used for social good. They also make a compelling case for how it can be adapted to meet commercial and business needs. Van Rijmenam and Ryan demonstrate in each of their proposals that they are adherents to the view that sustainable development is about ensuring transparency, fair trade, independent media, and financial inclusion. Indeed, we live in times when no one on the planet is immune to fake news, corruption, identity theft, counterfeit labelling, and bad data.

Starting with a clear and relevant explanation of how blockchain technology works, each chapter in this book builds on the one before. From identity to censorship and welfare fraud to tax havens, each analysis identifies a particular problem, the traditional or incumbent attempts to solve it, and the features of blockchain technology that can be applied to achieving those solutions. It is already well established that this revolutionary technology will transform systems and processes that manage payments, identity, and supply chains. However, until this book, it has been unclear how blockchain can also be applied for social good. There is a danger that not everyone will have access to the benefits that will flow from improved security and efficiency in tracking and storing information and assets, but Van Rijmenam and Ryan spell out how blockchain will help us build a better society for all.

It is refreshing that this work can be read as both a useful resource and a call to action. For governments, professionals, businesses, industry, and academics, this book offers an insight into blockchain technology, and makes accessible some of its more complicated features. For technologists, it lends purpose to their work and articulates the often-silenced expectations of the millions of unbanked, underemployed, and displaced peoples from countries plagued by corruption, political unrest, and natural disasters. These same people represent new markets of potential consumers keen to unleash their entrepreneurial potential in the world.

Just as the UN has called upon global leaders to work together towards the 17 Sustainable Development Goals, this book calls upon those working to reach those Goals to think about how new technologies like blockchain can help to achieve them. I found this book to be a thorough guide to the transformative potential of blockchain technology.

Patrick M. Byrne, PhD
CEO, Overstock.com

Acknowledgements

This book would not have been possible without the help of the following people who each provided valuable input and feedback on the different aspects of this book: Andrew Latchford, Andrew Tobin, Christopher Yong, Daniel Gasteiger, Daniel O'Quinn, David Peyronnin, David Birch, David Schrier, Haroon Oppal, Jason Williams, Jean-Marc Fisz, Jerry Qian, Jon Holmquist, Kaustubh Varade, Ken Bonar, Kevin Coleman, Martijn Bolt, Max Kaye, Nidhi Chamria, Olivier Rikken, Ott Sarv, Patrick Feeney, Phil Windley, Prahalad Belavadi, Robbert Naastepad, Ronald van de Meent, Samuel Brooks, Parag Jain, Sandris Murins, Duncan Brown, Shree Sule, Sina Ghazi, Sumit Sharma, Sushant Mayekar, and Virgil Griffith.

Special thanks to Cindy Lam for proofreading our book.

Chapter 1

Blockchain and Wicked Problems

Problem /ˈprɒbləm/: a thing that is difficult to achieve

1.1 Introduction

We live in a time of accelerated change and today's world is changing faster than we have ever seen before. The end of the 19th century and beginning of the 20th century were a period of technological upheaval and re-concentration of populations into urbanised centres. These shifts were made possible by the massive infrastructure projects that saw canals and railways connect cities and ports with producers of agriculture and mining. Communications systems were revolutionised by the laying of telegraph cable and the invention of flight. Now, in the 21st century, new technologies are driving even more dramatic changes in the way we live, work, and socialise. These developments and innovations challenge traditional ways of distributing goods and services, doing business, and making payments.

If our recent past is anything to go by, our immediate future seems set to change at a speed unlike any we have ever seen before. In fact, it sees a potential change in what it means to be human. Our interaction with automated processing, data, and the Internet of Things has changed how we store information, how we remember, and how we recall those memories. Decision-making has become something we do in concert with machines. With the advance of technology, we have the potential to create a world in which technology is used for good, while ensuring that the privacy of consumers is respected, a world where data is owned by individuals and used to improve the lives of all—essentially, a world that is better for all. In the future, it is all about algorithms, machine learning, big data, and artificial intelligence. This change comes about because of the development of robotics, 3D printing and augmented reality, nanotechnology, and quantum computing. There is disruption at all levels, resulting in system-wide innovations that can revolutionise an industry in years, rather than decades.

Blockchain technology will enable the decentralisation of the web and the disintermediation of many, if not all, of the services that are offered online.

The web was originally envisaged as a decentralised network, but somehow, in the past 25 years, it ended up in the hands of a select handful of very powerful companies. As Sir Tim Berners-Lee said during the Decentralised Web Summit in 2016:

> The web was designed to be decentralised so that everybody could participate by having their own domain and having their own webserver and this hasn't worked out. Instead, we've got the situation where individual personal data has been locked up in these silos.

Fortunately, Blockchain will allow us to bring back power to the users and create a decentralised society. Already, Blockchain challenges many industries, of which financial services will see the largest impact in the coming years. Accordingly, this necessarily begs the question—how will Blockchain have an impact on other global problems?

1.2 The problem

Despite the best intentions and efforts of well-meaning world leaders and non-government organisations, over-population, poverty, climate change, and political strife continue to create vulnerable and displaced populations. According to The World Bank's most recently published statistics (in 2017), 10.7% of the world's population has an income of just US$1.90 or less per day [1], whereas only 64% of adult men and 57% of adult women (aged over 15 years) have an account with a financial institution [2]. In the 55 years from 1960 to 2015, carbon dioxide emissions have quadrupled [3], and yet 15% of the world's population still has no access to electricity [3] and 56% has no internet access.

It has long been accepted that efforts to improve economic growth in developing countries are often hampered by government officials using their authority for private gain and implementing public policies from which they directly benefit [4, p. 417]. Corruption increases income inequality and poverty by reducing economic growth and rates of compliance with tax systems [5, p. 2]. It also distorts the government's role in distributing vital resources such as education, health, social security, welfare housing, and community amenities [5]. The direct causal relationship between corruption and disadvantage suggests that a reduction in corruption will alleviate poverty and its related evils [4, p. 426].

Eradicating corruption is not straightforward. In many developing countries corruption is culturally entrenched in the way that governments do business, both domestically and internationally. It is a symptom of institutional weakness and it reduces economic growth [6, p. 682, 7]. For this reason, many aid organisations send their own trusted people to deliver disaster relief in person, but these measures do not address the cultural problems that persist. Such issues must be addressed if there is to be meaningful long-term change. A key element in the equation is the rule of law, which, if embraced, will aid in the fight against corruption.

The law should afford adequate protection of fundamental human rights. The term 'human rights' was mentioned seven times in the United Nations' founding Charter. The Charter of the United Nations, which was signed on 26 June 1945, in San Francisco, at the conclusion of the United Nations Conference on International Organisation, came into force on 24 October 1945. Article 1 of the Charter identifies the purpose of the United Nations and includes the aim to achieve international cooperation in solving international problems of an economic, social, cultural, or humanitarian nature, as well as promoting and encouraging respect for human rights and fundamental freedoms for all, without distinction as to race, sex, language, or religion. In 1948, the Universal Declaration of Human Rights brought human dignity and fairness into the realm of international law. Since then, the UN has diligently protected human rights through legal instruments and on-the-ground activities. Human rights, as defined in the UN's founding Charter, remain a key purpose and guiding principle of the organisation.

The Universal Declaration of Human Rights was the first legal document protecting universal human rights. Included in the Declaration are the following: the rights to equal pay for equal work, privacy, freedom of movement and residence, freedom of thought and freedom of expression; the right to leave and return to any country; the right to nationality; the right to own property; the right to freedom of assembly and association; as well as special protection for motherhood and childhood. Seventy years later, many of these Universal Rights are under strain due to increases in world population and limited natural resources [8, 9, p. 31].

Seventy years ago, the population of the world was less than 2.5 billion [10]. Since then it has tripled. In 1948, the year that the UN published its Universal Declaration of Human Rights, the world's average life expectancy was just 45 years. It is now 65 years. From 1950 onwards, the world experienced rapid population growth mainly due to a reduction in mortality. The period 1950–1965 saw the fastest growth in world population, slowing since then mainly due to contraception [11]. However, with 7.5 billion people living mainly in urban areas, the pressure on the planet to feed and house its population is at an all-time high. The relationship between the environment and peace has never been more tenuous.

In recent decades, we have seen how environmental problems such as resource scarcity and climate change can create or exacerbate conflict. In 2007, UN Secretary General Ban Ki-moon described the conflict in Sudan's Darfur region as the world's first climate change conflict [12]. The assumption was that water scarcity from changed rainfall patterns, caused by climate change, contributed to this conflict. His thinking reflects the findings to date that the incidence of conflict is likely to be higher in years of lower precipitation [12, 13]. With rising water levels caused by melting polar ice caps, island nations and low-lying areas will soon need to move their inhabitants to higher ground. Island nations such as Kiribati and the Maldives, which have no natural high ground, will have to choose between sinking and shifting. To deal with these challenges and defend against changing conditions, these countries need to advance economically, although, in a seemingly paradoxical twist, their economic woes are underpinned by climate change.

As long as scientists cannot explain or predict climate change with precision, there will be room for deniers to exploit this imprecision as a basis for the argument that climate change is either non-existent or not man-made. This expectation that scientific discourse should be based on exact data undermines the overall message. A lack of political will in some parts of the world to accept climate change being caused by human activity is in part driven by the prohibitive cost of dealing with it. Political parties and politicians all over the world are prepared to include tackling climate change in their campaign speeches, but the harsh reality of how environmentally-friendly policies will impact on the electorate and the economy in any given election cycle is political poison. Manufacturing, transportation, fishing, the production of food, and the extraction of natural minerals are all resource-hungry activities. Global market forces and price competition make carbon emissions policies very unpopular.

There is strong evidence to support the view that poverty and human insecurity may arise as a result of climate change [14, p. 19, 15, p. 22]. Many important aspects of human development also relate to people's security. In this way, 'human security' can be defined as people's freedom from fear and freedom from want in a broad sense. Human security has always been tied to climate because want causes fear and conflict. Climate security focuses on the needs of individuals and communities and the idea of freedom from harm and fear. People need to be able to adapt in the face of any imposed harm. From this human security perspective, the central analytical issues are vulnerability, adaptation, and justice.

The issues of *human security* and conflict in relation to *climate* change have evolved to a place where they now constitute a recognised and important component in the *climate*-change conversation, and are being addressed at a diverse range of forums through meetings, reports, and changes in policy. Societies with more climate-sensitive economies, largely in the developing world, will be most affected because climate change acts as a 'threat multiplier' and adds to existing burdens. Decreasing availability of resources due to regional effects of climate change—such as drought and desertification—leads to intensified competition for these resources. And this, when compounded by pressures such as rapid population growth, tribalism, and sectarianism (as in Darfur and Somalia), could result in armed violence. As meteorological disasters become more frequent and intense with global warming, already struggling societies will be weakened further, making them more vulnerable to political instability, as in Haiti. It therefore follows that global warming may directly increase conflict. It is these issues that drive the UN's Sustainable Development Goals.

These goals, which were adopted by member countries in September 2015, were initially drafted to address 17 global challenges, with a view to protecting the planet and tackling climate change. At the top of the agenda are poverty, hunger and food security, health, water. and sanitation. Other aims include quality education, innovation, reduced inequality, sustainable cities and communities, strong peace and justice institutions, and responsible production and consumption. Blockchain technology can play an important role in achieving some of these goals fairly and transparently. For example, this book looks at how distributed ledgers can support Fair Trade by enabling transparency in the treatment of those who produce and distribute food and resources.

There is a basic core definition of human rights that has almost universal acceptance. It can be summed up in two points: (1) that the people and government should be ruled by the law and obey it; and (2) that the law should be such that people will be willing and able to be guided by it [16]. At the core of these principles are the notions that no one shall be punished except by a court of law and everyone is innocent until proven guilty. In addition to these process-driven values, there is a body of rights or truths within the rule of law that ensures dignity, free speech, and privacy. Of course, these private rights may from time to time compete with public interests. Where there is such a clash, it is important for the human actors in government institutions to know what the law is, and the extent and limits of their power to enforce those rules.

Upholding ethical standards of conduct and bringing those who fall short to account are all mechanisms that operate to motivate respect for the rule of law. Equally, the media and historians have a duty to report accurately and fearlessly the truth of what is observed and heard. Clearly articulated ethical standards have long played a key role in engineering practice and in recent years they have been extended to the work of computer scientists. Managed by the Institute of Electrical and Electronics Engineers (IEEE), the ethical foundation of science and technology dates back to the late 1870s with the invention of the electric light globe and the telephone. The IEEE's mission statement is that its core purpose is to foster technological innovation and excellence for the benefit of humanity. Significantly, the IEEE reviewed its Code of Ethics in November 2017 to include recognition and support for the UN's Sustainable Development Goals. Addressing its 430,000 members in 160 countries, the revised policy stipulates that members agree to hold paramount the safety, health, and welfare of the public, and to strive to comply with ethical design and sustainable development practices. This edict recognises that the fabric of our modern, technology-driven society is enmeshed in such a way that all of these forces and drivers play a part in ensuring stability and promoting peaceful and respectful debate in complex modern societies.

Technology has an important part to play in holding all actors to account. Blockchain has the potential to play an important part in how rule of law might be more readily discernible and therefore rooted in existing systems that are particularly vulnerable to abuse.

Meanwhile, fake news is more than just a political problem. Whether it is deliberate (disinformation) or inadvertent (misinformation), 'fake news' is a term that connotes manipulated reporting and information about political, historical, economic, or social events and phenomena. With the rise of social media and the ease with which news and current affairs are reported and distributed via the internet, reporting on the conduct of our institutions has become more problematic. News reporting has changed utterly over the past decade and traditional methods of disseminating what happens in parliament, in court, and in public have shifted to news consumers. With handheld devices that record with clarity both sound and video, people are instant reporters and publishers of events as they unfold in real time. The problem is that the lens of a phone has a limited point of view and it is difficult to reveal situation and context. Rationalising data and facts has become more challenging than ever. Distinguishing satire and parody from serious discourse can have significant consequences. Reporting on complex scientific or legal issues requires expertise [17]. In 2017, fake news became known to the larger public with the election of Donald Trump as President of the United States of America. With his constant remarks on 'The Fake Media', Donald Trump defined a new era in journalism, an era of which we should not be proud. His remarks demonstrate the significant influence that tech giants such as Facebook and Google have on the propagation of fake news. *Digital Deceit*, a 2018 report co-authored by Dipayan Gosh, previously a privacy and public policy adviser for Facebook, shows that the central problem is that an entire industry is founded on advanced technology that is purely focused on driving traffic and selling advertising. Of course, nefarious actors can benefit from this advanced potential to target specific demographics. Meanwhile, social media platforms such as Facebook benefit financially from these arrangements and so have no inherent motivation to prevent the distribution of fake news. Accordingly Gosh considers that disinformation operators can 'leverage this system for precision propaganda [and] the harm to the public interest, the political culture, and the integrity of democracy is substantial and distinct from any other type of advertiser' [18, p. 4].

As a result of this modern phenomenon, the factual and authoritative reporting and analysis of important matters has suffered. However, there are innovative ways to rate the veracity and usefulness of information. This technology has been tested on social media platforms such as TripAdvisor and Reddit.

It appears that Blockchain's capacity to monitor and report transactions and data has limitless potential to impact our online businesses, personal relationships, and interactions. This book explores censorship in light of the UN's expression of the right to freedom of expression and the right to privacy.

It provides examples of how blockchain is being used to disseminate and verify information, while at the same time protecting it from government manipulation and control. This capacity to track, monitor, and verify can positively impact the processes and information being managed by the use of blockchain technology. The technology underpinning blockchain can create trust where there has been distrust, and enable secure financial transactions and information exchanges in times of conflict and unrest.

1.3 The culture of Blockchain

The beating heart of blockchain technology is consensus and immutability. The participants in a distributed network can verify and authenticate other users' transactions and exchanges. For this reason, the community values its own worth and reputation. *Reputation* management across distributed systems is one of the most important protocol developments supporting *blockchain* applications. Although blockchain's reputation system has limitations in preventing fraudulent registration by participants, it is very powerful in detecting fraudulent activity by those participants. It is for this reason that many proponents of blockchain technology argue that the first priority is to solve how proof of identity can be digitally validated and authenticated, before moving on to its proof-of-work mechanisms. Blockchain's crypto-mechanism gives users in a digital network the power to rate, include, or exclude interactions and content. This essentially means that the social activity and values of the community can be 'watched' by the technology; this, in turn, provides cultural support for the network.

Reputation systems need to be built into (or on top of) blockchain protocols to ensure that both peer-to-peer human and machine ecosystems can sustainably survive strategic bad actors. It is important to note that, at the time of writing, blockchain technology is better equipped to detect false information than false participants. It is for this reason that proponents of blockchain technology argue for an identity solution before proceeding with the business of supply chains, smart contracts, and reliance on trust and governance protocols. At this time, fraudulent conduct is easier to detect than the responsible fraudsters.

A major barrier to addressing the problems identified in the UN's Sustainable Development Goals is the fact that action must be collective and popular. It needs to be coordinated by non-government organisations or governments. Either way, funding is required. In order to raise money to solve these problems, the institutions raising the funds must be trustworthy. However, trust in our institutions is at an all-time low. This lack of trust is particularly evident when you consider the criticism faced by governments following their responses to the 2008 global financial crisis, particularly with regard to their decisions to grant corporate bail-outs and their failure to bring the architects of the economic collapse to justice.

Meanwhile, globalisation has led to cheap manufacturing and food production in the developing world, which has forced car and technology manufacturers in developed countries out of business [19, 20]. The resulting unemployment and widening gap between the rich and poor are regarded as major forces behind the United Kingdom's Brexit shock and (to a greater extent) Trump's US presidential success in 2016. While the US Congress tries to roll back Obamacare, thereby stripping millions of Americans of healthcare insurance, the corporate tax gap created by the complex offshore financial arrangements is expanding. The most recent estimate of the Annual Tax Gap in the USA is US$406 billion [21]. In Australia, the tax gap figure for 2016 was approximately US$3.8 billion [22]. With revenue collection in the hands of government-controlled departments and the banking system regulated by legislation, it is understandable that negative sentiment about economic woes would be aimed directly at government.

1.4 Seven Wicked Problems

In this book, we propose ways in which blockchain technology can solve problems that we refer to as 'wicked'. This use of the term 'wicked' is a play on words. It has three meanings: first, 'wicked' can mean 'evil'. This is intended to connote a sense of evil that readers will accept as a fair description of some of the problems this book aims to solve. For example, tax evasion is despicable, particularly in societies where there is also chronic poverty and suffering. Second, 'wicked' is a modern slang term used oxymoronically by some millennials to mean 'awesome' or 'wonderful'. This use suggests the positive outcomes that can be expected if these problems are solved. Finally, 'wicked' is an adjective used to characterise a particular type of problem that is difficult or impossible to solve due to incomplete, contradictory, and changing requirements that are often difficult to recognise. It refers to problems wherein many stakeholders with conflicting values are involved and information is confusing.

The seven wicked problems that may benefit from blockchain-based technology are set out in five of the UN's Sustainable Development Goals. Just as education can influence outcomes for these Sustainable Development Goals [23], so too can some technologies. The UN's Goals set an ambitious agenda for the developing world. They aim to achieve discernible change by 2030, including the eradication of poverty, zero hunger, decent work and economic growth, climate action, reduced inequalities, peace and justice, and strong institutions. Whereas action in education can raise awareness of these issues and improve the economic prospects of women and children in developing countries and of vulnerable minorities, technology can enable and support these initiatives for change and key institutions for reform.

Blockchain technology offers the potential for us to establish the most sophisticated tracking and transparency systems that we have seen to date. It is possible to use such technology to establish robust personal identification systems, which are critical to the success of many development programmes. Traditionally, personal identification has been a two-step process: the person seeking to prove their identity produced a physical artefact (for example, a credit card with a data-loaded magnetic strip). In conjunction with using this, they rely on a pin or password or receipt of a four-digit code on their device. The problem with this process is that, if the person has lost or does not have the physical device or ID, then they may face being locked out of the service or system they seek to use. For this reason, many authorities are exploring replacing the card with the use of the person's mobile phone number. If you include the country code, all mobile numbers are unique. More recently, biometric identification (for example, matching data banks of fingerprint images with a given sample) and facial recognition technology have become very popular and proven particularly reliable. However, they still depend on an existing database against which to compare or match the human. Regardless of the methods used, proving identity is becoming a priority for governments around the world.

Blockchain technology also enables the tracking of assets and information in supply chains and across transactions. Accordingly, the use of blockchain has the potential to readily hold accountable recipients of aid and other funding, while at the same time protecting suppliers of Fair Trade agricultural products and natural resources from exploitation and the imposition of excessively onerous conditions in order to qualify or participate in economic and business networks.

The UN's aid efforts have historic problems with fraud, mismanagement, and bureaucratic red tape. Blockchain technology provides a mechanism to circumvent governments and banking institutions, and therefore transfer aid far more efficiently. In late 2017, several UN agencies identified the Ethereum blockchain as a potential solution for the distribution of aid to refugees across the world and for several other philanthropic purposes [24]. This idea is not novel. The World Food Program (WFP) is already using the Ethereum blockchain in a pilot programme called 'Building Blocks' to distribute food vouchers to refugees in Jordan. There are plans to expand the programme to refugees in the 80 other countries where the WFP operates. In addition, at the UN's 2016 Climate Conference in Germany, the Ethereum blockchain was proffered to help combat climate change.

Meanwhile, Alexandre Gellert Paris, an officer of the UN's Framework Convention on Climate Change, argues that 'blockchain could contribute to greater stakeholder involvement, transparency and engagement and help bring trust and further innovative solutions in the fight against climate change, leading to enhanced climate actions' [25].

In July 2017, the UN's Department of Economic and Social Affairs (UNDESA) published its Sustainable Development Goals Report. Based in New York, UNDESA is a secretariat that operates as the interface between global policies in the economic, social, and environmental spheres, and national action. Its work is guided by the 2030 Agenda for Sustainable Development.

The 2017 Sustainable Development Goals Report noted that progress has been uneven. For example, in the period between 2010 and 2015, the average global gross domestic product (GDP) grew more than in the previous five years (2005–2010). This apparently good news is soon tempered by the reality that only the USA, Canada, Europe, and eastern and south-eastern Asia are responsible for that statistic. Under-developed countries and developing land-locked countries lagged behind and recorded GDP growth rates behind the performance of the previous five years. The Report also identified that the effective tracking of progress is hampered by the lack of reliable, current, and available data. Although the quality and availability of data have improved worldwide, statistical capacity and analysis require strengthening. It is not only the UN and international aid organisations that face these challenges. The private sector and governments in the most developed countries also face challenges in relation to the accuracy and completeness of datasets.

It is important to note that small, big, and meta-data are all subject to manipulation. With this in mind, systems must be employed to address these vulnerabilities—bad data can lead only to bad decisions. In adding a layer of verification and transparency to data use, blockchain technology can be used to ensure that policies are formulated on the basis of accurate and reliable information.

1.5 Conclusion

Wicked problems are often composed of multiple interrelated issues. Accordingly, they cannot simply be resolved by addressing each issue on an individual basis. This description typifies some of the most challenging social problems addressed in this book. This book offers insights to organisations on how to apply Blockchain technology to develop products and services that will help the poor, combat climate change, and create a better world. It will help governments understand how Blockchain can be used to build a more transparent system, combat tax evasion and voting fraud, and reduce corruption.

Technology that verifies and authenticates human identity, scientific data, provenance, and transactions can also break down the barriers that have impeded previous attempts to end poverty, deliver sustainable energy, reduce inequality, and increase the accountability of institutions. Ultimately, what blockchain creates is a relationship of trust between users and content. Blockchain technology allows all users to see and verify all transactions and settlements, thereby removing the need for a third party or intermediary to manage counter-party risk or escrow funds. This capacity to manage and monitor exchanges can be applied to the exchanges of non-financial assets, including information, provenance, identity, and data.

We have formulated our solution to seven Wicked Problems in terms that reflect aims articulated in five of the UN's Sustainable Development Goals. These Goals are the eradication of poverty, availability of decent work and economic growth, support for industry innovation and infrastructure, systems for responsible consumption and production, and peace, justice, and strong institutions.

Poverty is more than the lack of income and resources to ensure a sustainable livelihood. Its manifestations include social discrimination and exclusion as well as the lack of participation in decision-making. Those who do not have access to education, land, or the labour market cannot fully contribute to society or the economy [26]. The social inclusion of people living in poverty is not just a fundamental moral imperative—it can also help to reduce economic and social costs by providing sustainable jobs. According to the UN, a key requirement for economic equality and progress is financial transparency [27]. Technological progress is the foundation of efforts to achieve environmental objectives, such as increased resource and energy efficiency. The relationship between human development and climate is inextricably linked. When climate is extreme and intemperate for long periods, resources become scarce. When resources are scarce, conflict and fear soon set it. Countries that rely on agrarian economies soon become vulnerable. Without technology and innovation industrialisation will not happen, and without industrialisation development cannot happen [28].

Blockchain's capacity to track workflows and supply chains via the immutable authentication of transactions can enable and ensure financial inclusion, respect for provenance, and the verification of human identity. However, before we examine each of the seven Wicked Problems and our proposed blockchain-based solutions, it is important first to understand the particular features of blockchain technology that make these proposed solutions possible.

Chapter 2

What is the Blockchain?

Blockchain /ˈblɒktʃeɪn/: a digital ledger in which transactions made in bitcoin or another cryptocurrency are recorded chronologically and publicly

2.1 Introduction

In 2008, while the rest of the world faced the biggest financial crisis in decades [29], a paper was circulated among a small group of cryptography enthusiasts [30]. In this paper, Satoshi Nakamoto [31] explained the concept of a cryptocurrency called Bitcoin[1] and a solution to the long-standing problem of double spending (where digital tokens representing unique value can be spent more than once) [32]. For years, double spending has been one of the main barriers to the widespread adoption of digital money. In 2008, the domain name Bitcoin.org was registered, and at the start of 2009, the *genesis block* for bitcoin—that is, the first block in a blockchain—was created [30]. At that point in time, nobody foresaw the impact that Nakamoto's [31] underlying technology would have on the world's largest organisations, trusted intermediaries, and society at large [33].

Since Nakamoto's paper, distributed ledger technology, also known as blockchain technology,[2] has rapidly gained popularity. Although ledgers have been around for millennia, for the first time in history they can be updated across multiple organisations and computer networks simultaneously through the use of blockchain technology. This functionality significantly reduces the possibility of 'gaming' the system, that is, the distributed and decentralised nature of the blockchain ledgers prevents any single party from controlling, and therefore manipulating, the ledgers. The cryptography underlying blockchain ensures a 'trustless' system, thereby removing the need for intermediaries to manage risk. This is a true paradigm shift and it is why so many organisations are exploring Blockchain's potential use to improve their tracking and audit systems.[3] Although blockchain technology has only been around for less than a decade, businesses, government organisations, and consortia alike have significantly invested in this modern phenomenon, with a view to exploiting it for their financial or political gain [31]. Marc Andreessen, from the well-known venture capital firm Andreessen Horowitz, calls it as big an invention as the internet. Palychata [34], a research analyst from BNP Paribas, compares the creation of Blockchain to the invention of the steam or combustion engine, whereas *The Economist* predicts that it will be as important an innovation as the invention of Limited Liability Corporations [35].

The extent to which Blockchain is affecting our world is evidenced by the R3 Partnership's investigation into how the distributed ledger technology affects players in the financial industry. The R3 Partnership is a consortium of 80 of the biggest financial institutions. The R3 Partnership described its December 2015 launch as the product of frustration among banks and other financial institutions with the multiple generations of disparate legacy systems that struggle to interoperate. In addition, six of the biggest global banks, led by Swiss bank UBS, have developed a 'Utility Settlement Coin' (USC) [36], which is the digital counterpart of each of the major currencies backed by central banks. Their objective is to develop a settlement system that processes transactions in (near) real-time, rather than days. The aim of the project is to enable global banks to conduct various transactions with each other using collateralised assets on a custom-built blockchain and to make financial markets more efficient [37]. A third example is Australia Post, which has released plans for developing a blockchain-based e-voting system for the state of Victoria, Australia [38]. The possibilities for the Blockchain are enormous and it seems that almost any industry that deals with some sort of transaction or tracking mechanisms can and will be disrupted by Blockchain. However, to understand how we should use Blockchain for social good, let's first take a deep dive into the technology.

A blockchain is a shared and decentralised public or private ledger that describes a single version of the truth of ownership [39–41]. It is a distributed ledger that uses database technology to record and indefinitely maintain an ever-growing list of data records [42], which cannot be tampered with and are irreversible, verifiable, and traceable [33, 42, 43]. At first, these data records were bitcoin transactions, but applications have now moved to any type of online transaction across any industry. Blockchains can serve as a record keeper for societies, including registration of any type of document or property [44]. Data records are stored chronologically in *blocks* that are *chained* together cryptographically. Every node in the network has a copy of the block and, in order for a transaction to be added to a chain, there has to be a consensus among the nodes in the network.

The result is that peer-to-peer transactions become possible, without the need for a centralised certifying authority, such as a bank, which usually takes a small commission to carry out the work. The removal of third parties, and the ability of organisations and consumers to execute peer-to-peer transactions almost instantaneously, is a true paradigm shift. In essence, this is what makes Blockchain so important.

There are different types of blockchains and the type of blockchain selected determines how actors in the network interact with each other [33]. There are permissioned and permissionless blockchains, each with different characteristics, rules, and actors. Permissionless blockchains are public blockchains. The best-known example is the bitcoin blockchain. Trust within the system is created through game-theory incentives and cryptography [33]. This means that anyone interested in joining a particular permissionless blockchain can do so by simply connecting his or her computer to the decentralised network, downloading the application, and starting to process transactions. It is not necessary to have a previous relationship with the ledger and you do not need to be approved to join. If you want to start mining Bitcoin and supporting the Bitcoin network, simply go to https://bitcoin.org/en/full-node and get started. A public, permissionless Blockchain is not owned by anyone and everyone can contribute.

On the other hand, permissioned, or private, blockchains do not require these artificial incentives because all actors in the network are known to each other [33]. New actors have to be approved by existing participants in the network, which enables more flexibility and efficiency in validating transactions [33]. Private blockchains are generally used by organisations that like to keep a shared ledger for settlement of transactions [45], such as within the financial services industry. They are owned and operated by a group of organisations and transactions are visible only to members of the network [45]. A good example of a private Blockchain is the *Blockchain Settlement System* developed by UBS and five other major banks in 2016 [36]. This Blockchain enables the four participating banks to discernibly improve settlement times among them and no other party has access to the Blockchain or can contribute to it.

Private and public Blockchains are the two flavours that have been around and, for both options, the main feature is that, once a transaction is approved and on the Blockchain, it cannot be changed or edited. Some of the larger fintech institutions (including China's first private and fully digital bank, WeBank) are considering layering their online banking on to combinations of public and private blockchain networks [46]. However, since 2016, a third option has been developed. Accenture has patented an 'editable Blockchain', the history of which can be adjusted by a central authority. This is a bit of a contradiction, because the power of the Blockchain is that data, once validated, cannot be altered. However, Accenture claims that this type of Blockchain would be for private permissioned Blockchains only—used, for example, by the banks, where a central authority can manage the network under agreed governance rules [47]. This type of Blockchain would offer a 'safety button' that could, in fact, make the Blockchain safer to use.

The type of blockchain that an organisation could opt for depends on the objective of the organisation and the type of transactions that need to be stored on a blockchain. Some transactions, such as financial transactions, should not be visible for the general public, whereas other transactions, such as ownership of (digital) goods and land titles, benefit more from a public blockchain

[48]. Regardless of the type of blockchain, the data stored becomes immutable, verifiable, and traceable, due to four key components of Blockchain: cryptographic primitives, consensus mechanisms, transactions, and smart contracts. We address each of these components separately below.

2.2 Cryptographic primitives

Cryptography is a key component of any blockchain system. Among other things, it consists of two important features: the digital signature and the Hash Algorithm.

2.2.1 Digital signatures

Digital signatures are based on public key cryptography, also known as asymmetric cryptography. Asymmetric cryptography means that two keys, a public and a private key, are mathematically related to each other. This relationship means that any data encrypted by one key (public key) can be decrypted only by the other (private key), and vice versa. It is impossible to encrypt data with a public key and use another public key to decrypt that data [49]. As a result, you can use a key pair to identify the owner of a certain digital asset. As the public key is publically available, any data encrypted with a related private key can be decrypted only by the corresponding public key. It works like a mailbox, where everyone has a key to deposit a letter to that mailbox, but only one person has the right key to open the mailbox and take the mail out of it.

Public Key Infrastructure has now been widely deployed. Almost anything online uses the Public Key Infrastructure, from sending emails to visiting websites (a website is encrypted using the Public Key Infrastructure if it has an SSL certificate and the website shows *https*). It means that we can be certain that the data that is sent between you and the server is not interrupted. Public Private Key Infrastructure is also used to ensure authenticity of a certain document, which is done using the Hash Algorithm.

2.2.2 Hash Algorithms

Each block of data on a blockchain receives a *hash ID, as a database key,* calculated by a Secure Hash Algorithm. A block's hash is fixed. In other words, the hash ID allocated to the block never changes. Hash algorithms are used in a variety of components of blockchain technology, one of them being the hash ID, which is a unique string of 64 numbers and letters linked to data in each block. The US National Security Agency (NSA) has designed a second generation of cryptographic Hash Functions called Secure Hash Algorithms 2. It includes SHA-256, a highly efficient Secure Hash Algorithm that creates a unique hash ID for every piece of data. Hash Algorithms create the exact same hash if the data is exactly the same [50]. Altering only one bit in the data will result in a completely new hash ID. The hash ID of a block that is added to a blockchain is the starting data for the next block, and as such the blocks are chained together. This means that if data in a block is changed, it will change the hash of that block, which in turn will change the hash in the subsequent block, etc. To tamper with the data, the blocks would have to be revalidated by consensus. This will not happen because the other nodes in the network do not have an incentive to work on 'old' blocks in the chain. Besides that, a blockchain keeps on growing, so it requires considerable computing power to revalidate old blocks, which simply makes it not worthwhile [51]. The hash makes data on a blockchain immutable and that it has not been changed over time verifiable.

2.3 The consensus mechanism

Consensus decision-making has been used by humans for many years [52]. Although it began as a concept applied to politics and societies, it has become an important part of computer science [53]. Consensus algorithms ensure that connected machines are able to collaborate independently without the need to trust each other and can continue working even if some members of the network fail [53, 54]. There are a multitude of consensus algorithms that take different approaches to authenticating and validating values and transactions on a blockchain. Consensus mechanisms are key to any blockchain; due to the consensus algorithm, there is no longer the need to trust the other party and, as a result, decisions can be created, implemented, and evaluated without the need for a central authority [44, 54, 55]. The result is intermediary-free transactions, whether they be human to human, human to machine, or machine to machine [44].

Consensus is vital to blockchains, because there is no trusted central authority. Actors in the network have to agree on the rules that govern the blockchain, and how these rules must be applied, before a blockchain is deployed. The nodes in the network execute an agreed-upon algorithm and a predefined majority must agree on the outcome. Consensus algorithms use cryptography to validate transactions (and thus decisions) and at the moment,[4] the two most common consensus algorithms are Proof of Work (PoW) and the Practical Byzantine Fault Tolerance (PBFT), although new consensus algorithms are being developed constantly [56]. PoW is commonly used in permissionless blockchains, whereas PBFT is used in permissioned blockchains. In addition, Proof of Stake (PoS) is another consensus mechanism that is currently being developed. It is highly experimental, used only in a few altcoins, and not yet mature. Although Ethereum is looking into switching to PoS and the EOS Blockchain will use a delegated Proof of Stake consensus mechanism.

A consensus algorithm solves the long-standing problem of double spending related to digital currencies. Double spending refers to actors who want to cheat the system by spending the same digital token more than once. With fiat money, this problem is solved through the usage of a central authority (that is, a bank). In a decentralised system, without a central authority, it can be solved by consensus. To understand the issue, Lamport and Shostak [57] proposed *The Byzantine Generals' Problem*, a thought experiment about a group of generals who are each commanding a different part of the Byzantine army and need to agree upon a plan to attack and conquer an enemy city. The generals can communicate only via messenger, but the problem is that at least one general is a traitor. The question is how many traitors can the army have and still function as one force? Every consensus algorithm is a Byzantine Generals' Problem solution and the first algorithm that came up with a solution was the PBFT algorithm [58]. Since then, many PBFT algorithms have been developed, before Bitcoin was introduced. PBFT algorithms can be applied in a decentralised, permissioned network, meaning that a central aspect to PBFT algorithms is that a membership is required, which has to be approved by a centralised authority. The PoW algorithm solved this problem [31, 54]. This consensus algorithm operates in a decentralised network, without a central authority, but it assumes that most of the actors are 'honest' actors and reduces the risk of dishonest actors.

2.3.1 Proof of Work

The PoW algorithm solved the requirement for a centralised authority. The technical innovation of a PoW is that it does not require membership. For this reason, a central authority is no longer required. The PoW algorithm is, therefore, used in public or permissionless blockchains, where actors do not have to know or trust each other. As such, it is used in the bitcoin blockchain, which is a public blockchain. This consensus algorithm requires participating actors to solve a difficult computational problem to validate the blocks. The validation is done using cryptography, which means that the actor has to find the solution of an inequality, which requires considerable computing power (and energy). When a solution is presented, it is immediately clear that it is correct. This can be compared with a crossword puzzle, which can be difficult to solve, but once completed you immediately know that it is done correctly. The moment an actor has solved the equation, the solution is presented to the whole network and the actor receives bitcoins as a reward (in the case of the bitcoin blockchain).

2.3.2 Proof of Stake

Proof of Stake (PoS) is another common consensus algorithm that takes a different approach. Within PoS, as within PoW, validators are selected randomly, but, where validators within PoW have a larger chance of being selected if they have more computing power, within PoS the amount of money (that is, the number of tokens or the amount of cryptocurrency) that a member holds determines the likelihood of being selected [59]. Once a block has been produced, a transaction fee is paid to that validator and signers commit the block to the blockchain. These signers can all be nodes in the network or a randomly selected group of nodes that do the signing for the complete network. To 'incentivise' nodes to hold a larger stake, the more stake a node has in the network, the less complex the puzzles the node has to solve. As a result, nodes that already have a large stake can easily become larger. PoS still requires a consensus agreement on the current state of the network, but the more crypto-coins an actor owns, the higher the stake in the success of a blockchain. As a result, PoS requires far fewer computer processing unit computations and therefore is more energy efficient [60]. The assumption underlying PoS is simple: if an actor has a higher stake in the system, they have a higher incentive to ensure that the network is secure and correct because of the pain felt when the price and reputation of the cryptocurrency are damaged, due to attacks. It is expected that the Ethereum network will implement a PoS consensus mechanism in 2018.

2.3.3 Timestamp

A consensus mechanism implements a timestamp service [31], which ensures that every block that is added to a blockchain is timestamped to prove temporal relationships between different events [31, 61]. The timestamp basically confirms that a certain transaction occurred on the blockchain at a certain time. If an actor tries to cheat the system and offer the same transaction again, nodes will check the transaction against the timestamp and, if the transaction is found in a previous block, the nodes in the network will come to a consensus that the transaction is invalid. In addition, the timestamp feature, in combination with the hash, enables users to prove at any given moment that a certain document was owned by a particular user at a certain moment in time and that since then the document has not been altered [44] (that is, it makes the data fully traceable).

2.4 Transactions

Intermediary-free transactions [44] are key to Blockchain because they remove the need for trusted centralised third parties, who generally take a commission for verifying transactions. Taking out the middlemen (that is, the intermediaries) will completely change how actors interact with each other and how decisions are developed, implemented, and evaluated [60]. Bitcoin transactions are still the most common transactions that are recorded on a blockchain. However, other financial transactions related to any other currency, financial contracts, or hard and soft assets can also be recorded on a blockchain [44]. In fact, any type of transaction, whether related to digital or physical goods, can be recorded on a blockchain. This includes land registrations [62], tracking of goods throughout a supply chain [48], Internet of Things devices exchanging transactions [63], identity, reputation, natural resources [64], as well as peer-to-peer exchanges such as taxi rides or home sharing [65]. The list is endless and a complete overview can be viewed at the website of Ledra Capital, which is collecting the wide range of potential uses of the Blockchain on an ongoing basis [66]. In 2016, for the first time, a transaction took place between two organisations across the globe that was paid for using the blockchain and smart contracts [67]. The Commonwealth Bank of Australia and Wells Fargo from the USA used blockchain in, what was hailed as, the world's first global trade transaction between independent banks for a shipment of cotton from Texas to Qingdao in China. Further, in December 2017, Dutch agriculture trading house Louis Dreyfus Co. collaborated with Dutch banks ING and ABN Amro, and French bank Société Générale SA to sell a cargo of US soybeans to China using a blockchain platform. They digitised documents, were able to match data in real-time, prevented duplication, and handled the entire transaction in half the time it normally took [68].

Ownership of physical products can also be transferred and stored on a blockchain when owners sell their assets (such as art) by transferring a private key attached to that asset [44]. When this is done automatically using smart contracts, it is called smart property [44]. Smart contracts are a special branch of transactions that can be stored on a blockchain, using, for example, the Ethereum Blockchain [69]. Smart contracts, it is proposed, will have a major effect on organisational design and decision-making [44, 65, 69].

2.5 Smart contracts

The term 'smart contract' was first coined by Szabo [70] as 'a computerised protocol that executes the terms of a contract'. It can be seen as a traditional agreement that is automatically defined and executed by code, leaving no room for discretion [44]. Smart contracts are analogous to scripts for processing transactions and/or decisions. They run on a blockchain and are considered 'the killer application for the cryptocurrency world' [71]. With the arrival of smart contracts deployed on a blockchain, the concept of what defines an organisation and how organisations can achieve competitive advantage will change drastically.

Smart contracts can be seen as *If This Then That* statements compiled into bitcode (although a lot more complicated). They are software programs that will execute certain transactions or decisions, which were agreed upon by two or more actors [72]. They are created by choosing events or preconditions, and by providing what needs to happen when those preconditions are met. The protocol is then recorded on a blockchain and, once deployed on the blockchain, these scripts can no longer be altered and will always execute once the preconditions are met [73].

Smart contracts have three distinctive characteristics: they are *autonomous* (after deployment on a blockchain they can no longer be altered); they are *self-sufficient* (they can accumulate and spend value over time); and they are *decentralised* (they are distributed across multiple nodes within a network) [39, 44]. Once a smart contract is on a blockchain, it is final and cannot be changed (that is, they become immutable, verifiable, and traceable). However, certain parameters can be altered only if the original code allows for this. Therefore, it is vital for organisations to ensure that the code is 100% correct and that no bugs or errors remain in the smart contract when it is recorded on the blockchain. Mistakes can be extremely costly, as we have seen with The DAO Hack which lost US$50 million due to a mistake in the smart contract [74]. The only way to fix a bug in a deployed smart contract is through a 'hard fork' on the blockchain, which is exactly what happened with The DAO. Nevertheless, do not expect blockchains to create a hard fork every time an organisation deploys a faulty smart contract.

Smart contracts not only have a potential impact on contract law but also, more broadly, on social contracts within society and organisations. This is because smart contracts are automatically and autonomously executed, thereby taking out the need for human judgement and minimising the need for trust [44]. In addition, smart contracts remove the need for developing, implementing, or evaluating decisions by management or employees—when multiple smart contracts are combined, together with artificial intelligence and big data analytics, it becomes possible to automate decision-making capabilities [44, 69]. This will result in a 'fundamentally new paradigm for organising activity' [44], automating (strategic) decision-making, and corporate and data governance, and creating new organisational designs [33] that are completely run by computer code, so-called Decentralised Autonomous Organisations (DAOs) [69].

Smart contracts may seem revolutionary, but they are nothing new and have been around for a long time. As explained by Vitalik Buterin, founder of Ethereum, smart contracts are already in place in most modern office buildings. For example, access cards that determine whether you are allowed entry to a certain area are predefined by a piece of code and linked to a database [75]. The example of the access card shows that smart contracts have already been around for a long time. The only difference now is that, when they are deployed on the blockchain, they remain accessible indefinitely and will carry out their predefined tasks whenever certain conditions are met. Smart contracts offer tremendous opportunities for organisations, but it is vital that they are deployed on the blockchain only when they are correct. In the coming years, we will probably see a wide variety of applications using smart contracts that will change how we work, how we do business, and how we run our daily lives. It will be interesting to see how this will increasingly take away the middlemen, managers, and employees.

When managers or employees are no longer required to run an organisation, it will significantly change organisation design and how actors within the organisational network interact with each other [44]. Even if an organisation does not move to a completely DAO design, the usage of blockchain and smart contracts will affect how actors interact with each other [76] and change decision-making capabilities. Blockchain reduces opportunism within networks, due to the trustless system based on cryptography [55], and automates decision-making. In addition, organisations become more intensely connected with each other, because they share the same database across time and space, thereby increasing the actors, and interactions, within the network.

Organisations adopting blockchain technologies can be viewed as Human–Machine Networks (HMNs), where combinations of humans and machines interact with each other to produce synergistic effects [77]. Depending on the level of blockchain integration within the organisation, it could affect strategic decision-making capabilities. The more an organisation moves towards a DAO design, the more efficient and autonomous it will become. Ultimately, organisations can operate completely independently using a blockchain, smart contracts, and big data analytics, and a DAO will not have any management or employees [69]. The interactions between actors will be guided purely by autonomous software algorithms [39, 44, 62], increasing the need for careful deployment of smart contracts on a blockchain by shareholders of the DAO. The immutable, verifiable, and traceable characteristics of blockchains mean that steps would need to be taken to avoid the considerable damage that would ensue if smart contracts were deployed with bugs [73]. Incorrect smart contracts are, however, not the only challenge facing organisations wanting to move to a blockchain. The Blockchain is still a nascent technology and many (technical) challenges remain that need to be solved before wide-scale adoption becomes possible.

2.6 Changing organisation design

Although Blockchain is the underlying technology of Bitcoin, cryptocurrencies are not the only possible application. Any transaction can be recorded on a blockchain [39]. Smart contracts can enable a wide variety of applications, not just those related to financial markets and/or 'self-enforcing autonomous governance applications' [73]. The possibilities of Blockchain are, therefore, almost endless for organisations to create new, distributed products and services that will result in efficiency gains in existing organisational structures [33]. Such Blockchain-enabled products and services are commonly referred to as Decentralised Applications, or DApps. A DApp has at least two distinctive features [44]: (1) any changes to the protocol of the DApp have to be approved by consensus; and (2) the application has to use a cryptographic token, or cryptocurrency, which is generated according to a set algorithm. There are already quite a few examples of DApps, of which Bitcoin is of course the best known. An extensive list of all known DApps at the moment is available at dapps.ethercasts.com.

The development of such decentralised products and services will change organisation design. Blockchain does not require a centralised authority for maintenance, because the database is stored on millions of decentralised computers, and its decentralised infrastructure ensures that a single case of mismanagement, resulting in a point of failure, does not affect the entire network [45]. In addition, due to the trustless system based on cryptography, the usage of Blockchain and smart contracts will enable an organisation to control and reduce opportunism, while automating decision-making. This will, in turn, have a direct impact on organisation design [55] and any legal, regulatory, IT, and accounting frameworks [72]. Blockchain removes the need for trust in the absence of a centralised governing body. It therefore follows that any organisation developing DApps should still have a strong focus on data governance. After all, only data authenticity can be ensured; reliability and accuracy cannot. With Blockchain, it becomes possible to embed data governance directly within the network, bringing the code to the data [45]. Laws and regulations can be programmed into a blockchain itself, so that they are enforced automatically, which makes governance easier [78]. Hence, the ledger can act as legal evidence for data and increase the importance of data ownership, data transparency, and auditability. The resulting effect on organisation design could eventually result in the establishment of DAOs.

A DAO is a combination of smart contracts linked together, possibly connected to Internet of Things devices, big data analytics, and artificial intelligence. It is run by immutable code under the sole control of a set of irreversible business rules [39]. A DAO will have different actors from today's organisations; it will require extensive data governance processes that ensure data reliability and accuracy, and it will result in a fundamentally new organisational structure [44, 79–81]. A DAO is a self-organising framework that uses automated decision-making based on consensus in which actors interact with each other without the need to trust each other. Within a DAO there is no traditional organisational hierarchy because hierarchy is determined by ownership (that is, how trusted an actor is as well as the merits earned by that actor as a result of behaviour). This change in organisational structure affects the balance of power. In traditional organisations, power is distributed either by hierarchy or by knowledge, and often these are related; the higher up the hierarchy, the more information you have and the more power you have within the organisation [82]. Within a DAO, this works differently. Power is determined by the number of tokens an actor owns, an actor's trust level, and their achieved merits. This will shift the power balance within an organisation from a hierarchical structure to a distributed structure, thereby affecting the governance structure [83].

In its simplest form, a DAO is just immutable computer code: one or more smart contracts linked together and deployed on a blockchain, encouraging actors to self-organise. The code defines governance within the DAO, because governance is the rules that are implemented within the smart contracts. With the functionality of blockchain technology, a DAO can be seen as a self-organising structure that uses consensus mechanisms to make automated decisions, without the need for trust. As a result, within a DAO, there is no traditional hierarchy (because there are no employees or managers), no traditional governance (because the code is the governance as the rules are embedded within the smart contracts), and it is not possible to email or call a DAO, except for interacting with chat bots (because the entire organisation operates automatically, without the need for people being involved). DAOs can, however, operate as traditional organisations, although they do this autonomously; they can order products and services, have customers and suppliers, and make profits or losses. It has the same activities as a traditional organisation; it needs to make money, it has costs, it has customers, shareholders, and even employees (although these are independent contractors), it offers a product or service, and it is subjected to regulatory requirements (although being a distributed company this becomes a lot more difficult since regulatory requirements could be contradictory across jurisdictions). Therefore, governance is important when developing a DAO and a governance structure should be incorporated within the DAO (within the code). In addition, one should ensure that the code of the DAO works and continues to function correctly for an indefinite amount of time because, once deployed on a blockchain, it becomes irreversible. Lack of governance or quality assurance can have major consequences, as was shown in The DAO Hack in 2016 [84]. Therefore, in summary, actors who want to establish a DAO have to ensure that the right governance structure is implemented within the code and that the code works correctly to guarantee that the DAO can operate properly once deployed.

So far, we have not yet seen any true, and successful, DAOs. The first attempt of a DAO, 'The DAO', was stopped after a bug in a smart contract enabled a hacker to siphon away US$50 million. However, there have been several other attempts to create a DAO of which DAX and Digix are the most well known. Digix is an asset-tokenisation platform built on Ethereum. They leverage the blockchain's immutability, transparency, and auditability by applying it to precious physical assets such as gold (on a separate note, Digix raised US$5.5 million in just 12 hours with their Initial Coin Offer—or ICO—in 2016 [85]). Dash is an open-source, peer-to-peer cryptocurrency that offers instant and private transactions. Some people would also classify bitcoin as a DAO, although this classification is a point of contention.

To gain a better understanding of how a true DAO would look like for society, let's look at a futuristic example of how a DAO could operate in the real world several years from now:

> Imagine a self-driving taxi company in the not-too-distant future. Consumers can call the taxis using an App, similar to the Uber App. Once the taxi has been ordered, it automatically picks up the passenger and drives him or her to the requested destination. The car automatically

> takes the best route, avoiding traffic and detours. Once the passenger leaves the taxi, the money is automatically transferred using a smart contract. The money that is received with the service is used to automatically service the cars if needed. Once a car notices that service is required, it automatically books an appointment with a car service station. The repairman automatically and immediately receives a report on what needs to be done and if any parts need to be ordered. After years of great service, the car notices that it has reached the end of its life and automatically drives itself to the car-recycling company. Some time before that, smart contracts ordered a new self-driving car, based on the demand it sees in the market. The moment the old car is recycled, the new car leaves the factory and picks up the first passenger. No manager, no employee will be involved in the entire process. Big data analytics is used to automatically improve the service, understand the customers, and monitor the cars.[5]

Although it will be a while, probably a decade or so, before such a DAO exists, it is just a matter of time. The process of completely automating a company using smart contracts, big data analytics, artificial intelligence, machine learning, and the Internet of Things not only can be done within the taxi branch, it could also be achieved in retail, banking, manufacturing, or even the hospitality industry [86]. Obviously, governance will always remain important and there are quite a few challenges to be solved. After all, within a DAO, multiple actors, human and non-human, have to cooperate interdependently. Within such systems, mathematical models of conflict and collaboration can incentivise actors to act in the best interest for the system as a whole. DAOs are an exciting opportunity to redesign our society and how we do business, and to create more efficient organisations that offer better products and services for lower prices.

2.7 ICOs—every company its own central bank

An important aspect of a DApp or DAO is the cryptocurrency, sometimes referred to as the cryptocoin or token. For years, start-ups have been looking for investors to invest in their venture to build the next Facebook or Google. However, money is expensive and any start-up that raises money has to give a share of the company to the investors. The earlier an investor joins, the higher the risk, and the more expensive it becomes for the entrepreneur. That has been the paradigm for the past decades. Not anymore. Since the rise of the Blockchain, times are changing. The latest method to raise funds for a new start-up has become the Initial Coin Offer, or ICO (also known as a Token-Generation Event).

An ICO is increasingly being used by Blockchain start-ups to raise money by distributing a percentage of the initial coin supply [87]. Basically, with an ICO a start-up plays the role of a bank; it digitally creates money out of nothing and sells that to 'investors'. The tokens, or cryptocoins, which are sold during the crowd sale will be used on the platform to pay for transactions and distribute value across the stakeholders. 'Investors' who purchase these coins during the ICO do not get a share in the start-up, but they hope that the price of the coin will rise and as such they can get a (substantial) return on their investment.

Some ICOs can be very successful. For example, the ICO of Filecoin, a blockchain data storage network, raised US$257 million in their ICO in September 2017. Filecoin raised the record-breaking amount in less than a month. However, one of the earlier ICOs was that of Ethereum. In 2014, Ethereum raised US$18.4 million via the ICO of their cryptocoin Ether (ETH). At the time of the ICO, 1 Ether was worth ≈ US$0.31 (2000 ETH for 1 BTC) and, at the moment of writing this book, 1 Ether has increased in value from US$11.27 to US$1228 and consequently dropped in value to US$600.[6] Two other very successful ICOs have been Bancor, which raised US$153 million in five hours, and Block, which raised US$185 million in five days. At the end of 2017, the secure messaging app Telegram announced their ICO to enable them to develop a decentralised ecosystem. In March 2018, they had already secured US$1.7 billion in funding through their private token sale and, by the time you read this, it will be known how much they eventually raised. Of course, these fundraising activities also raise questions about purpose, trust, and governance. Notoriously, some ICOs and exchanges have operated Ponzi Schemes and other scams. Wherever there is money to be made, fraud and deceit are likely to follow. Some examples of these are discussed later in this book.

The coins that are sold during an ICO are often used to fund the development of the platform that is built. In many cases, a platform has not even been built yet and the founder(s) of the start-ups only have an idea or whitepaper that explains the objective of the platform. As a result, ICOs are extremely high risk and, because they often take place outside the realm of government regulators, there is no safeguard or guarantee at all for those who invest [88].

Start-ups that want to do an ICO should take it very seriously and ensure that the ICO complies with all relevant regulations. Often, start-ups naively think that, because they are incorporated outside of the USA, they do not have to take into account the SEC (Security and Exchange Commission) requirements [89]. However, failure to comply with the SEC is illegal and could affect the founders of the start-up.

Nevertheless, currently an ICO is a very popular way to raise millions. In the past months, there have been ICOs that raised millions of dollars in days, hours, or even minutes. Some of the most successful ICOs are: the DAO (raising US$160 million in three weeks, and subsequently losing US$50 million in the DAO Hack) [90], Bancor (raising US$153 million in three hours), Block.one (raising US$185 million), Sirin Labs (raising US$157 million in December 2017 to build a blockchain-based smartphone), Polkadot (raising US$145 million in October 2017 to allow people to use multiple blockchains at the same time), and Status (raising US$107 million in June 2017 to offer an interface that makes it easier to use Ethereum). These massive ICOs are a long way from earlier ICOs, which were deemed very successful at the time. For example, in 2016, Lisk raised US$5.7 million in four weeks whereas Synereo managed to raise US$4.7 million in four weeks, and SingularDTV raised US$7.5 million in just 17 minutes. Back in 2015, Augur raised US$5.2 million, of which the first 2000 BTC in only 12 hours. By the time you read this, these numbers will pale against more recent trends and records. A list of ongoing ICOs can be found at www.smithandcrown.com/icos/ or https://tokenmarket.net/ico-calendar

However, it is not all good news. There have been a few scams with ICOs. Quite a few ICOs are more like Ponzi Schemes and try to lure people in with the promise of high returns. OneCoin was one of the largest digital currency scams exposed recently as a Ponzi Scheme [91]. Another scam was GAWMiners, which raised US$19 million in their ICO based on nothing but lies [92]. If there is no working beta, or worse if there is only limited documentation and/or it is unclear who the developers are and what their background is, participating in an ICO is extremely risky and consumers can be scammed out of their money. Even if everything seems fine, as was the case with the massive ICO of Tezos, which raised US$232 million in July 2017, things can quickly turn bad. In December 2017, a class-action complaint was filed on the basis that Tezos allegedly violated US securities laws and committed investor fraud.

After an SEC investigation into The DAO Hack, the SEC ruled that some coins for sale are actually securities and that investors should be careful in deciding whether to invest in them. It is likely that the SEC will announce more guidelines in the future [93]. China went a step further and completely banned ICOs in 2017; this was a result of the Chinese community voicing concern that some ICOs are financial scams and pyramid schemes [94].

The scams organised by maleficent 'entrepreneurs' are one way that investors can lose their money when taking part in an ICO. Unfortunately, there are many more types of cryptocurrency scams. The most common is the so-called Pump-and-Dump schemes, where members of private groups on, for example, the messaging app Telegram, decide to promote a coin they own so they can sell it at a higher price. Within the stock market, such practices are illegal, but the crypto-market is still unregulated in many jurisdictions. Such behaviour can result in volatile fluctuations and ordinary investors suffering hefty losses. Criminals also try to steal money by copying websites of popular ICOs and trying to direct people to the wrong website. When people then transfer money to a given address, they never receive any tokens in return. In addition, there have been examples of fake exchanges, Ponzi schemes, fake wallets, and phishing attempts.

As a result of these scams, there has been a crackdown on cryptocurrencies by various countries including China and South Korea in 2017 and 2018. Of course, this caused mayhem among cryptocurrencies, with some coins losing almost 50% of their value in a few hours and Bitcoin dropping 25%. Many government bodies and regulators are trying to understand cryptocurrencies and developing regulations for them. However, the outright banning of cryptocurrencies, crypto-exchanges, and ICOs is not the solution. Instead, what we need are global regulations focused on exchanges complying with Know Your Customer-Anti Money Laundering (KYC-AML) regulations and ICOs complying with regulations similar to Initial Public Offerings (IPOs). Only then will we get a more educated and regulated market that does not limit innovation and benefits all.

As is the case with any new technical innovation, especially in the IT space, regulators always lag behind new markets and disruption to old systems. By the time laws and regulations have been implemented, they are often no longer relevant to the digital space. As soon as new regulations are announced, the community moves ahead and develops new solutions. In addition, as much as governments cannot prevent hacking, spam, or phishing, they will not be able to prevent hacks and robberies in the cryptocurrency market. Furthermore, as cryptocurrencies are inherently decentralised, virtual, and borderless, attempts to regulate such a phenomenon in one part of the network will not work. As Joachim Wuermeling of the Bundesbank stated, at the start of 2018, the only way to regulate a decentralised phenomenon is through global agreements:

> Effective regulation of virtual currencies would therefore only be achievable through the greatest possible international cooperation because the regulatory power of nation-states is obviously limited.[7]

The problem with global regulations is that they take time and a lot of countries have different motivations to ban or regulate cryptocurrencies. Nevertheless, there are two areas that regulators can focus on in attempting global regulations: crypto-exchanges and ICOs.

Regulations can force crypto-exchanges to comply with KYC-AML obligations to prevent cryptocurrency being traded by people who are not allowed to do so (although due to the inherent decentralised nature of it, they can never prevent users from making transactions outside exchanges). Regulations can also enforce exchanges to take the right security measures. Unfortunately, it is impossible to completely prevent hacks or digital robberies.

In addition, regulators should focus on the ICO. A more streamlined process around ICOs can definitely prevent scams and Ponzi Schemes. Similar to existing IPO regulations, ICOs should comply with certain regulations to protect investors and keep promoters accountable. However, regulations should not prohibit ICOs completely, because they are truly an innovation with tremendous potential. Therefore, similar to the General Data Protection Regulation (GDPR) compliance developed by the European Union (EU), a global standard should be developed for ICOs. These regulations could include requirements such as:

- Disclosing financial, accounting, tax, and other business information before an ICO;
- Implementing escrow functionality with smart contracts to ensure that funds are released only on reaching certain milestones. If those milestones are not met, funds will be returned automatically;
- Having a board of advisers that are involved with the company, instead of having stock photos as advisers or even stealing other people's identity;
- Having a prospectus that informs potential investors of the risks involved with the ICO.

Apart from regulations, another area that governments and regulators should focus on is educating citizens about the risks involved when dealing with cryptocurrencies and helping consumers understand how they should deal with them. By 2017, Russia had already announced a programme to educate its citizens on cryptocurrencies and the dangers associated with investing in them. More countries should follow to help citizens understand what this new phenomenon is and what risks involved are.

Nevertheless, it seems that ICOs are here to stay. Start-ups have discovered this lucrative way of raising money and are acting as their own central bank, although it is very likely that regulators will attempt to regulate the ICO and impose restrictions or rules on doing an ICO. Cryptocurrencies will fundamentally change how we perform transactions online and as such how we use and build new products and services. They will have a big impact on Blockchain for social good and could hold the key to solving some of the Wicked Problems, but more on that in the following chapters.

2.8 Blockchain platforms

This section considers some of the organisations that are developing the new technology for Blockchain. Of course, this is not an exhaustive list of the technology that is already available. The number of companies developing new tools and solutions is constantly expanding and here we provide three examples of different types of blockchain start-ups. The companies mentioned below are only for the purposes of illustrating what is already out there.

2.8.1 Ethereum

Ethereum aims to reinvent the internet and has been around for a few years now. It is a decentralised platform to develop DApps that run through smart contracts. These smart contracts are small software programs that execute a task, a sort of *If This Then That* statement (but a lot more complex). They run on a custom-built blockchain and as such there is no chance of fraud, censorship, or third-party interference. Ethereum has developed an enormously powerful, shared, global infrastructure, the Ethereum Virtual Machine, which can execute code of arbitrary algorithmic complexity. They are continuously expanding the infrastructure and building new solutions for the distributed web.

2.8.2 Ripple

Ripple is a Blockchain start-up focused on the financial services industry. They claim that they are not using blockchain, but rather use Distributed Ledger Technology. They have developed a Distributed Ledger Technology to enable banks around the world to send real-time international payments, without the need for a centralised authority. It is in reality a payment network to instantly transfer any type of currency across the globe. They have developed a distributed global network that hosts payment nodes to transfer value around the world. Banks can monitor and coordinate the transfer of funds across distributed ledgers, with minimal risks and delays, contrary to the amount of time it takes today to settle international transactions (which can be up to a week).

2.8.3 IOTA

IOTA is a completely different cryptocurrency from the above because it does not use a blockchain, but rather uses a Directed Acyclic Graph called Tangle. It is developed especially for Industry 4.0 where connected devices have to be able to perform micro- or nano-transactions with each other. As such, it offers the following characteristics:

- Infinite scalability as it does not use blocks or miners. Instead, every party that wants to perform a transaction has to validate two transactions;
- No transaction fees, thereby enabling nano-transactions among connected devices;
- Proof of Work consensus mechanism that requires minimum computing power and can be performed by connected devices;
- Completely decentralised, in contrast to the semi-decentralised networks such as Bitcoin.

2.8.4 Other start-ups

In 2016, the amount of investment in Blockchain start-ups crossed the US$1 billion mark for the first time and in the first quarter of 2018, ICO funding exceeded US$ 6 billion, as such it is impossible to give a complete overview of Blockchain start-ups [95]. However, we set out below, in no particular order, a list of some more interesting start-ups working in the decentralised and distributed space. By the time you read this book, it is likely that some of these start-ups may no longer exist:

Everledger: a permanent ledger for diamond certification and related transaction history.

Cardano: a smart contract platform that seeks to deliver more advanced features than any protocol previously developed.

Stellar: a platform that connects banks, payments systems, and people. Moves money quickly, reliably, and at almost no cost.

NEO: a competitor to Ethereum, NEO is developing an open network for a smart economy.

Coinbase: a platform to buy and sell bitcoin and ether.

Lisk: a platform that enables the development and publishing of blockchain applications with your own sidechains.

Blockstream: offers software and hardware solutions using the Blockchain.

tØ: a blockchain-based trading platform.

OpenBazaar: a decentralised marketplace.

BitFury: one of the biggest bitcoin mining infrastructure providers.

Augur: a decentralised prediction market built on the Ethereum blockchain.

Neureal: open source and decentralised artificial intelligence.

Maidsafe: a distributed platform that enables the creation of fast and secure applications.

IPFS: a peer-to-peer distributed file system that aims to replace http.

Imagjn: developing a reputation protocol to enable collaboration among individuals, organisations, and things.

EOS: a smart contract platform for DApps that raised over $4 billion in their token sale.

Of course, there are many more Blockchain start-ups establishing their roots in this market every day.

2.9 Blockchain challenges to overcome

Blockchain follows the same path as many disruptive technologies that could have a major impact on the world. As such, it still faces some challenges, which will require time before they will be overcome.

With the attention moving away from Bitcoin and towards the enormous potential of Blockchain, it may seem that Blockchain will solve many of the world's problems, but it is still a very young technology. Below is an overview.

2.9.1 Scalability issues

Scalability is a major issue for blockchains, at least for public blockchains. The most popular blockchain, the Bitcoin blockchain, is by now 170 Gigabytes[8] and is growing steadily at 1 MB per block every ten minutes. The idea of Blockchain is that every node in the distributed web has a complete copy of the blockchain. So, if you wish to start validating transactions on the Bitcoin blockchain, you first have to download the entire blockchain.

A potential solution to the issue of scalability could be 'blockchain pruning'. This basically means that nodes in the network use only a verified representation of the blockchain that contains the last few hundred blocks. The entire blockchain would still be available, but only on a few nodes. At the time of writing, there is a lot of discussion in the Bitcoin community regarding whether the size of the block should be increased to 2 or 4 MB. It is likely that scalability will remain an issue as the popularity of Bitcoin increases. In 2017, this scalability challenge resulted in a division among bitcoin miners. As a result, some miners decided to hard fork and create a new cryptocurrency, Bitcoin Cash, which enables up to 8-MB blocks. The size of the Bitcoin Cash Blockchain has since grown to 159 GB.[9]

Scalability is less of an issue for private blockchains, such as Hyperledger, because they contain only nodes that have a direct interest in processing transactions. Although private blockchains are more expensive than a single centralised database, if you add up the costs involved in all those centralised databases replaced by the blockchain, it is still a lot cheaper.

2.9.2 Transaction speed and costs

Transaction speed and costs are also a major issue for some blockchains (although not all). IOTA's distributed ledger (Tangle) is infinitely scalable at zero costs. However, the bitcoin blockchain does face significant transaction and cost challenges and, as it is the most-developed blockchain, we focus on the bitcoin blockchain. When Bitcoin was launched, everyone was excited about the almost negligible transaction costs. Sending money almost instantaneously across the globe was almost free of charge; this created a completely new world that bypassed the need for banks when it came to transferring money across the globe. However, things have changed. On 21 December 2017, the average transaction fee reached its highest level of US$54.90 per transaction.

Obviously, if you wish to perform a small transaction, let's say buying a coffee with bitcoin, this becomes impossible. If you use bitcoin to transfer large sums of money across the globe, hundreds of thousands or millions of dollars, such a fee is relatively cheap compared with what you would have to pay a bank. However, for a cryptocurrency to be widely accepted and potentially replace fiat currency, it should be usable by everyone for every type of transaction.

The cause for the high transaction fees lies in the fact that the sizes of the blocks are currently limited to 1 MB per block and almost each block is completely filled. For example, on May 4, 2018, the average block size[10] was 974 kB, which means that every block is filled up with transactions. Bitcoin was created in such a way that miners who validate transactions have to use a tremendous amount of computing power (that is, energy). If there is an increasing demand for transactions to be validated, miners will prioritise transactions that pay a higher fee. Economics 101 dictates that, if the demand increases, but supply remains the same (number of transactions that can be validated per block), the price increases.

Another reason for the increased transaction fee is the newly created cryptocurrency Bitcoin Cash that split off from Bitcoin on 1 August 2017. Bitcoin and Bitcoin Cash are very similar cryptocurrencies, which means that miners can easily switch from Bitcoin to Bitcoin Cash, if it becomes more profitable to mine Bitcoin Cash (the rationale behind this has to do with how the Bitcoin and Bitcoin Cash protocols have been developed; if there are fewer miners, the mining difficulty goes down, and the possibility to make more money increases). Fewer miners on the Bitcoin network means less supply, which means an increased transaction fee.

Of course, the Bitcoin community is aware of this and is attempting to implement solutions to increase the size of the blocks, thereby increasing supply and lowering transaction fees. There is an ongoing debate in the Bitcoin community related to block size, with multiple arguments in favour of and opposed to an increase in size. The reality is that, without a solution to this problem, the number of transactions per second remains limited, and the transaction fees will continue to increase. Or, as Vitalik Buterin [96], founder of Ethereum, said: 'If [the niche of digital gold] is what Bitcoin users want, then they should keep the limit, and perhaps even decrease it. But if Bitcoin users want to be a payment system, then up it must go.'

2.9.3 Negative image due to security concerns

Clearly, the decentralised approach that blockchain offers has some advantages. It becomes a lot more difficult to hack and/or censor data, and the usage of the Hashcash Algorithm ensures that it is impossible to retrieve the hashed content. The Bitcoin blockchain itself has not yet been hacked, despite the fact that it has been around for almost a decade. However, many of the services surrounding it have. The DAO was hacked and subsequently almost lost

US$50 million [90]. This was preventable only thanks to a 'hard fork'. Mt Gox, the (at the time) world's largest bitcoin exchange, was hacked and as a result US$460 million disappeared [97]. Further, Bitfinex, a Hong Kong-based bitcoin exchange platform, lost US$70 million [98]. More recently, in January 2018, the Japanese exchange Coincheck was hacked, resulting in a loss of US$660 million in NEM tokens. These hacks do not help the image of bitcoin and other cryptocurrencies. Although bitcoin is only one application of Blockchain, these hacks distract the general public from its true value. People might not feel comfortable with these security concerns surrounding blockchains.

2.9.4 Energy consumption and costs

Validating transactions requires computers to solve complicated puzzles. This, in turn, requires a tremendous amount of computing power and is very expensive. Bitcoin is a particularly unsustainable coin in terms of its energy consumption. The Proof of Work consensus mechanism requires tremendous amounts of computing power. According to VICE, in 2015 a single Bitcoin transaction used roughly enough electricity to power 1.57 American households for a day [99]. This results in an estimated annual energy consumption of approximately 16 terawatt-hours.

CERN (the European Organization for Nuclear Research) uses approximately 1.3 terawatt-hours per year to power the Large Hadron Collider [100], an amount equal to the annual energy consumption of Iceland. This is almost 30,000 times the energy consumption of VISA [101] (which processed 82.3 billion transactions in 2016 [102], compared with the approximately 100 million Bitcoin transactions in 2017). With the potential increase in block size, the amount of energy required to solve the puzzles would continue to increase. In addition, given that most of the mining pools are in China, most of this energy consumption is driven by unsustainable coal-powered energy plants. Although it is possible that miners may switch to clean energy, there is still the problem that the mining of bitcoin is literally a waste of energy [103], because the complex computer calculations as part of the Proof of Work consensus protocol have no value at all. No world problems are being solved by the calculations, except to show that the calculations have been done. In an ideal world, we would see the development of a consensus algorithm that actually contributes to the public interest, similar to what was done with reCAPTCHA, which was used for training neural networks.

In times of climate change, the energy consumption of Bitcoin is a serious problem. Of course, different consensus mechanisms, such as Proof of Stake, do solve these issues, but many blockchains, including the Bitcoin blockchain, continue to use Proof of Work. Unless Bitcoin switches to a different consensus protocol, the energy consumption of Bitcoin will rapidly become unsustainable.

2.9.5 Lack of talent

Blockchain technology remains nascent and as a result not many developers have mastered working with blockchain-related technologies. Already, there are hundreds of Blockchain start-ups that all want fish from the same talent lake. As a result, it becomes increasingly difficult for organisations that want to move to the distributed web to attract the right talent. As was the case with big data a few years ago, it will take time before universities catch up and start developing the right courses for the distributed web. This delay in training the right graduates may slow down the development of new applications.

2.10 A word about doubt and criticism attendant upon blockchain adoption

In 2017, the Australian Government's data research and engineering centre—Data61—produced two reports detailing the long-term scenarios and immediate technical applications for blockchain technology[11]. The Data61 reports describe some of the possible opportunities for the use of Blockchain in Australia, including monitoring the outbreak of pests or animal and plant diseases, conducting border surveillance, tracking intellectual property, and establishing identity systems that provide greater certainty over entitlements, benefits, and tax obligations. The reports also provide some well-researched insight into why some of the major blockchain projects that were launched in 2015 and 2016 stalled. It is useful to consider here the problems facing blockchain-based solutions, because these issues have garnered media attention and resulted in some negative sentiment surrounding blockchain's promise as a solution to some of the fundamental problems facing our globalised world.

Since 2015, banks, regulators, tech giants, and start-ups from across the world have raised billions of dollars to explore the potential of Blockchain. But, so far, the only really successful, 'scale-able' use of Blockchain remains cryptocurrencies. The problems that have hampered attempts to apply the Blockchain's capabilities to other applications are all risk based, and fall into three broad categories: privacy and fraud.

When it comes to blockchains and privacy, it is important to begin with a distinction between private and public ledgers. Public ledgers do not afford privacy. Privacy inside the Bitcoin system has proved to be highly porous and heuristic, with nothing even close to approaching high guarantees. This is because transactions are globally published and are not encrypted in most applications. If this data is personal data, for example 'medical or financial data', this brings the regulatory and legal issues into the light, particularly in

Germany, which has some of the strictest privacy regulations. Even if there is an attempt to encrypt and hide personal information, it is still possible to glean statistical or meta-data. One solution is to store only encrypted data on a blockchain, but this leads to another problem: if the key to decrypt specific information is lost, the data may not be recovered accurately. Furthermore, if a key is stolen and published, all the data is forever decrypted in the blockchain because the data cannot be altered. For more information on Public Key Infrastructure, see Chapter 3.

In a speech delivered to the Africa Blockchain Conference in March 2017, Andreas Antonopoulos warned that many recent 'blockchain' projects are fraudulent attempts to raise capital under the guise of innovation and disruptive technologies. The use of blockchain in financial transactions also poses problems for compliance with anti-money-laundering legislation, which requires that anyone providing financial services (for example) must satisfy themselves as to the identity of their client or customer. At this time, a problem with smart contracts and cryptocurrencies is that they are susceptible to manipulation. This was a key reason for the US Security and Exchange Commission's refusal in March 2017 to approve the registration of the Winklevoss Bitcoin Asset Trust.

These shortcomings may explain why a number of high-profile blockchain projects stalled in 2015, 2016, and even 2017. For example, in mid-2017 the Bank of Canada announced that its blockchain project, Jasper, was not yet fit to handle settlements. Citing transparency and privacy issues, the bank found that the benefits of using blockchain did not outweigh the risks [104].

Risk was not the only reason that blockchain projects stalled. In February 2017, the R3CEV consortium of banks and technologists announced, after more than 18 months of investment, innovation, and testing, that they would not be using blockchain for their project because they did not need it. This decision does not amount to an attack on the Blockchain's promise or reputation. It is simply a practical decision based on the fundamental question of whether or not an application is fit for purpose.

Finding a solution to the real risks and challenges facing the Blockchain is a priority for developers, investors, and promoters who want to attract the number of users needed to make running a network reliable and profitable.

At the Third Global Blockchain Summit held in Shanghai in September 2017, Vitalik Buterin acknowledged these problems and offered a road map for the Ethereum Project's proposed solutions. In his presentation to an audience of 1200 government, industry, and academic experts, he suggested that security and privacy issues can be readily addressed by creating user accounts (for networks managed by central authorities), or via zero knowledge proofs known as SNARKS and STARKS which may resolve issues for public networks.

A SNARK is a succinct non-interactive argument of knowledge that enables the extraction of verification so that it can be published to the network as an additional proof. Meanwhile, STARKs are scalable transparent arguments of knowledge. This zero knowledge proof improves the verification process by providing a statistically (probabilistically) checkable proof. These measures will improve the mathematically defensible verification of each block in the chain.

In order to resolve the problems arising from the demand for security and scalability, the Ethereum developers have looked to Sharding as a possible solution. A blockchain cannot process more transactions than a single node can. In large part, this is why Bitcoin is limited to three to seven transactions per second and why Ethereum can only manage seven to fifteen transactions per second. The promise from Ethereum is that Sharding will change the way that the Blockchain can be validated. Referred to as Sharding, a small subset of network nodes will validate every single transaction. This means that the Ethereum blockchain will remain secure while also allowing for better scaling. There are also completely new solutions in production, such as the internet of things Blockchain start-up IOTA which offers a new version of blockchain, called 'the Tangle', offering infinite scalability.

There are still issues that remain unresolved and questions that remain unanswered. For example, the timeframe for the implementation of these innovations remains unclear and their performance has yet to be tested. Importantly, technologists are as invested as users in the way forward. This moment is reminiscent of the routing security problems that dogged the development of the internet in 1989, when it was little understood, hard to explain, and described amusingly in terms of surfing and super-highways.

Ultimately, blockchain technology can help to improve defensive cybersecurity strategies, especially in terms of identity and access. Solutions are being explored and they promise to provide greater security and privacy than yet experienced on the internet. Cybersecurity threats emerge every day, whereas older threats still linger around and wait to be exploited once again. Blockchain technology will not be the holy grail of cybersecurity, but it is a powerful tool that can help to harden systems.

2.11 A decentralised and distributed society

In recent years, technology has drastically changed many elements of how we do business and lead our lives. Unfortunately, our economic, legal, and political systems have not kept up with the changes [105]. As a result, our administrative controls have also not kept up and our economic, legal, and political systems still operate in a bureaucratic way. Hence, these systems are often ineffective, lack transparency, and are open to fraudulent actions. Blockchain technology can change this and the opportunities of a decentralised and distributed society are enormous. Marco Lansiti and Karim Lakhani, both professors at Harvard

Business School, view Blockchain not as a 'revolutionary technology but a foundational technology, which has the potential to create new foundations for our economic and social systems' [105]. Building new foundations for our economic, legal, and political systems takes time (possibly decades), and will present many different challenges. However, once we make it to the other end of this transition, it will result in better, more transparent, and fairer economic, legal, and political systems.

A decentralised and distributed peer-to-peer world will offer many benefits, which our economic and social systems are currently lacking. The cost of doing business will be reduced by removing intermediaries, (smart) contracts will be executed automatically based on predefined conditions, society will be reshaped, and we will need to rely less on intermediaries, whether these are governmental or for-profit organisations. Of course, organisations that want to move to Blockchain will also reap all the benefits of this technology; it will help them reduce costs, reduce fraud, offer better services, become more transparent, and all in all, become a better company. However, this book is not about how companies can use the Blockchain. If you are interested in how your company can become more profitable using Blockchain, we recommend you put aside this book and read one of the many, often very-well-written, books on Blockchain for businesses. In Chapter 10, we do provide a roadmap for organisations how to implement blockchain technology within their business. This book is all about solving the many Wicked Problems our society faces, because of the economic, legal, and political systems that have lagged behind. Our objective is to explain how Blockchain can help these systems catch up and we sincerely believe that, if governments and organisations focus on Blockchain for Social Good, we can create a better world for all. Therefore, we focus on those problems that affect our society negatively, and for each of these problems we discuss the identity and nature of the problem. What is the scope and impact of the problem and why should we actually care? What attempts have been made to solve the problem so far and how can Blockchain solve the problem? How can a decentralised and distributed approach offer new insights for solving the Wicked Problem? We dive into some of the best practices that are already out there, as well as the barriers and possible solutions to those barriers. The seven Wicked Problems that we discuss in this book are:

- Identity;
- Poverty;
- Climate change;
- Corruption, tax evasion, and money laundering;
- Fair Trade;
- Voting fraud and disenfranchisement; and
- Censorship.

If we can solve the above Wicked Problems, using a decentralised and distributed solution, we will create a peer-to-peer world that offers many advantages to our current system. Although the technological developments will take up at least a decade or more, once we have created a decentralised and distributed society based on peer-to-peer collaboration, we will have created a better world.

2.12 Conclusion and takeaways

Blockchain is the Distributed Ledger Technology that ensures that data and contracts are stored in transparent and shared databases, and protects data from removal, corruption, or modification using a consensus mechanism and cryptography. The *Hash Algorithm* ensures that we can always control whether a document, ownership, or transaction has been altered. The immutability of records on a blockchain ensures that we can always go back to the origin of a transaction, to control or monitor who has been involved in that transaction across time and space. Apart from transactions, a blockchain can also store *smart contracts*, so-called *If This Then That* statements, albeit a lot more complex. These contracts are written in code, understandable across jurisdictions, and ensure that a certain action will automatically take place once certain pre-set conditions have been met. When you start combining one or multiple smart contracts with technologies such as big data analytics and artificial intelligence, it becomes possible to create DApps or even DAOs. A DAO is an organisation without management or employees, run completely by code, where (data) governance is enforced in the code. In this way, existing paradigms of how we should run an organisation are changed completely.

The Blockchain, and with it the hundreds of DApps that have already been developed, offer a glimpse of what the future holds. Blockchain is still in its early development and a lot of development work has still to be done. However, decentralised applications that are run by smart contracts, without the need for a centralised governing power that generally takes a large commission, offer tremendous advantages. They are cheaper and more efficient to run, more difficult to control by governments or centralised organisations, and more secure and transparent than existing applications. It is these technologies and applications (Blockchain, smart contracts, DApps, and even DAOs) that could contribute to solving *Wicked Problems*.

Notes

1 This book follows industry practices in the writing of Bitcoin vs bitcoin. When written as Bitcoin, it relates to the technology, and, when written as bitcoin, it relates to the cryptocurrency.

2 Blockchain is only one form of a distributed ledger technology. There are more versions of distributed ledgers, for example the Tangle developed by IOTA. However,

in this book we focus on the distributed ledger technology called Blockchain and, for the sake of the argument, include other variations of distributed ledger technologies under Blockchain (although technically these variations of course differ, sometimes even significantly).

3 This book follows industry practices in the writing of Blockchain vs. blockchain. Blockchain refers to the technology/trend as a whole, whereas blockchain means one or more blockchain(s)—a distributed ledger database.

4 It should be noted that the technological developments around Blockchain are so rapid that, by the time you read this, this could be outdated.

5 This example was originally created by Vitalik Buterin, founder of Ethereum and has been adapted for this book.

6 Price as of the beginning of February 2018—https://blockchain.info/charts/blocks-size.

7 www.reuters.com/article/us-bitcoin-regulations-germany/any-rule-on-bitcoin-must-be-global-germanys-central-bank-says-idUSKBN1F420E.

8 As per March 2018—https://blockchain.info/charts/blocks-size/.

9 https://bitinfocharts.com/bitcoin%20cash/—as at March 2018.

10 https://blockchain.info/charts/avg-block-size.

11 See 'Distributed Ledgers' (2017) and 'Risks and Opportunities for Systems using Blockchain and Smart Contracts' (2017), which can both be found here—www.data61.csiro.au/en/our-work/safety-and-security/secure-systems-and-platforms/blockchain.

Chapter 3

Blockchain and identity

Identity /ʌɪˈdɛntɪti/: the fact of being who or what a person or thing is

3.1 Introduction

At the start of 2010, Nicole McCabe was happily living in Israel with her husband when she became one of the main suspects of a political assassination in the United Arab Emirates. At the time, the Australian was six months pregnant. She was out driving on a Wednesday when she heard her name read out as one of the assassins responsible for the murder of the Hamas chief Mahmoud al-Mabhouh in a Dubai hotel room a few days earlier [106]. However, she had never been to Dubai and being six months pregnant she was not a likely suspect of an assassination. Nicole had become victim to identity theft. Somehow the thieves had used her personal identifiable information to create a fake passport and used that to enter Dubai [107]. As a result, she was now wanted for murder in Dubai, along with 17 other westerners, whose identities were also stolen by members of a hit squad believed to have acted on the orders of Israeli spy agency Mossad [108].

In early 2012, American Helen Anderson[1] was living in Seattle when she had to pay a visit to her daughter in Portland, Oregon. The then 64-year-old retired nurse had to care for her daughter who was having health problems and she had asked her niece, Samantha, to house sit. When Helen came back in October 2012, she found out that her niece had given Alice Lipski, a meth addict, shelter in Helen's house for a few days. Helen told Alice to leave, but the damage had already been done, as she later discovered. While she was away, Alice had stolen personal identifiable information from mail and receipts that Helen kept in her house and Alice used that information to take over Helen's identity. Alice signed up to a credit monitoring service, which is intended to help protect citizens from identity theft, and subsequently reported every inactive credit card as stolen in order to get new cards, usernames, and passwords. With these new cards, Alice purchased food and clothes, paid for gas bills, went to the casino, and racked up a total bill of

$US30,000 in just six months. In total, before Alice was arrested, she had stolen almost $US1 million by using Helen's information and that of dozens of other victims [106, 109].

When Axton Betz-Hamilton's mother died in 2013 she discovered that she had fallen victim to identity theft. Axton's father and grandfather were also victims of an identity theft that had started almost 20 years earlier. Becoming a victim of identity theft is a nasty experience, but it is made much worse when you find out that your mother was the one who perpetrated the crime. For almost two decades, Axton's mother lived a secret life, while she was (seemingly) happily married. During those years, she stole the identity of her husband, daughter, and father-in-law—defrauding her own family of thousands of dollars. For 20 years, her mother had committed a breach of trust that left Axton and her father in deep trouble. As a consequence of this identity theft, Axton's credit rating was degraded and she had to pay hundreds of dollars in fees, interest rates, and deposits. In addition to all the trouble that comes with identity theft, Axton also had to deal with discovering that her mother was not whom she thought she was [106, 110].

Nakeisha Hall had been working for the IRS Taxpayer Advocate Services for over a decade and her job was to help people who had fallen victim to identity theft. However, Nakeisha was not only helping the victims, but also helping herself. With the access she had to the IRS databases, she was able to steal names, birth dates, and social security numbers. She used this personal identifiable information to submit false tax returns and requested the refunds on debit cards, which she used to fund her lifestyle. In total, she managed to steal over $US400,000, although she intended to steal almost a million dollars from the people she was supposed to help. Today, she is serving a nine-year sentence in a federal prison after pleading guilty to identity theft and tax fraud [106, 111].

Nicole, Helen, and Axton are not the only victims of identity theft from the likes of Nakeisha. In fact, identity fraud and theft are a problem that over 15 million people in the USA alone encounter every year, resulting in annual financial losses of up to $US50 billion [112]. Identity theft comes in a wide variety of forms and can have a big impact on someone's life, sometimes disrupting it for several years. Unfortunately, with most of our communication being done digitally, thieves and hackers have become increasingly sophisticated at stealing personal identifiable information. As such, it has become relatively easy to steal someone's identity and commit all kinds of crimes. However, identity is becoming more and more important and, nowadays, it is almost impossible to purchase any service, subscription, or financial product without revealing your identity and disclosing your personal identifiable information. Even when you want to enter a bar or buy alcohol, you have to prove who you are, although, in fact, the only thing they really need to know is your age.

Identity has become flawed as too often our privacy is breached unnecessarily and too many people fall victim to identity theft, that is, if you at least have an identity. Article 6 of the Universal Declaration on Human Rights stipulates that 'Everyone has the right to recognition everywhere as a person before the law'. As such, identity is a fundamental human right. Unfortunately, according to the World Bank, approximately 1.5 billion people live without an officially recognised identity, most of them in Africa or Asia. These people do not own a government-issued and -recognised document, and often are the most vulnerable people who cannot access basic services because they lack an official identity. In the digital society in which we live, it is therefore time for change and, if we want to solve some of the Wicked Problems discussed in this book, we first need to solve the identity problem. As it stands, Blockchain might be a suitable technology to do so. Before we dive into how to solve this identity problem and what the role of Blockchain could be, let's first discuss what identity actually is, because it might not be as straightforward as you think it is.

3.2 What is identity?

Know thyself was inscribed in the forecourt of the Greek Temple of Apollo at Delphi, and since then philosophers, psychologists, scientists, poets, authors, artists, and politicians have discussed and debated the topic. Plato referred to it as long-standing wisdom, which was given as advice by the Gods, and, according to Socrates, 'to know thyself is the beginning of wisdom'. It seems so easy to answer the questions 'Who am I?' and 'What is my identity?', but it is a lot more difficult than one would expect and many people disagree as to what identity is. Is your identity what is stated on your government-issued identity document such as a passport or driver's licence, assuming that you have such a document? Is identity your name that your parents gave you or is it the nickname that your friends gave you? Is identity your Facebook, Twitter, or LinkedIn username, is it your employee number at your work, or is it your social security number or your credit card number? If your credit card number has been stolen, has your identity been stolen as well? What about the pseudonyms that you use when you comment on different forums on the web, or is the username that you created for that dating website your identity? What if those websites get hacked? If you suffer from dementia and forget your name, have you then lost your identity? If you are schizophrenic, do you have multiple identities? These are just some of the questions that come up when thinking about identity. But that is not all. Once you have identified who you are, we have to deal with the persistence of identity; which you *is* you? Is your identity who you are today, yesterday, or tomorrow? Is it your physical appearance, your perceived identity, your feelings and thoughts, or your actions? If you change your attitudes, behaviour, or even your physical body (your cells are replacing themselves constantly), does it change who you are? In addition, is your perceived identity different from your real identity? Your feelings about yourself and your characteristics might be perceived differently by you than by others. You might identity yourself as a shy, introverted person, whereas others view you as a confident and extraverted person. The way in which we perceive our identity, however, determines how we experience life—does this mean that it is part of your identity or is your identity how others see you? As hard as it may seem to answer this rather philosophical question in the analogue world, it seems a little bit easier to address in the digital world, as we shall see. Nevertheless, as you may have discovered by now, identity is a lot more complex than you might have thought, bearing in mind that we have not yet embarked on questions about group identity and all those devices that you can connect to the internet: do they have an identity as well? As it happens, they do, but we will get back to that in a bit.

3.2.1 Attributes

As may be clear from the questions raised above, identity is built up of many different attributes, which are constantly changing and evolving in terms of priority and durability. Some attributes, such as your name and social security number, might stay with you for your entire life. For a number of reasons, a person might change their name one or more times. Others, such as your employee number, your student number, and your address or phone number, will come and go on a constant basis. Some attributes stay with you for several years or more, whereas others can be very short-lived, such as a username on a forum or website. Each of these attributes has different, uniquely identifiable characteristics and their combination makes up who you are, although you might perceive that differently.

One characteristic of most of these attributes is that they are digitally recorded, that is they are data. Your social security number, name, date of birth, or address is recorded in a government database, whereas your certificates and employee number are recorded by educational institutions or your work. Usernames, phone numbers, credit card details, and many more attributes are recorded by commercial, or not-for-profit, organisations such as your bank, your telecom provider, or your local supermarket. Even your physical appearances and attributes may have been recorded in your Electronic Health Records. As a result, your identity is scattered in thousands of pieces and stored across thousands of databases around the globe, over which you have only limited, if any, control. Some may only record a username, whereas others, such as the US Customs, might want your biometrics, social security numbers, address, and much more. This immediately reveals one of the challenges of identity; it is digitally distributed across the virtual world and who owns your identity is not always clear.

Not all attributes may be recorded in a database; your personality traits such as your sense of humour or your trustworthiness are known only to those who know you personally and are not usually recorded. They are a very important aspect of your identity. However, this is changing rapidly as online services such as Uber, Facebook, eBay, LinkedIn, or even Tinder record your sentiments, trustworthiness, or reputation, in large databases, and this reputation plays an increasingly important role if you want to use those services. For example, if your Uber, or Lyft, reputation score, as either a driver or a passenger, hits below a certain threshold, you can no longer use the service. As such, these companies have a powerful control mechanism over you and you have an incentive to behave, if you wish to continue to use the system. As it appears, with the possibility of recording every transaction and every interaction, reputation is rapidly increasing in importance.

3.2.2 Reputation

The first real known use case of online reputation does not, however, come from a service that many of you have used and, if you did, you probably would not want that information to be made public. We are talking about Silk Road, an anonymous website on the dark web that was used to trade illicit goods and services, including drugs, weapons, and even murders for hire. It was named after the trading routes linking the East and the West in the 13th century and, as with the original Silk Road, trade was the main activity at the platform. However, when you are dealing with illegal goods and services, you are dealing with criminals who, by their nature, are difficult to trust. With trade, trust is vital, even among criminals. If you ordered some drugs on the platform you needed to be sure that you got what you ordered and the seller needs to be certain that he or she got paid. In order to solve this problem, Silk Road used a reputation system, an eBay-style, peer review system [113], which allowed buyers and sellers to review the other party, and their goods or services, before a transaction would take place. The system incentivised good behaviour, which worked remarkably well until Silk Road was shut down in October 2013. In recent years, online reputation has gained traction and most of the well-known online services use some sort of reputation score: TripAdvisor rates hotels and destinations, Uber rates its passengers and drivers, AirBnB rates its hosts and guests, Netflix rates its movies and documentaries, Tinder rates its singles, and Glassdoor rates organisations. As such, reputation has become an important aspect of our lives, thereby incentivising good behaviour, and we foresee that this will only increase in the years to come, thanks to Blockchain, which will make reputation traceable and immutable.

However, it is not just individuals who have identities and a reputation to maintain. In a similar way, groups of people, that is organisations, companies, and institutions, also have an identity and a reputation. We call this brand identity and it is important to consider how you identify with brands and how organisations build their identity and reputation, as well as how they use your identity and reputation. Naturally, organisations also have a wide variety of attributes that make up their identity: their culture, the people who work there, the brand image, company symbols and icons, their leaders, the rules and regulations, the products and services offered, customer service, etc. Each of these attributes interacts with others to create a company identity and reputation that directly influence your identity and reputation when you deal with that company. Think of Apple; for many people Apple is like a religion [114]. People want to be identified by the products and they value the attributes that are linked to the Apple brand, such as *innovation, power to the people, passion, aspirations* [115]. In addition, Apple has a certain reputation, built up over decades of creating products and interacting with billions of customers. In fact, in 2017 Apple landed in 20th place in the Reputation Institute's Global RepTrak 100, a ranking that measures public perception of major companies around the world [116]. As such, organisations have a certain identity and reputation, which directly influence our own identity.

Finally, as already briefly mentioned, machines are also being ascribed an identity. This is especially relevant for the Internet of Things, where devices and machines are connected to the internet and can interact with other devices as well as people. As with people and organisations, machines have a variety of attributes as well as a reputation that make up its identity, for example, the type of device, such as a car; which version, such as model ABC; and the characteristics of the device, such as it is red, has four wheels, is electric, and three years old. In addition, the car has a reputation: is it responsive in the communication, does it talk to other actors on the road (in the case of a self-driving car), does it do what it says it will do (for example, it communicates that it will overtake a car, but, if it does not do that, this could cause trouble on the road)? All these aspects make up the reputation of the car and the higher the reputation the more likely other devices, and humans, will want to deal with the machine. Would you like to enter a self-driving taxi with a very low reputation? Probably not. When machines start interacting with each other, for example as part of a smart grid, which we discuss in Chapter 6, the price of, in this case a kilowatt, could go up or down based on the reputation of the device. Or to come back to the self-driving taxi example, a car with a very high reputation could become more expensive than a car with a lower reputation.

Machine identities can become very complicated. Consider that the typical car today has around 30,000 parts [117] and, if each part had an identity, with multiple attributes and a reputation, it would rapidly become extremely complicated. Of course, probably not all of these parts will be connected to the internet, yet, but it shows that machine identity and interactions between machines can very quickly become complicated, which is why Blockchain is important to ensure immutability and traceability among all those connected things.

3.2.3 Shadow reputation

A final aspect to identity, which becomes increasingly important due to the network economy in which we live, where people, organisations, and machines interact in a continuously changing network, is what we like to call *shadow reputation*. Within networks, reputation is made up by those with whom you interact (the people, companies, and machines, that is the actors in your network). Dealing with trustworthy actors increases your reputation and as such changes your identity. The opposite is also the case, dealing with untrustworthy actors, for example criminals, will negatively affect your reputation and as such your identity. You can compare this as 'having the wrong friends' and, when you become too closely linked to 'the wrong friends', it will directly affect how people view you and as such have an impact on your identity. This shadow reputation is intrinsically linked to who you are and how others identify you.

Shadow reputation not only influences people, but also affects organisations and machines, and is inherently connected to identity. An interesting example of this happened during the Global Financial Crisis (GFC) in 2008. Those people who worked at a bank at that time, and especially one of those banks that had to be bailed out, preferred not to talk about what they did and where they worked when they were at a party, because it would result in strange looks and difficult questions, and people would change their perception about them almost instantly. This is an example of shadow reputation: where the negative reputation of the bank at that time directly influenced how people perceived the bank's employees. Of course, what goes for people and organisations also goes for machines. If too many machines within a smart grid have a bad reputation, the reputation of the smart grid will go down. Or if a machine is connected to a machine infected with malware, it will directly affect the reputation of that device.

3.2.4 What is identity?

So, what is identity? We have discussed the different aspects of identity; not only do people have an identity, but also organisations and machines. Identity is made up of countless attributes, changing over time and always evolving. It is also made up of your reputation: your actions and behaviour towards others. Finally, your identity is made up of your shadow reputation; the reputation of other actors in your network that influence your reputation while you interact with them. The concepts of attributes, reputation, and shadow reputation are forever linked to identity and with the Blockchain they will become immutable, traceable, and as such verifiable. Figure 3.1 demonstrates the identity diagram. This changes everything, but, before we get there, there are some challenges to explore before we can move on to what identity on the Blockchain would mean.

3.3 Identity challenges

Let's go back to the examples of Nicole, Helen, and Axton who became victims of identity theft. Identity theft is only one of the many challenges within the current identity system that we have developed with each other. Our global identity system was developed in and for an analogue world and,

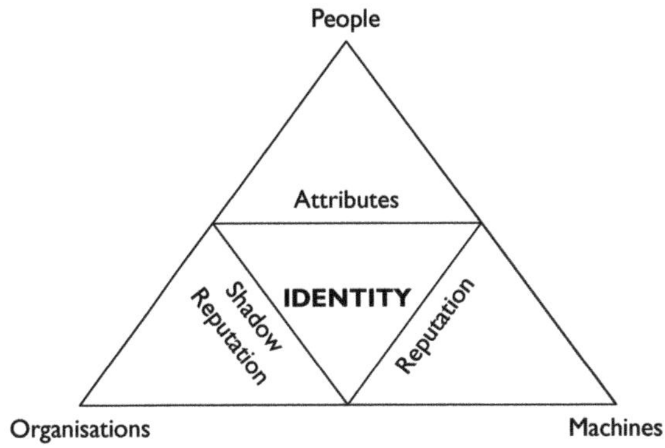

Figure 3.1 Identity diagram

although we have entered the digital world, our identity systems have not yet followed. The existing problems with identity relate to security (personal identifiable information is scattered around thousands of, often insecure, databases) and routines (the hotel where you are staying making a copy of your passport) resulting in the relative ease with which an identity can be stolen. In addition, with identity still residing in the analogue world, verification of identities is expensive and difficult and can easily result in flaws. On the other hand, online identity verification is hopelessly outdated, with many websites still allowing passwords such as *abcd1234* or *password*. Offline verification, meanwhile, requires all kinds of additional personal identifiable information, which are not relevant but, as there is no other way, inevitable. For example, when purchasing alcohol at a shop, your name really is not relevant to determining whether you are legally allowed to buy alcohol. Finally, the biggest challenge of them all is the 1.5 billion people without a proper identity, who as a result of this do not have access to banking, job security, education, and other human rights. If we wish to solve some of the Wicked Problems as discussed in this book, all humans should have a personal, verifiable identity. Let's discuss each of these challenges briefly:

3.3.1 Identity theft

Identity theft is a serious problem and it exists in a wide variety of forms. The examples of Nicole (criminal identity theft), as well as of Helen and Axton (both financial identity theft), are the most serious forms of identity theft, affecting the victims over long periods of time and costing the global economy billions of dollars. However, there are also other forms of identity theft including grave robbing, social media fraud, medical identity theft, synthetic identity theft, tax identity theft, and commercial identity theft [118–120]:

- Criminal identity theft: your identity is stolen to commit a certain crime, in the case of Nicole McCabe the murder of a high-profile person;
- Financial identity theft: your credit card or bank details are stolen through phishing or skimming, and the criminal will charge purchases to the limit of the credit available on those cards or steal money from your bank account;
- Grave robbing: millions of dead people have their identities stolen and the thieves use this to apply for credit cards, credit lines, or other products. Often the results can be devastating for the family members of the deceased;
- Social media fraud: millions of people put personal identifiable information on social media networks: phone numbers, addresses, dates of birth, school names, pet names, or even pictures of a newly received credit card. When this information is visible to all, it makes it very easy for criminals to steal your identity;
- Medical identity theft: criminals use your medical information to apply for 'free' medical care, which could result in financial damage for the victim and a corrupted medical record;
- Synthetic identity theft: one of the most sophisticated forms of identity theft, where criminals use your social security number, combine it with fake information and create a new identity;
- Tax identity theft: this is the works of people like Nakeisha, who use stolen personal details to make fraudulent tax refund claims;
- Commercial identity theft: using fake identities to obtain information or to bill for services or products that have not been delivered. This happens to all types of organisations and, as recently as April 2017, Facebook and Google admitted being the victims of a $US100 million commercial phishing scam [121].

Identity theft can have serious consequences for the victims, ranging from financial losses, having difficulty getting credit, having difficulty getting jobs, to experiencing stress and not being able to get rid of fake records. Unfortunately, it seems identity theft is becoming easier. Personal identifiable information is scattered around the web, across thousands of databases and too often organisations make unnecessary copies of your identity. In Australia, for example, many bars and registered clubs require patrons to produce a government-issued identity document, which is then scanned, before they allow you in. In addition, many hotels still require your passport upon check-in and then they take (digital) copies of it before they hand over the key. In the European Union, hotels are even required to collect personal identifiable information such as names, nationality, and the state-issued identity number, enabling law enforcement to cross-check for wanted individuals, criminals, or missing persons [122]. It is unclear how this information is stored, for how long, and, more importantly, if it is stored securely.

The more details a criminal can obtain from a potential victim, the easier it becomes to steal their identity and use it in a variety of ways. Identity theft is still a major problem and will remain so until we have brought identity into the 21st century.

3.3.2 *Identity verification*

Verifying your identity can be as simple as showing an ID card or a laborious and time-consuming task, involving multiple documents from a variety of organisations, as well as verification questions to prove who you are. Verifying your identity happens all the time, online and offline. 'In the physical world, there are fairly accepted ways to verify who you are, like a driver's licence or a passport', says Cameron Gough, digital delivery centre general manager at Australia Post. 'But in the digital world we don't have this. So, . . . organisations have a trade-off between fraud and friction, and convenience. They would love to decrease the level of fraud but usually the mechanisms available to do that result in an increase in inconvenience or friction for customers' [123]. Organisations such as banks, telcos, social media websites, or online retailers need to verify your identity when you want to do business with them, often because of regulation such as Know Your Customer or Client (KYC). KYC is the process that financial institutions, in particular, need to have in place in order to verify the identity of customers to prevent money-laundering activities or even financing of terrorism. It consists of multiple checks and the production of specific documents. Every time you open up an account at a new bank, you will have to go through the same process again, even if you have already been verified by a different institution. KYC requires the financial institutions to know who you are and what your activities are, and to assess money-laundering risks [124]. However, banks are not the only institutions that employ KYC; other companies use it to make sure that they deal with legitimate persons or companies. In recent years, KYC has been expanded to KYCC, or Know Your Customer's or Client's Customer or Client. It takes the KYC requirements to a higher level, because it requires knowledge of whom your customers are dealing with, what their sources of funds are, and their risk of money laundering. The only way to comply is to demand proof of the legitimacy of the funds and transactions. As a result, as of 11 May 2018 Customer Due Diligence (CDD) Final Rule will come into effect in the USA. In June 2017, the 4th AML Directive went into effect in Europe. Both regulations require companies to continuously monitor customers and customers' customers to mitigate suspicious transactions, risks, and financial crime [125]. As you can imagine, complying with these regulations will be time-consuming and expensive, although not complying can be a lot more expensive due to heavy fines and reputational harm.

Identity verification is so engrained in our lives that we might not even see how outdated the system of identity verification is. Despite all those safety measures such as KYC and KYCC (and in the future KYCCC?), verification of identity is still not secure, as evidenced by the scale of global identity theft and the ease with which identity can be faked or purchased. For example, the price of a fake US passport on the dark web starts at just $US938 [126]. In addition, the more companies have to store customer and customers' customer data, the higher the risks become that such data will be stolen by hackers, because not all companies will ensure the highest level of security. At the same time, people constantly have to provide their details on the web and remember details such as usernames and passwords. As a result, people often use very simple passwords, increasing the risks even more.

As providing your identity at so many different places has become so normal to us, we forget how not normal it is to provide your identity at all those places. After all, if you are buying alcohol at a shop, there is absolutely no need for the shop owner to know your name, or even your age. All he or she is interested in is if you are above or below the legal age to purchase alcohol. This is just a Boolean expression, which results in a Boolean value, that is in a value that is either true or false. Nothing more. Why then does the shop owner need to see your government-issued identity, with a lot more personal identifiable information than necessary, and as such potentially breach your privacy? The answer is simple and disturbing: because there is no other solution available, at this moment. As may be clear by now, identity verification offers plenty of challenges and the current system is not built for the 21st century.

3.3.3 Identity exclusion

Identity theft and identity verification are two big challenges related to identity, but the biggest challenge that we are facing is the identity exclusion that millions of people face every day. As it is necessary to show proof of your identity to participate in social and economic activity, not possessing one can have deeply damaging consequences for individuals. Yet, around 1.5 billion people, or 20% of the global population, does not have any proof of an officially recognised identity. Most of these people live in developing countries and are already dealing with multiple other Wicked Problems. Not having an identity only increases these problems, because it prevents them from joining the modern economy, to vote, and to have access to basic services such as opening a bank account or having a telephone subscription. In addition, the 'unidentified' face increased human trafficking risks, because they are invisible before the law and as such cannot claim any rights. Although having an officially recognised identity is a basic human right recognised by the United Nations' Universal Declaration on Human rights, too many people still live without one.

Apart from the personal problems associated with not having an officially documented identity, not having up-to-date population data prevents (local) governments from developing and executing proper social services.

According to ID2020.org, a public/private partnership for solving the problem of identity exclusion, over 100 countries do not have functional civil registration and vital statistics systems [127]. As a result, approximately 230 million children are not registered at birth and as such officially do not exist. Not having accurate population statistics prevents business, governments, and non-government organisations (NGOs) from conducting frictionless business. It precludes proper planning and budgeting if you do not know who and how many people you are dealing with. For countries that already face multiple other Wicked Problems, this poses a real challenge and solving those challenges often starts with solving the identity problem. Only people who have proof of their identity can open a bank account, vote, and participate in the economy, thereby stimulating the economy and creating a better world for themselves and the country as a whole.

One country that is working hard on giving all their citizens an identity is India. In 2009 the government launched the project AadHaar, which is the world's largest biometric identity system. The objective of the system is to provide every Indian with a government-issued identity card, linked to their biometric details and with a 12-digit number based on their biometrics and demographics. As of April 2017, 1.133 billion people had been enrolled, or 99% of Indian citizens aged over 18 years. It is the world's most sophisticated identity platform and has a capacity to enrol 1 million people per day [128]. This proof of identity enables Indian citizens to have easy, online, and portable access to government services, and the system is linked, through Application Programming Interfaces (APIs), with other, non-governmental services such as banks. As such, it enables those organisations to comply with KYC. AadHaar is a great example of how a government brought their identity system into the 21st century, although, as is always the case with projects of this scale, various parties have their concerns about whether the design is secure and private.

Despite projects such as AadHaar, millions of people still exist without a formal, government-issued proof of identity, and as such face difficulties in their lives. The challenges that we face with identity prevent us from solving many of the Wicked Problems discussed in this book. It is therefore time to upgrade our identity system to the 21st century and bring identity to the Blockchain. This will not only help solve problems such as poverty or fraud, but also enable organisations to create better products and services, without having to invade their customers' privacy.

3.4 Identity on the Blockchain

Although AadHaar has been built for the 21st century, it is not based on the Blockchain and as such all the problems that currently exist with identity still remain. Blockchain offers enormous potential to solve our identity crisis. Having 'an identity on the Blockchain' will make it immutable, traceable, and verifiable, thereby significantly reducing the possibilities for identity theft, making identity verification seamless, and giving power back to the user. Building a digital identity on the Blockchain would act as a digital watermark, similar to the way that traditional identity documents such as passports have a watermark to verify the document's authenticity [129]. This digital watermark then enables any organisation with access to the Blockchain to check identity on every transaction, in real time. If you can check someone's identity on every transaction, this would eliminate the possibility of fraud. As such, enabling identity on the Blockchain is a $US4.2 trillion opportunity, that is the global annual cost of fraud, according to research from the University of Portsmouth [129]. Contrary to today, verification of someone's identity would be at almost no cost, because the customer would simply 'lend' their digital identity when necessary, without revealing any information that is not necessary for that particular transaction.

However, before we delve further into this topic, the first thing we need to make clear is that putting your identity on the Blockchain does not mean putting personal identifiable information, such as your passport, social security number, or any other attribute, on the Blockchain. Blockchain is used to manage keys, anchor data records in time, and make them immutable, as well as to discover those records when necessary. It is, and should never be, used to store personal identifiable information and the reason is simple. Linking personal identifiable information to, for example, coins means that information will remain there indefinitely and becomes always traceable. If you were to do so, it would mean that you would use one or only a few coins to link those attributes, which would immediately expose it to discovery of correlations among them, even if you would not be able to decrypt the data. In addition, as we already established earlier, your attributes constantly evolve over time, so that is not something that you should want to be immutable because attributes that are legal today can become illegal tomorrow. Instead, if we want to put identity on the Blockchain, we should remove all data related to the person and store only the token on the Blockchain, and allow the user to store their personal identifiable information on their own device of choice, which will probably be a smartphone or something of that sort. As a result, consumers will get back control of their own identity. Meanwhile, attributes scattered across thousands of databases will become a thing of the past and the unidentified can obtain a digital identity, simply by collecting and controlling their attributes, reputation, and shadow reputation using a blockchain.

How does that work? In order to explain this we first need to clarify something about Public Key Infrastructure, because it is intrinsically linked to identity on the Blockchain and, to do so, we have to go back in time to the 1970s. In 1976, two Stanford mathematicians, Whitfield Diffie and Martin Hellman, discovered an advanced mathematical relationship called asymmetric cryptography. They identified a relationship between large prime numbers, where data encrypted with one key, could be decrypted by its paired key. At the same time, in 1978, three other mathematicians named Ron **R**ivest, Adi **S**hamir, and Leonard **A**dleman identified the same relationship and published it as the

RSA algorithm [130]. They were able to monetise this algorithm and build a company around it (RSA Corporation), which was eventually sold to EMC and now belongs to Dell.

Asymmetric cryptography means that two keys, a public and a private key, are mathematically related to each other. This relationship means that any data encrypted by one key (public key) can be decrypted only by the other (private key) and vice versa. It is impossible to encrypt data with a public key and use another public key to decrypt that data [49]. As a result, you can use a key pair to identify the owner of a certain digital asset. As the public key is publically available, any data encrypted with a related private key can be decrypted only by the corresponding public key. Hence, if Alice encrypts a file with her private key and sends it to Bob, who uses the corresponding public key, he can be certain that Alice was the one who encrypted the file. The other way is also possible: if Bob wants to send Alice a private message, he encrypts the file with the public key that is mathematically linked to Alice's private key. If Alice receives the message, she is the only one who can open the message using her private key. Therefore, it is vital that she keeps her private key really private. It works like a mailbox, where everyone has a key to deposit a letter to that mailbox, but only one person has the right key to open the mailbox and take the mail out.

Since then, Public Key Infrastructure has been widely deployed. Almost anything that you do online uses the Public Key Infrastructure, from sending emails to visiting websites (a website is encrypted using the Public Key Infrastructure if it has an SSL certificate and the website shows https). It means that we can be certain that the data that is sent between the user and the server is not interrupted. Public Private Key Infrastructure is also used to ensure authenticity of a certain document. This is done using the Hash Algorithm as discussed in Chapter 2. Hash Algorithms are special mathematical formulae that will turn any input into a unique fixed-length output of numbers and letters. Changing the input will completely change the output. If you want to secure a message or data file, you hash the data and then encrypt it using the Public Key Infrastructure. As a result, the identity of the sender can be proved and the authenticity of the data file verified, revealing whether or not the file has been tampered with. In the traditional and centralised internet, Public Key Infrastructure relies on centralised trusted third parties, called Certificate Authorities (CAs). These CAs issue, revoke, and restore the key pairs, for every stakeholder involved. Apart from the fact that these are centralised companies exerting a lot of control, hackers can potentially spoof user identities, perform man-in-the-middle attacks, and thereby intercept communications [131]. As of May 2017, there are several research projects working on decentralised version of the Public Key Infrastructure, each taking a slightly different approach. Of course, there is a lot more to cryptography in terms of technicalities, but this is enough to know. The combination of Public Key Infrastructure and Hash Algorithms is used extensively on the Blockchain and is, more or less, what enables identity on the Blockchain.

Another concept that we need to cover is tokenisation, before we can tie it all together. Every Blockchain uses tokens to help validate transactions and create the blocks, which are subsequently chained together. A token on a blockchain can mean several things. Either they are referred to currency tokens, such as bitcoin (BTC), or they are referred to asset tokens. Currency tokens are the most well-known tokens, simply because the first crypto token ever, Bitcoin, is a currency token. A currency token is a medium of value exchange, and the value of the token is determined by supply and demand. Contrary to fiat money, which is backed by gold, currency tokens are only backed by the demand in the market. The other type of token is 'Asset Tokens', which are claims to an underlying asset that belongs to a certain issuer or user. They can be best compared with an 'I Owe You' (IOU) when you, for example in the old days, could bring gold to a goldsmith who would write an IOU, which you could then trade. Anyone who owns that IOU could go to the goldsmith and trade it for the original gold. Asset-backed tokens are the digital equivalent of an IOU and it enables you to track a certain asset as it moves from person to person. Once you have 'tokenised' an asset (either tangible or digital), you can track its movements. New digital tokens are created every day to track new assets from diamonds to music to art. Asset-backed tokens can be traded and eventually someone can trade it back to the original asset [132]. Apart from physical items such as paintings or digital assets such as music, you can also tokenise an identity attribute, since it is also an asset, albeit an intangible one. However, instead of transferring the token from person to person, you 'lend' it to the other party and retain ownership of the token. We also have security tokens and utility tokens. A security token is a token that allows the owner of that token a (future) stake in a company, while a utility token is a token that has a use case and has not been developed as an investment. Most of today's Blockchain startups aim to develop their token as a use case.

So, how can we put identity on the Blockchain? There are a variety of cases of use and different start-ups have developed different solutions. We show only one generic solution to explain how identity on the Blockchain works. Please note that, in this example, any messages that are sent between different parties are, at all times, encrypted and secure (to ensure authenticity and that the message has not been tampered with), precisely as email works nowadays:

1 If you wish to store an attribute (or a reputation or even shadow reputation for that matter) on a Blockchain, you use a combination of tokenisation and encryption. First you create the attribute. This can be done by the user, who we can call Alice or by an organisation, who we can call Gov. Alice can create an attribute, for example *female*, and Gov can create an attribute, for example '*Is allowed to drive a car*' or '*Social Security Number is 71231236*'. Of course, an attribute created by an official institution is more trusted than one created by the user.
2 Second, the attribute is tokenised, that is turned into a random string of numbers and letters. The Key Value pair that links the attribute to the

token is either stored by Alice (if she created it) or stored by Gov on a public ledger, encrypted, and time-stamped (if Gov created it). Notice that this ledger stores only unidentifiable attributes: '*Is allowed to drive a car*' does not say anything about *who* is allowed to drive a car. In addition, Gov can add messages such as *Expired* or *Revoked.*

3 The token is encrypted by the actor who created it, with the respective key to enable authentication.
4 The encrypted token is time stamped.
5 The time-stamped, encrypted token is added to the Blockchain, making it immutable, verifiable, and traceable.
6 Gov sends Alice the encrypted token + the pointer where the Key Value can be found.
7 Alice receives the encrypted token + pointer and encrypts both with her public key. She then stores it at a location of choice, which will probably be on her smartphone as well as in the cloud. If Alice were the one who created the attribute, step six would of course not be necessary.
8 Organisation 2, let's call it the Police, wants to verify something, whether this is a certain attribute or a Boolean value of that attribute (True/False). For example, the Police want to know Alice's Social Security Number and whether or not Alice is allowed to drive.
9 The Police determines the level of trust that is required. In this case, Alice herself stating that she is allowed to drive will not be sufficient. The Police want to know from Gov if she is allowed to drive.
10 The Police send a request to Alice. This request can be done using a QR code that Alice scans with her smartphone. Alice verifies the authenticity of the request and checks that the message has not been tampered with.
11 Alice looks up the respective encrypted token + pointer in her smartphone. If the Police wants multiple attributes, Alice sends multiple tokens + pointers. She sends this message to the Police.
12 The Police goes to where the information is stored, in this case Gov, and uses the public key of Gov to decrypt the token, to ensure that the token is authentic. The Police sends the request to Gov who can do two things:
    a Gov sends the encrypted attribute, for example '*Social Security Number is 71231236*', to the Police. The Police now has Alice's Social Security Number and can link them together;
    b Gov checks the request against the attribute. If the request is '*Can Alice drive*', Gov will return *True* and send it to the Police.

The entire process from request to receiving the attribute is likely to take only one or two seconds. Enabling identity on the Blockchain ensures that the user, Alice, remains in full control of who receives what information about her and her identity remains protected. This is called a *self-sovereign identity*. Even if hackers were to steal all Key Value pairs from Gov, the information would be useless because they cannot link it to persons, so there is no problem with storing the information in a public ledger. In addition, whether Alice is a person or a *Thing* really does not matter. The connected device performs the same actions as Alice would do. As such, identity on the Blockchain has many advantages, which we turn to next.

3.5 Advantages of self-sovereign identity

The advantages of having such a self-sovereign identity system are enormous, as much for a consumer or organisation as for a machine. It will make identity personal, private, persistent, portable, and protected (let's call it the 5Ps of self-sovereign identity—see Figure 3.2) and as such protects consumers, organisations, and machines from identity theft and fraud.

Personal: It will make identity personal, because you control your own data and who gets access to certain attributes. Even more, you can have many different attributes and for different platforms you can combine different attributes, effectively creating multiple identities for different organisations. For Organisation 1 you use Attributes A, B, and C, whereas for Organisation 2 you use Attributes D, E, and F. Self-sovereign identity allows you to create purely personal identities.

Private: It makes identity private, because organisations no longer have access to personal identifiable information that is not relevant. Going back to the supermarket, when you want to purchase alcohol, the supermarket

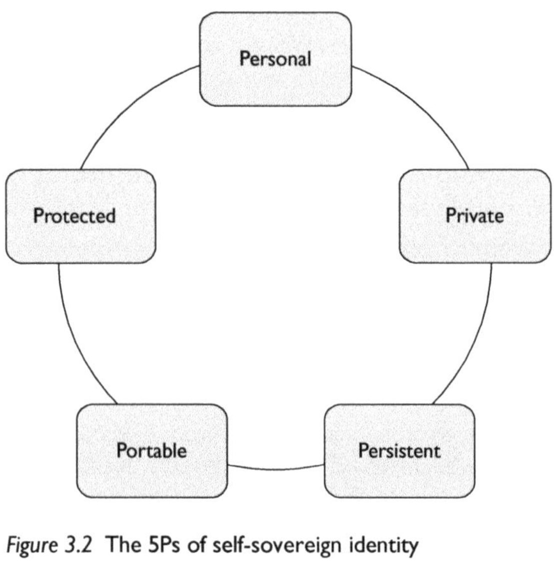

Figure 3.2 The 5Ps of self-sovereign identity

needs to receive only a True or False value on whether or not you are allowed to. Any other information is irrelevant. In addition, if they want an age, the more personal date of birth is not required. Of course, you could state that, taking your dad's phone would solve the issue, but a government-approved and -provided image, securely stored on your phone could be matched to your face using the camera's phone and facial recognition in real time. If the two do not match, a False value will be returned.

Persistent: Third, identity needs to be persistent, which means that an identity and its corresponding attributes should last forever, or at least as long as the user wants. This must not contradict the 'right to be forgotten', because a user should be able to remove attributes whenever wanted [133]. Self-sovereign identity removes the possibility of centralised organisations, such as Google, Facebook, or LinkedIn, simply deleting a user and brings that power back to the user.

Portable: Next, identity on the Blockchain will be portable. If Alice, for example, was a seller on Amazon and had built a great reputation, and as such was a trusted identity, that identity would be worth a lot to her. However, if Alice decided to leave Amazon and move to eBay, normally she would lose her reputation and have to start from scratch. Using this system, eBay can verify at Amazon that Alice had a great reputation and link that to Alice on eBay, making identity portable, verifiable, and in Alice's full control. In addition, compliance with KYC processes becomes a lot easier. Once a user has been verified for the first time by a bank, that information can be moved to another bank, without exchanging any private information, making dealing with such processes a lot simpler and cheaper.

Protected: Finally, self-sovereign identity is protected and highly secure. As the ledgers of organisations store only non-identifiable attributes, it does not matter whether the ledger gets hacked and the attributes stolen. As such, the information that criminals can steal is useless to them, because a string of numbers without any other details does not mean anything and cannot be used for anything. Therefore, self-sovereign identities are highly secure. An additional advantage of self-sovereign identity is that it removes the need for usernames and passwords to login on websites. It would solve the problem of passwords and usernames. You could create unique usernames and complicated passwords, which basically are an attribute linked to your identity. These attributes are stored encrypted on the user's device. If the user needs to login on a platform, the user scans a QR code which is a request to verify the user, after which the user is logged in.

Of course, the *5Ps of self-sovereign identity* apply not only to human actors, but also to organisations, machines or connected devices. In the world of the

Internet of Things, the connected device, or machine, will control who gets access to its identity data (*Personal*); the device only has to show relevant identity information when being verified and not all (*Private*); its corresponding attributes should last forever, unless the device decides otherwise (*Persistent*); it should be able to move its identity from one network to another (*Portable*); and a self-sovereign-connected device is highly secure (*Protected*).

3.6 Blockchain and your social media identity

The need for a new identity system that empowers consumers became very clear in March 2018, with the Cambridge Analytica/Facebook scandal. Those who value their privacy should think carefully about their usage of Facebook as well as other social media networks. For example, Cambridge Analytica is the data mining and data analysis company that played a pivotal role in the US Presidential Election of 2016, the Brexit vote, and many other political races. Behind the company are the key figures of President Trump, including Steve Bannon, Trump's former strategic adviser, and Robert Mercer, founder of the Government Accountability Institute, which uses the dark web and bots to denigrate political opponents.

In 2014, the company used personal information obtained without users' authorisation to develop a highly effective system to target individual US voters. Under the pretence of academic research, they harvested 87 million profiles without the users' approval, and then used that data to influence the US election. It is a privacy breach on an unprecedented scale and shows that Facebook's attempts to protect their users are not working.

Scandals like these show that we need to rethink our (online) identity system, and Blockchain offers us a chance to give back the control of our online social media profiles and data that we create. To achieve this, we would need to delete existing social media networks such as Facebook and re-build them from scratch. In a world with decentralised social media networks, your online presence becomes yours again and, with that, your online presence becomes private, protected, and portable:

3.6.1 A private decentralised social media profile

Currently, your social media profile is anything but private. Facebook determines how others can view your profile and how advertisers can use your data. Despite extensive privacy settings, the company constantly creates new ways to breach your privacy, with the latest being their creepy facial recognition option that tags you in photos that people upload even if they do not tag you. Although Facebook announced that this setting would be *off* by default, when we checked the Facebook privacy settings recently, it was *on* by default. You might want to check your settings.

A decentralised social media network, on the other hand, would ensure complete privacy of your personal details. The company developing the decentralised social media network will simply have no option to use your personal information without your consent as your data will be encrypted and only you will have the key. As a consequence, within a decentralised social media network, you own your own social media presence and you determine who gets access to what data.

3.6.2 A protected decentralised social media profile

The Cambridge Analytica/Facebook privacy breach shows that your data on a centralised social media network is anything but protected. Once hackers have access to the centralised server, they have access to all the data on that server. A self-sovereign identity is, however, a protected identity, because your personal data is not stored on a centralised server for any hacker to access or any analytics firm to harvest. Instead, your tokenised data is stored decentralised on millions of servers.

As decentralised social media networks store only non-identifiable attributes, it does not matter whether or not the database gets hacked and the attributes stolen. As a result, the information that criminals can steal is useless to them, because a string of numbers without any other details does not mean anything and cannot be used for anything. Therefore, blockchain enables a protected decentralised social media profile that is owned by you.

3.6.3 A portable decentralised social media profile

If you have used Facebook for a long time and you are an active user, you have created a massive portfolio of thoughts, images, conversations, videos, and other pieces of content. Although you can download your data file, you cannot take it somewhere else. This is a problem of any social media network currently out there. As a result, if you wish to leave Facebook due to the existing scandals, you will have to start from scratch at a new platform. To us, this does not make sense, because it is your data and your content. Why should that not be portable to another platform if you wished to leave the social media network?

Fortunately, within a decentralised social media network, your data and content are yours and you will be able to take it to wherever you want. When you have the ability to leave a network at any time, it forces the social media network to deliver features that benefit you rather than the advertiser or the shareholder.

3.7 Disadvantages of self-sovereign identity

There are not many disadvantages of self-sovereign identity because almost any system would be better than the current model. However, the main disadvantage of a completely new identity system would be the cost of building the infrastructure, resulting in an initial hiccup in the set-up. In addition, it would be a complex infrastructure to build and implement, but, as we shall see, multiple organisations are already working on solving this. Another disadvantage of a self-sovereign identity is that the average user might not want to deal with storing private keys on a smartphone and/or in the cloud. This is something intangible that consumers are not used to. In addition, all too often smartphones are stolen and, if the smartphone is not secured with biometrics, the thief can access the encrypted identity information. If the user had not created a back-up in the cloud, he or she has a serious issue. The way around these two issues is to always require users to use biometric security on their phone and a secure back-up of the identity information on the smartphone.

3.8 Challenges of self-sovereign identity

As the disadvantages already show, it will be quite a challenge to develop and globally implement a self-sovereign identity system. There are four main challenges, which focus on adoption, governance, regulation and scalability:

> **Adoption:** Self-sovereign identity gives responsibility to the consumer to digitally secure their identity. Of course, as discussed, organisations should build-in safety measures such as requiring biometrics and back-ups. Nevertheless, it will take a dramatic change in how consumers deal with identity, moving from having a tangible document, that is a passport or driver's licence, to an intangible and incomprehensible string of numbers. Change is always difficult and such a dramatic change will require time and patience from organisations and governments, as well as a gradual move to self-sovereign identity.
>
> **Governance:** Currently, companies make billions of dollars by leveraging private consumer data. It is unlikely that they are willing to give up this treasure trove without a fight. In addition, when the new system is built, we do not want a few commercial organisations running the infrastructure, or nothing meaningful will have changed or improved. It is therefore important that global self-sovereign identity is run and governed by a global, not-for-profit institution similar to how we run DNS, TCP/IP, and domains online (ICANN). Development of these institutions requires global consensus and will therefore take time to achieve. Finally, we need governance to prevent individuals from selling (part of) their identity to others. Selling (part of) your identity will become as simple as transferring your private key and this should be prevented at all times.
>
> **Regulation:** Whenever you deal with a global product you deal with global standards and regulations. Self-sovereign identity can offer tremendous

benefits if it is implemented globally across countries. Meeting the wide range of global regulations and conforming to all the different jurisdictions will be a massive challenge which we need to overcome. However, only when a self-sovereign identity has the same rights and can be operated across the globe can we truly benefit from its potential.

Scalability: Finally, as mentioned in Chapter 2, Blockchain has some challenges that need to be solved, including its scalability. The technology is still very nascent and—as discussed earlier—the Bitcoin Blockchain can handle only a few transactions per second. However, when you have billions of attributes linked to 7.5 billion people, 100 million organisations, 50 billion connected machines, and 1 trillion sensors, it becomes rather big quite quickly. In these circumstances, we face a massive challenge to prepare the infrastructure for the massive amount of data and transactions that will occur once we have a global self-sovereign identity system in place.

The technology of Blockchain is still emerging and over time these challenges will probably be overcome. Over the past hundreds of years, humankind has been very flexible and innovative in adopting and adapting to new technologies. It will not happen overnight, but a global self-sovereign identity system will eventually become a reality.

3.9 Self-sovereign identity applications

Self-sovereign identities are still in development and there are many start-ups working on solutions to bring identity to the Blockchain. Each solution is slightly different from the others and has a different approach in terms of tokenisation, hashing, and encryption. These start-ups focus on digital identities related to passports, birth/wedding/death certificates, e-residency, online account logins, etc. Some of the pioneers in digital identity are as follows, in alphabetical order[2]:

2WAY.IO: a peer-to-peer reputation and identity platform that puts the user back in control. They offer services, which are blockchain agnostic, to organisations looking to implement an identity solution—http://2way.io/;

Banqu App: a Fintech company focusing on economic identities and extreme poverty. They offer a secure, portable digital identity that maintains transaction history through a proprietary blockchain-based platform for the poorest people—www.banquapp.com/;

BitNation: a platform company that offers the same services as traditional governments, but based on the Blockchain. They call themselves the first decentralised borderless voluntary nation—https://bitnation.co/;

BlockAuth: BlockAuth is developing a framework to verify user authenticity while also enabling an easy-to-integrate OpenID authentication system—http://blockauth.org/;

Bron Tech: a blockchain-based identity platform that aims to redefine the interrelationship of people, personal data, and money—http://bron.tech/.

Cambridge Blockchain: a start-up that aims to put control of personal identity data back in the hands of the end-user. The platform focuses on the financial industry and enables them to comply with KYC regulations—http://cambridge-blockchain.com/;

Civic: an identity platform that uses identity verification and protection tools to provide business and individuals with control over their identity—www.civic.com/;

HYPR: they build an identity and security platform for the Internet of Things (IoT), to secure users across mobile, desktop, and IoT systems. They use tokenisation to secure private keys using biometrics—www.hypr.com/;

KYC-Chain: a platform using Distributed Ledger Technology to enable users to manage their digital identity securely, while offering organisations a reliable and easy way to comply with KYC regulations—http://kyc-chain.com/;

Procivis: a start-up that aims to develop and offer an 'e-government as a service' solution, where digital identity empowers citizens and gives them control over their identity data—http://procivis.ch/;

ShoCard: they are building a digital identity platform to protect consumer privacy and make it easy to use. It is built on a public blockchain data layer and, as such, they do not store any data or keys—https://shocard.com/;

Sovrin: a self-sovereign identity blockchain developed initially by Evernym, who have since then open sourced the platform. They aim to build the missing layer for secure identity on the internet—www.sovrin.org/;

Sphere: a next-generation social network, separate from big corporations, where users are in full control—https://sphere.social/;

Tradle: they are building a global trust provisioning network to offer KYC on the Blockchain, which aims to lower KYC costs and improve customer experience—https://tradle.io/;

Traity: this offers a way to build, protect, and manage your reputation, which is backed up on the Blockchain. They aim to be the credit score of the future—https://traity.com/;

UniquID: this has created a decentralised, blockchain-based identify access management platform for connected things using private key storage and biometrics security—http://uniquid.com/;

uPort: they aim to develop an open-source, self-sovereign, blockchain identity system based on Ethereum; they partnered with Microsoft and it is developed by ConsenSys—www.uport.me/.

These start-ups, and many more, aim to develop solutions around identity for all industries. It can be foreseen that any industry can benefit from digital identities that are verified using the Blockchain. However, three early adopters are most advanced in the development of applications for digital identity: the financial services industry, healthcare, and government.

3.9.1 Financial services industry

Already, the financial services industry is investigating how Blockchain, or distributed ledgers, can be applied to improve a sector that is known for using legacy hardware and software. If you accept that banks, in their purest form, exist to facilitate financial transactions, it is easy to see how Blockchain could make banks redundant. There are multiple benefits for the financial services industry through use of Distributed Ledger Technologies and digital identities. Traditionally, the financial services industry is known for its legacy systems and it is, therefore, not surprising that the it has embraced Blockchain to improve many of their outdated systems. It will also go a long way to saving a lot of money (which, not surprisingly, might be the main reason for them moving to the Blockchain). Using a distributed ledger, banks can trade faster and cheaper and become more efficient, among other things by improving their KYC processes. Banks ignore the Blockchain at their own peril.

Transactions can be completed in minutes or seconds, whereas, currently, settlements can take up to a week. This is due to long and complex internal and interbank processes. Often the settling of transactions, especially large transactions across countries, can take three to seven days. With Blockchain, settlements become user optimised, which will save a significant amount of time and money, for both parties involved. Blockchain will remove the need for a lot of middle office and back office staff at banks, as transactions settle instantly. Digital identities are essential if banks want to truly benefit from Distributed Ledger Technologies.

One of the main features of Blockchain is that it removes the need for a trusted intermediary and makes peer-to-peer transactions possible. When Blockchain is applied to the financial services industry, it could render obsolete the fee-charging intermediaries such as custodian banks (those that transfer money between different banks) or clearing houses (those vouching for counterparty's credit positions). As such, Blockchain offers better capital optimisation, due to a significant reduction in operational costs for banks. In addition, when banks share a Blockchain, the total costs of that Blockchain and the surrounding ecosystem might be higher than the individual costs of managing transactions at a bank. However, the costs are shared among all participating banks so there is a significant cost reduction. Finally, according to research by Accenture, financial reporting costs could drop 70% due to optimised data quality, transparency, and internal controls. Compliance costs could drop 30–50% due to transparency and better auditability of transactions, as well as improved and more efficient KYC processes. Finally, business operation costs could drop 50% due to the reduction and removal of unnecessary processes [134]. When transactions are settled almost instantly, it removes a significant part of the risk of a counterparty not meeting its obligations (otherwise a substantial expense for banks).

When banks and financial institutions start using smart contracts, this will improve contractual term performance, because smart contracts execute automatically according to certain pre-set conditions. Smart contracts and digital identity are a powerful combination offering a lot of new possibilities for banks. It is important that those smart contracts are firmly rooted in law and comply with any regulatory provisions, across jurisdictions, as required. As a result of these requirements, R3CEV had to tailor-make the smart contracts within their distributed ledger platform. Particularly complex financial asset transactions can benefit from Blockchain, due to automatic settlement with smart contracts under the control of an incorruptible set of business rules.

It is vital for the financial services industry to innovate and investigate how digital identities, smart contracts, and distributed ledgers can improve their products and services. If the incumbents do not change their offers and innovate, newcomers will disrupt their business. We have already seen this with a variety of Blockchain Fintech start-ups that are building new ways to handle your finances. It is time for financial institutions to change and benefit from the possibilities of distributed and decentralised networks, technologies, and digital identities.

3.9.2 Healthcare

Healthcare records always ensure a healthy debate in almost any country. After all, nothing is more personal than your health details, recorded in a database, which is prone to attacks and privacy breaches. This prospect scares a lot of people. However, the benefits of digital healthcare records that are shared among important stakeholders such as doctors, hospitals and pharmacies could save many lives and make healthcare a lot cheaper. In addition, anonymised healthcare records, or even Genome data, can contribute to improving healthcare, resulting in better medicines and treatments. Already, it is possible to analyse your genome data for around $US1400 [135] and the cost is likely to drop in the future. Each sequenced genome produces roughly around 100 GB of data [136]. When you unleash big data analytics and advanced artificial intelligence on to these large datasets, it will offer invaluable information for creating better healthcare. However, your genome data is as personal as it gets and, when linked to your identity, you want to make sure that it is secure and only the right people have access to it. This is where Blockchain and self-sovereign identity come in: enabling researchers and healthcare specialists to use your genome data, without breaching security and your privacy.

Already, multiple companies are investigating the potential of combining healthcare data with Blockchain, including Google's DeepMind, which seems very promising. In March 2017, Google announced that they wanted to apply their advanced deep learning technology to UK healthcare data to enable patients, doctors, hospitals, and the National Health Service, combined with blockchain technology, to track personal healthcare data [137]. According to DeepMind co-founder, Mustafa Suleyman, this has been called 'Verifiable Data Audit' and it will 'record the fact that a particular piece of data has been used, and also the reason why, for example, that blood test data was checked against the NHS national algorithm to detect possible acute kidney injury' [138]. They are building an auditing system for healthcare data [139]. As a result, any access of and changes made to the patient's data are immediately visible and can be tracked by the system. Contrary to public blockchains (such as the bitcoin blockchain), the distributed ledger that will be used provides access only to trusted stakeholders such as hospitals and national institutions for verification of the integrity of the ledgers. However, the result is the same: any entry to the ledger is immutable, verifiable, and traceable by those with access to the ledger. The system could become a federated patient-identified information database that allows relevant stakeholders to perform valuable research to create better healthcare, without breaching patient privacy. Instead, it puts humans back in control of their healthcare data. Imagine the possibilities, when the system that DeepMind is developing is combined with a global self-sovereign identity system? This would mean that you would carry your own digital healthcare records across the globe, in a secure and private way. Whenever you need healthcare, anywhere in the world, you could provide local caregivers with secure access to your relevant healthcare data, ensuring that you have the best possible care. When you get home, your own doctor can see exactly what happened, what treatment was given and any testing or analysis conducted by the treating physician. This would dramatically improve healthcare, reduce costs and—more importantly—save lives.

3.9.3 Governments

Blockchain offers tremendous potential for the commercial world, but has as much potential for government services. Governments exist in a competitive, rapidly changing, and uncertain environment, where companies are attracted by efficiency and cost reductions. Attracting these companies requires a different attitude and governments increasingly need to be run like a business. As a consequence, those governments that can apply the latest technology to offer innovative services for companies operating around the globe will develop a competitive advantage that could be worth billions. Therefore, digital identities can have a big impact on how governments are organised. If pushed by governments, it could provide those excluded with a much-needed proof of identity and allow them to improve their services. A well-known example of a government working hard to bring identity to the 21st century is the government of Estonia. This small country in eastern Europe has been digitising its government since it restored its independence in 1991 and they have become a global role-model for e-government. When they developed their e-government they focused on four principles:

1. Decentralisation: there is no central database and every stakeholder can select its own system;
2. Interconnectivity: all systems work together smoothly;
3. Open platform: the platform is open to all stakeholders, who can use the Public Key Infrastructure;
4. Open-ended: the platform will be developed and improved continuously.

As a result, Estonia built an e-residency program based on the Blockchain, which enables anyone in the world to become an e-resident of Estonia. Although this does not allow you to vote in the country, it does, once accepted, enable you to benefit from the digital government services that have been developed in Estonia. Once accepted, it allows the e-resident the possibility of starting a company and opening a bank account. This enables anyone to benefit from the efficient services of Estonia, while bringing new revenue streams to Estonia. To achieve this, they are collaborating with Bitnation to offer public notary services to every Estonian e-resident. This enables Estonia to open up their government services globally and move towards the idea of a country without borders. It is a revolutionary approach, which focuses on efficiency benefits for companies rather than tax benefits, which can be a lot more lucrative for organisations. Furthermore, having an identity on the Blockchain solves the longstanding issues of identity theft, identity verification, and, hopefully in the long run, identity exclusion.

Estonia is not the only country that sees the enormous potential of a Blockchain government. In 2017, Dubai announced the development of the first city built on the Blockchain. Although Estonia is ahead of Dubai, Dubai aims to achieve their bold vision by 2020. Their vision is to become the world's happiest city and be ranked first in the digital world. By 2020, they aim to have moved all government services and transactions to the Blockchain, making them immutable, traceable, and verifiable, while reducing bureaucracy and inefficiencies. No bureaucracy and efficient government services certainly contribute to that vision, although they still have long way to go.

In order to achieve their vision, Dubai has developed a public–private partnership called Smarter Dubai. This is a citywide effort to implement Blockchain across the city for a multitude of services. The objective is for collaboration of government, semi-government, and commercial organisations to speed up the development of blockchain applications in the Emirate city. They have partnered with IBM and ConsenSys to guide them in this objective. As with any ambitious project in Dubai, they have pledged investment of millions and already the first blockchain services have come into being. For example, the Department of Economic Development is moving its entire processes of business registration and licensing services to Blockchain. In addition, Dubai's largest bank, the NBD, is developing a smart contracts platform to reduce complex documentation for moving, shipping, and tracking of goods [140].

In the coming years, we will probably see more governments that move to the Blockchain and develop identity solutions on it. As a result, we will see governments start to compete for the best companies, not based on tax benefits, but on the efficiency gains that can be achieved. This will change the playing field and those governments that focus on an open, inclusive, e-identity system, connecting government and commercial services using Blockchain, will be in the best position to win.

3.10 Conclusion

Identity is the combination of many different attributes, constantly changing over time, and linked to your reputation, that is how trustworthy you are, as well as your shadow reputation (who you are dealing with). It is not only humans that have identities. Organisations and many things are also uniquely identifiable. With the rise of the Internet of Things, which will connect billions of devices and trillions of sensors, an upgrade to our identity system is long overdue. Our existing identity system has some serious flaws: identity theft is commonplace, costing us billions of dollars and leaving victims traumatised; identity verification is expensive and a hassle, seriously breaching our privacy, and millions of people are excluded from obtaining a government-issued proof of identity, leaving them vulnerable and without access to basic services. However, we can bring identity to the 21st century by creating a digital identity, a self-sovereign identity, that uses distributed ledgers to make identity data immutable, verifiable, and traceable. A self-sovereign identity can be described according to the 5Ps; personal, private, persistent, protected, and portable. It uses tokenisation as well as encryption with the Public Key Infrastructure to prevent identity theft, improve identity verification, and help those who are excluded by giving them a digital identity. Those who are excluded can use different personal data traits and digital social connections to verify who they are, simply by using an App installed on their phone [141]. Once they have been verified, it will enable them to open bank accounts, apply as a refugee, and apply for many more services that will improve their lives. Of course, it is vital that personal identifiable information is never *as it is* put on a blockchain. Putting an address, biometric data, or even a passport on a blockchain is a serious privacy risk, which is why tokenisation is so important. Once we solve the Wicked Problem of identity and create digital identities that bring control back to the individual, this offers us a chance to solve some of the other Wicked Problems. Therefore, in the next chapter, we explore this more closely and see how Blockchain can contribute towards ending poverty forever.

Despite the enormous potential of a self-sovereign identity for any industry, there are still some major challenges ahead of us. These challenges include ensuring global adoption, scalability, and governance, as well as compliance with local regulations and jurisdictions. Nevertheless, a number of players (including the financial services industry, healthcare, and some governments) are already working on developing a digital identity and/or self-sovereign identity, and it seems we are indeed at the forefront of an identity revolution.

Notes

1 Some of the names of the victim and perpetrator have been changed, those that have not been changed where publicly known already.
2 Please note, this list was constructed in May 2017; by the time you read this book, some start-ups might have gone out of business, changed their name, or gone on to great fame.

Chapter 4

Blockchain and poverty

Poverty /ˈpɒvəti/: the state of being extremely poor

Over the past 100 years, the world has seen an extraordinary growth in welfare. Across the board, the world today is in a much better state, economically, than it was 100 years ago. Although it may seem that the world is on fire at the moment, with ongoing wars in Syria, the Yemeni crisis, or the terrorist threat from ISIS that killed thousands of people and left millions fleeing their country, or the Mexican Drug war that has killed over 80,000 people since 2006 [142], nothing can be further from the truth. On almost all levels, life on earth has improved in the past 100 years from our life expectancy, the number of people living in democratic countries, to the number of people living in extreme poverty. Thanks to significantly improved healthcare, as well as better living and working conditions, life expectancy has increased rapidly in the past 100 years, from 34.1 years in 1913 to 71.4 years in 2015 [143]. In addition, the child mortality rate fell from 43% of the world's newborns who would die before their fifth birthday in 1800, due to the poor health conditions, to only 4.3% in 2015. Although 4.3% of all newborns who die in childhood is still too high, it is quite an achievement [144]. Thanks to better food production, the number of famine victims fell drastically from 578 global deaths per 100,000 population in the 1950s to 3 global deaths per 100,000 population in the 2000s [145]. Also, the number of people living in a democracy increased significantly over the past 100 years. In 1900, almost 200 million people, or 11.97% of the world's population, lived in a democracy. In 2015, that number grew to 4.1 billion people, or 55.8% of the world's population [146]. Finally, thanks to technological advancements, global poverty has also been reduced significantly in the past 100 years. The percentage of people living in extreme poverty[1] [147] dropped from 94.4% in 1820 to 9.6% in 2015 [147]. This achievement is predominantly attributable to the past three decades, because only as recently as 1980 the percentage was still 44% [147]. The third industrial revolution, the information age, which started in the 1970s and brought us mainframe computing, personal computing, and the internet, has enabled millions of people to leave poverty and become connected to the global economy. Unfortunately, 9.6% of the world's population still live in extreme poverty—that is, 700 million people, which is still 700 million people too many. The vast majority of these people live in Sub-Saharan Africa and South Asia [147]. However, developing countries also still experience poverty, which, unfortunately and interestingly, has been on the rise in recent years, especially in Europe. The International Labour Organization estimated that, in 2012, over 300 million people in developed countries were living in poverty [148]. This high number is linked to the wave of refugees who have fled to Europe in the past three years [149].

There is a wide variety of causes for poverty, which differ by country, but in general the causes for poverty include: lack of education, environmental problems, lack of access to banking facilities, lack of legal ownership of property, lack of rule of law, overpopulation, epidemic diseases, weather-related events, war, and changing trends in a country's economy. Overcoming poverty is vital if we want to create a world that is peaceful and fair for everyone. Besides which, in 2015 the United Nations adopted its Sustainable Development Goals that challenge global leaders to help end poverty in all its forms, everywhere, by 2030. Therefore, it is time to get to work and lift the remaining 700 million people out of extreme poverty.

4.1 The impact of poverty

The effects of poverty reach every level of our society, and often the things that cause poverty are also the effects of poverty. For example, when hurricane Sandy moved over Haiti in 2012, it displaced over 18,000 people, many of whom were still living in UN camps after the devastating earthquake of 2010 [150]. Those displaced people have to live in poor conditions, directly affecting their health. If they become ill, their capacity to work will be negatively impacted and, with a lack of a social security system in place, the line to poverty is easily crossed. It is often a vicious circle that is difficult to break and the effects of poverty are often passed on from one generation to the next. The effects of poverty are often interrelated, rarely occurring alone, and are, therefore, difficult to solve. Poverty is a true Wicked Problem, which will require the involvement of all stakeholders, collaborating with each other, using the latest technologies to try to break the vicious circle of poverty. Poverty has an impact on different levels within a person's life or within a country and, to break the vicious circle of poverty, each of these aspects should be approached, ideally simultaneously. That is what makes this Wicked Problem so difficult to solve.

Poverty has a direct impact on the ability of someone to purchase sufficient nutritious food and water. Whether in developing or developed countries, malnutrition as a result of poverty is also a catalyst for poverty. Often, the healthiest and most nutritious food is also the most expensive. For these reasons, people with small budgets often have less nutritious diets due to their dependence on cheaper 'fast' food. Thus, their children grow up without the required nutrition, which has an impact on their ability to learn, play, and grow. In addition, too much fast food results in obesity, with all the associated health consequences. Poverty will, therefore, almost always result in severe health effects, whether in developing or developed countries. The lack of nutrition and proper medicine, the (easy) access to healthcare facilities, or the lack of proper sanitation conditions negatively influence people's life expectancies. In addition, lack of healthcare insurance stops people from seeking care because they cannot afford the treatments or medicine, thereby making their situation deteriorate. Children who are sick or suffer from malnutrition will have difficulty concentrating at school, if they get the chance to attend a school at all. In developing countries, many children are sent to work as soon as they can stand, in order to earn money for the family. Lack of education results in illiteracy, which can haunt them throughout their lives. The effect of illiteracy is that they will have difficulty getting a job, resulting in rising unemployment rates, uncertainty, and a growing informal economy, which limits a government from improving the situation for the country as a whole, due to lack of income. Many of the poor people living in informal economies do not have a documented identity, thereby limiting them from access to many (government) resources and activities. In addition, the rise of robots and automation will make things worse in the coming years, reducing even further the number of available jobs for those who are uneducated. Consequently, social unrest can develop and quickly derail a society. This effect played out during the Arab Spring in early 2011, where a series of anti-government protests, uprisings, and armed rebellions spread across the Middle East. The chaos and lawlessness were fuelled by political uncertainty and quickly led to increased job insecurity and higher levels of poverty.

Breaking the cycle of poverty starts with investing in children and providing them with sufficient high-quality food, a proper education, knowledge, and skills to enable them to realise their full potential. Next to education comes access to affordable proper healthcare (including insurance), access to clean water and sanitation, and, last but not least, economic security and connecting poor people to the (global) economy by offering them an identity, access to banking facilities, and the right of ownership. Economic security includes registration of property ownership, access to banking facilities, and a fair and transparent rule of law, which includes rules that everyone understands and respects. Especially in developing countries these three economic securities (property ownership, access to banking facilities, and rule of law) are often lacking. As a result, these countries often have a large informal economy, which results in less respect for ownership or financial and legal rights, making it expensive to abide by the law.

4.2 Informal economies

Informal economies exist in every country of the world, but take up a larger chunk of the gross domestic product (GDP) in developing countries. The informal economy is the part of the economy that is neither taxed nor controlled by any form of government. The larger the informal economy, the more insecurity there is for citizens, which can result in unrest and poverty. Due to a lack of data, determination of the size of the informal economy is difficult. However, Mexico determined in 2014 that the informal economy contributed on average 26% to their GDP over the decade from 2003 to 2012 [151]. That's a large chunk of the economy that is not controlled or monitored, and therefore affects millions of people.

An informal economy often exists due to a lack of economic security and the high costs of doing business legally. According to research by McKinsey, emerging-market businesses face administrative costs three times higher than their counterparts in developed economies [152]. In addition, the famous Peruvian economist Hernando de Soto Polar, who is a known for his work on the informal economy, views property ownership rights being vital for a strong market economy. De Soto argues that, without adequate participation in an information framework that records ownership of property and other economic information, poverty is difficult to overcome. Next to the absence of property rights, the lack of rule of law [153] and of access to banking facilities facilitates the growth of an informal economy, because it drives up the cost of doing business legally [154].

Unfortunately, economic insecurities and poverty have a negative side effect. Many different organisations try to help poor people, all with the best intentions. However, these organisations operate in isolation, each of them having their own database with information on the citizens whom they try to help. As a result, there is no centralised overview, leaving the person in need without any information or credit history that could be used to improve their situation, while requiring each organisation to maintain their own database. Thus, being poor is often very expensive, resulting in a negative vicious circle and an increase in poverty in already poor countries.

4.3 Reducing poverty with technology

Worldwide, two billion people remain unbanked [155]. This is because traditional systems require that all parties to every transaction be known to the system. However, populations in poorer and developing nations, and those displaced by war, famine, and climatic events, often lack the means to identify themselves formally. If the system can manage the authentication of participants and then handle the exchange, people with no formal identity documents can conduct online exchanges and thereby enjoy the benefits that come with having a secure online financial wallet or bank-like account. As Andreas Antonopoulos observes, Bitcoin may not be as sophisticated as an international banking system, but it delivers freedom and it allows us to unleash creativity [155a].

Of the two billion people who are unbanked, a quarter have access to the internet. By simply downloading a free app, they can have access to an international financial transaction network. For all its faults, this is something that no banking system anywhere in the world can offer.

Increased access to banking, availability of rules of law, and respect for property ownership reduce the size of the informal economy, which has significant advantages including increased government protection for consumers, accumulating government pensions for workers, increased job security for workers, and enabling companies to grow bigger, all contributing to a reduction in poverty. In addition, creating a centralised database for poor people makes being poor a lot less expensive. But that is not sufficient. In order to be able to end poverty in all its forms, we should focus on the different levels of poverty: nutrition, health, education, economic security, and society. If we can use technology, such as big data analytics, Blockchain, and artificial intelligence to give people better access to better and cheaper food, give them good healthcare and a reliable healthcare insurance, give them an education that they can use anywhere, and reduce their economic insecurity, then we have a chance at ending poverty in all its forms globally. There are several ways in which emerging technologies can help end poverty.

4.4 Healthy nutrition for poor people

Eating healthy food is often a challenge for poor people; it is expensive and often difficult to obtain, because not every store will sell it. In developed countries, poor people, therefore, often opt for fast food or food with limited nutrition, which is the worst food possible to eat on a daily basis. In developing countries, the problem is more persistent and often the question is whether there is enough food at all, let alone healthy and nutritious food. Although Blockchain might not at first seem to be a technology that can help, it does offer some advantages. However, most advantages can be achieved by focusing on emerging technologies such as big data analytics and precision agriculture.

One company that has developed an innovative solution from San Francisco follows the adage: 'Give a man a fish, and he has food for one day. Teach a man to fish, and he has food for the rest of his life.' In 2009, Brandi DeCarli and Scott Thompson met and worked on the Kisumu Youth Empowerment Center. They worked on modified shipping containers built around a soccer field to offer basic services and resources in education, health, and sport for the local youth [156]. Their work at the Kisumu Youth Empowerment Center resulted in a plug-and-play model for agriculture, developing self-sustaining, smart, modified shipping containers for agriculture. The 'Farm from a Box' is a unique concept that offers all the necessary equipment to run a small, off-the-grid farm in a single shipping container. The container is fitted out with solar panels and batteries for creation and storage of renewable energy. It also has water filtration and micro-drip irrigation equipment, sensors, and an on-board computer for soil monitoring and land mapping. The self-sustaining container can be placed anywhere in the world and is sufficient to support farms one hectare in size, which happens to be the size of most farms in the world [157]. The Farm from a Box costs between US$25,000 and US$40,000, depending on the level of technology inside, but it offers the farmers a way to grow more food and more types of food, and become less dependent on the weather or power local power supply. The Farm from a Box is capable of feeding 150 people.

Farm from a Box brings together emerging technologies such as precision agriculture (which is a farming concept based on detailed monitoring of the crops and constant adjusting of the precise nutrition to optimise the output), Internet of Things, and big data analytics. The shipping container offers a farmer everything that he or she needs to create healthy and nutritious food for the community, while creating a steady stream of income. Although the Farm from a Box does not require integration with blockchain for it to be a success, doing so could improve its outcomes even more. Now imagine that the Farm from a Box is connected to the local power grid and the farmer can give back any excess energy to the local energy grid, as we shall see in Chapter 6, which stores the records of these transactions on the Blockchain and instantly pays the farmer in bitcoin or another cryptocurrency. It would offer the local farmer an additional stream of revenue, while at the same time offering the local community clean and inexpensive energy. In addition, if the farmer could accept bitcoin, or any other cryptocurrency, he or she could avoid dealing with banks and cash money. This would improve the farmers' financial security, because digital money cannot be robbed in the traditional way, and give the farmer full control over his or her digital money.

In 2016, the concept of Farm from a Box planned several pilots: one in California and one in Ethiopia as well as another unit with resettled refugees from Nepal, Bhutan, and Afghanistan in California [158]. The shipping container empowers the local community by decentralising the food production. When a local community is empowered to grow and sustain their own crop, whether in developing or developed countries, it will be better off and more resilient.

4.5 Access to healthcare

Healthcare is an industry that offers tremendous scope for improvement thanks to emerging technologies. Healthcare organisations tend to have a vast array of data stored across the organisation, ranging from patient, medicine, and supplier data to financial, insurance, and staff data. Healthcare organisations can mix and match their data, combine it with valuable external data sources, such as social media data, to enable the healthcare organisation to better determine risks (including financial risks, clinical risks, or operational risks), predict operational performances and act accordingly, and create a single view of the healthcare organisation as well as the patient at any given moment in time. However, at this time, much of this information is stored and conveyed in handwritten notes or faxed between healthcare professionals and centres and their support organisations. This old-fashioned system satisfies regulatory requirements for protection of patient data, but is plagued by delay, handling failures, and errors. This is a security problem in need of a reliable and trustworthy solution. A complete overview of the patient can eventually lead to personalised medicine that will offer the patient better treatment than standard medicine. Combined with emerging technology such as artificial intelligence, Blockchain and drones, healthcare can be significantly improved.

Imagine a future healthcare organisation for rural Africa that created a Blockchain-based Electronic Health Record for patients in Africa. The organisation, let's call it *AHealth*, has partnered with many local doctors and provided them with tablets to record any patient data, which will be stored on a permissioned, private Blockchain. The first time someone visits a doctor who is a partner with *AHealth*, the doctor will create a new patient record that will include a variety of personalised identifiable information such as name, address, age, height, weight, blood type, and perhaps even a DNA sample. All the information will be tokenised, encrypted, and stored on the Blockchain. The patient is in full control of who has access to his or her personal data, similar to the self-sovereign identity discussed in Chapter 3. Using a centralised storage system, as is common these days, would not be sufficient, because it would take away control of the data from the patient. Only the patient and the doctor will be able to view any patient-specific data and, if another doctor or organisation needs to get access to the data for health reasons, the patient can release only information that is required, cryptographically, using the private key on a smartphone. No longer does the patient or doctor have to carry paper documents on different patients, with the risk of losing them or mixing up records.

Next to this, *AHealth* has deployed, in many rural villages, self-scanning connected devices that enable a patient to monitor a variety of physiological parameters: blood pressure, temperature, heart rate, and pulse oximetry. The system uses artificial intelligence to understand what is wrong with the patient. If a patient does not feel well, he or she can login with his or her smartphone, perform several tests, and the data is automatically added, securely (tokenised and encrypted), to the details on the Blockchain. The doctor will get a ping to view the results if approved by the patient and, in case medicine is required, the doctor will order the medicine, via a smart contract deployed on the blockchain, at the local or regional pharmacy which has also partnered with *AHealth*. The pharmacist will prepare the personalised medicine and a secured drone will automatically deliver the medicine to the patient.[2,3] The patient can retrieve the medicine only through a biometric verification and, as soon as the medicine has been taken out of the delivery drone, the delivery is confirmed and the smart contract will automatically transfer the crypto-funds from the patient's healthcare insurer to the pharmacist, ensuring that everyone in the supply chain is paid a lot sooner than is currently the case. The patient uses the medicine and will report any progress back to the doctor, which will be added to the Electronic Health Record on the blockchain. In cases of more severe health problems or when a patient needs to be transported to hospital, the advantage is that the hospital has access to all the records of the patients, including any medicines that have been delivered by drone, and so can develop a better treatment for the patient. Thanks to the Blockchain, *AHealth* has created an efficient healthcare system that spans vast areas of land and delivers cheap and reliable healthcare to the far corners of Africa.

At this time, this scenario is of course still science fiction—albeit inspirational—and will probably remain so for the coming years. However, it shows the power of blockchain technology by securely (tokenising and encrypting) storing any patient data on a blockchain, and giving full control to the patient who has access to that data, while at the same time preserving any private information about the patient (as mentioned, any personal data such as biometrics or DNA should never be put *as is* on a blockchain). Blockchain technology, or more specifically a self-sovereign healthcare identity system, would give patients and doctors all the advantages of digital records while ensuring privacy for the patient. Of course, any company dealing with health data on blockchain should ensure privacy for its users by giving full control to the user and ensuring that data remains private. This could be achieved, for example, by using Zero Knowledge Proof (ZKP). ZKP ensures that data can be shared without leaking personal information and one party can prove a certain fact without revealing that information. However, giving full control of healthcare data to the patient also creates a significant challenge, because, as discussed in Chapter 3, the Public Key Infrastructure is an important aspect of this. Loss of the private key would cause problems for the patient to remain in full control. Therefore, any start-up working in this field should offer solutions for when individuals lose, for whatever reason, access to their private keys.

Although this particular fictional scenario is still far away, fortunately different Blockchain start-ups are developing solutions to improve healthcare for poor people. One of these companies, BanQU, focuses on the 'last mile' of healthcare. Often, the last part of the healthcare supply chain is the least developed, resulting in poor infrastructure, inaccurate records, and inadequate storage and tracking mechanisms [159]. Blockchain can help improve the health supply chain, by creating a reliable, controllable, and effective connection between patient and health provider. The company BanQu, which according to their website, are on a mission to end poverty using Blockchain technology, is already capable of creating a smart contract that will automatically release funds to a drug manufacturer for medicine required by a patient. The smart contract will automatically pay the state health worker if needed and there is a reduced inventory because medicines are shipped only when actually needed [159]. Although the imaginary company *AHealth* may seem far away, parts of it are already possible and in action today.

4.6 Access to education

Africa is the world's youngest continent, with over 50% of people aged younger than 15 years [160]. Unfortunately, in a fifth of the African countries, less than 30% of these children are enrolled in school [161]. Reducing poverty is a long-term process and starts with children having the ability to learn and use that knowledge to create a better life for themselves and their families. In most poor families, especially in developing countries, children have to work to support their family. They do not have the time to go to school, play with friends, and learn new things in the same way that children in developed countries can. A lack of education is the starting point of the vicious circle that keeps people poor, because, if you cannot become educated, you cannot climb the social ladder. Therefore, if we wish to solve poverty for good, there needs to be a focus on improving access to education as well as improving the quality of education itself. There are already a lot of charities and initiatives that focus on education for poor people and provide help in building schools, providing materials, educating teachers, and offering scholarships for talented children.

If we truly want to enable children, as well as adults, in developing countries to be educated, we need a new system, one that is scalable and offers personalised learning for children, particularly in rural areas. However, access to education is only one aspect of this Wicked Problem. Next come the limited availability of qualified teachers, sufficient materials and schools, lack of energy to run schools, and many more, smaller and interrelated issues.

Another major aspect of this Wicked Problem is proof of education, which is almost as important as the education itself. If you cannot prove that you have a degree from a certain college or university, you will still encounter difficulties in obtaining a job to match your skills. Fortunately, Blockchain and emerging technologies such as big data and artificial intelligence seem to offer a good shot at solving many of the different interrelated problems. Blockchain for educational purposes is very new and, at the time of writing, there have been very few examples of organisations or start-ups applying Blockchain for educational purposes, let alone using it to improve education for poor people. Nevertheless, the potential for Blockchain to improve our educational systems is vast. Blockchain can completely revolutionise education by making it more accessible to anyone, and giving children a fair chance to learn and prepare themselves for the real world.

The education foundation KnowledgeWorks, which focuses on personalised learning and strategic foresight, released a report in 2016 that explores the impact of emerging technologies such as Blockchain, big data and artificial intelligence on the education system. The report gives an insight into how these technologies can transform the model of education delivery from a centralised to a distributed one—and in so doing can make learning much more personalised [162]. The report considers four scenarios over the next decade on how technology can revolutionise the education system. Although the report focuses on the USA, it does give us an idea of the possibilities of what Blockchain can do for the education system. In brief, the four scenarios are [163]:

1 Blockchain-enabled administrative and financial backend for schools to optimise and automate managing student/employee/school records in a private and secure way. The actual delivery of education remains the same, with a focus on in-person teaching;
2 Education-as-a-device delivered as a plug-and-play content delivery service. Machine learning delivers customised lessons and any achievements and activities are recorded on a blockchain. Smart contracts automate everything and mediate across students, teachers, parents, and the schools. The rich data can be sold, securely and privately, to offer schools more profit;
3 A DIY education system built on a permissioned blockchain, where smart contracts help students to access resources, enable membership decision-making, and automate payments. It operates as a Decentralised Autonomous Organisation (DAO) separate from classrooms, districts and teachers;
4 Blockchain-based ecosystem management tools enable schools to deliver a unique, decentralised education programme for the students. Students can define coursework and hire experts or seek guidance. All data, including certificates, is recorded on a blockchain and smart contracts automate everything.

The four scenarios show the different possibilities that emerging technologies offer for the education system. In each of the four scenarios, Blockchain plays an important role in enabling the record of progress, achievements, and certificates. In some of the scenarios, big data and artificial intelligence will automatically and autonomously develop personalised learning programmes. Of course, this is still far away and the closest we currently have are the Massive Online Open Courses that are developed on multiple platforms such as the Khan Academy, EDx, or Coursera. The future offers great possibilities for developing true personalised learning and Blockchain will be able to record any of the achievements. Some of the first organisations and start-ups that are experimenting with such possibilities at the time of writing are set out below [164]:

- BadgeChain is an open community discussing uses of blockchains for education;
- The Sony Global Education division developed a platform for educational assessment and testing scores based on the Blockchain, which can securely share data with other services or third parties [165];

- otlw.co developed a Blockchain system to secure universal assessment of skills and knowledge. They also developed otlw-publish, which facilitates the distribution of micropayments;
- Various universities are experimenting with authentication and delivery of academic certificates on the Blockchain, including MIT Media Lab (in 2016 they released a new open standard, 'Blockcerts' [166]), University of Nicosia, Holberton School, and Ecole Supérieure d'Ingénieurs Léonard de Vinci.

The future of education offers poor people a new shot at leaving poverty through becoming educated. The current rate of technological developments is exponential, also in the educational sector, and Blockchain and AI could revolutionise education in the coming decade. In fact, the World Economic Forum predicts that, in 2030, the largest internet company in the world will be an educational DAO—a company that uses big data analytics and artificial intelligence to develop personalised learning courses on the spot, based on a detailed profile of the student [167]. Add Blockchain and smart contracts to the equation and you have an educational DAO that can help reduce poverty by offering poor people a chance to become educated.

4.7 Ensuring property ownership

Correctness and completeness of property ownership registration are vital, as is the prevention of unauthorised and fraudulent changes to data records. As such, blockchain technology is perfectly suited to register ownership of property, of anything digital and non-digital. It will protect the rights of the owner (in the case of theft), enable easy resolution of disputes, enable correct transfer of ownership after sale, and prevent fraud, because any records are immutable, verifiable, and traceable.

Already, multiple countries are considering the possibility of adopting blockchain technology to register and record land title ownership. Countries such as Sweden [168], Honduras [169], and Georgia [170] are testing Blockchain technology, although Honduras's attempts have recently stalled [171]. They are developing a land registry that is transparent, enables easy registration, and respects land ownership. Registering property ownership, such as land titles, on the blockchain has multiple advantages, such as significantly reducing manual errors, while improving security processes for transferring documents, mortgage, or contracts [168].

Blockchain enables irreversible records of ownership, because, once data is on the blockchain, it can no longer be tampered with. In addition, the usage of smart contracts will enable automatic transfer of ownership if the right conditions have been met, protecting the seller as well as the buyer from fraudulent actions. Therefore, Blockchain ensures easy and safe registration of property ownership. When property ownership can be proven easily, the person has a better chance of prospering in a capitalist society:

> With titles, shares and property laws, people could suddenly go beyond looking at their assets as they are—houses used for shelter—to thinking about what they **could be**—things like security for credit to start or expand a business.
>
> (Hernando de Soto [172])

Once owners have been able to document their ownership, it gives them a possibility of proving their existence, which in turn increases the possibility of accessing banking facilities. Recording ownership can also help solve corruption, which is also a large problem related to ownership in many countries, but we turn to that in Chapter 5.

4.8 Access to (cheap) banking facilities

Financial inclusion is an important step towards reducing poverty, because it offers people more freedom to save and spend money how, where, and when they like. Unfortunately, for poor people it has become very difficult to open a bank account and/or get a loan to improve their lives or build a business. Either they do not have the right ID, which can be solved using a self-sovereign identity, or they do not have a credit history, which makes it almost impossible to access banking facilities. As a result, they are forced to save in livestock, which is obviously not very liquid if essential items such as medicine need to be bought. In addition, a transaction fee of US$0.50 on credit card purchases represents almost a third of the daily income for extremely poor people who live on US$1.90 a day.

Blockchain technology is rapidly changing this, something that we can already see with Bitcoin. Bitcoin enables everyone with an internet connection to open a wallet and start receiving and sending money, without the need for an ID or a credit history. For many developing countries, this might be nothing new. They have been using pre-paid mobile phone minutes as a currency for years. Mobile airtime minutes, or credits, can be transferred between phones or dealers, or shown to owners to purchase or barter for goods and services [173]. This is similar to tokens or crypto-coins on a blockchain, albeit less secure and more open to fraud.

When Blockchain and crypto-coins are used, they offer a wide variety of new products and services for poor people, for a fraction of the cost, which could significantly improve their lives. Examples include microloans, or payday loans, for a fraction of the cost of traditional (payday) loans. The company Wayniloans developed a bitcoin-lending platform, which is gaining power in Latin America. They offer multiple loan services, including cash advances, peer-to-peer loans, and business loans, using the bitcoin blockchain for a much lower rate than traditional lending companies.

Another area that can drastically improve the lives of poor is people Blockchain-enabled remittances. Today, over US$410 billion [174] in remittances flow to developing countries, with an average cost of 7.4% [175] and up to 12% [176] in certain regions. Remittances are expensive, opaque, and recurring transactions of necessity, with the costs borne predominantly by poor people [177]. Blockchain can offer enormous improvements in cost savings for poor people who send money to families in another country. Not surprisingly, there are multiple start-ups and organisations [178], including the United Nations, that are developing blockchain-based remittance services [179]. A blockchain-based remittance service uses a crypto-coin to transfer money instantly across the globe for a fraction of the cost, and uses local agents to exchange the crypto-coin into the local fiat money that can be used by the receiver. Instead of a transaction taking days to process and costing a fortune, it takes minutes and is significantly cheaper (despite the challenge of high transaction costs currently linked to Bitcoin, as explained in Chapter 2).

Finally, trustless lending can enable smart property and smart contracts for the delivery of financial products to poorer customers. Use of the property owned by individuals or the combined wealth of groups of borrowers as collateral can make the provision of credit more widely available, more competitive, and therefore cheaper. These mechanisms ensure that lending is available to a greater percentage of the community. Smart contracts can also automate repayments, thereby reducing the risk of contractual disputes [180, p. 15].

4.9 Society and reducing uncertainty using rule of law

Rule of law means that a country and its people, including the government, should be ruled by law and obey that law. In addition, the law should be such that people will be able, and willing, to be guided by it [16]. In other words, both the government and the citizens know the law and obey it [181]. Rule of law is the principle that law should govern a nation and not the arbitrary decisions of individual government officials. Therefore, a lack of rule of law will increase the informal economy because it becomes more expensive and difficult to do business legally.

Obviously, a country's law cannot be stored and enforced through a blockchain in its entirety, but separate aspects of it can when adopting smart contracts. Already, Blockchain is having a profound impact on the legal industry and lawyers are trying to understand how it will affect their business. Blockchain and smart contracts can be used to transform legal contracts into code, which is understandable and indisputable across legal jurisdictions.

As mentioned earlier, smart contracts can be viewed as software programs that use Boolean expressions and algorithmic determination to perform certain actions. Smart contracts automatically execute when a predefined condition is met and, as a result, cannot be ignored. All too often contracts are simply ignored, payments delayed or bluntly refused, and disputes need to be resolved in court, costing a lot of time and money for the parties involved. Smart contracts, if developed correctly and securely, could prevent this, because the contract will automatically execute only once certain pre-set conditions have been met. As such, it becomes easier for organisations and citizens to obey the law and abide by agreements that have been made, making it cheaper to play by the rules and reducing the informal economy.

Of course, there are many technical and organisational challenges that need to be solved and not all contracts can be transformed into Boolean expressions. Smart contracts cannot operate in a vacuum and the legal framework remains important. However, when smart contracts become common in developing countries, the potential is enormous.

4.10 Decentralised identity

Blockchain enables multiple stakeholders to access, as well as add to or update, records in a shared database. The major advantage is that those organisations that are part of the public, or private, blockchain always have an up-to-date, single version of the truth. For the financial services industry, this reduces settlement times, costs, and the risks of fraud and errors. However, those same benefits apply to (not-for) profit organisations that aim to help poor people.

Multiple organisations, especially in developing countries, try to help poor people and sometimes they assist the same people over prolonged periods of time. However, as data about these relationships is stored in silos, it cannot be used to build up a credit history or other important evidence needed to get things done, access money, or transfer ownership of property. If multiple organisations would use the same, distributed database, and citizens would have a self-sovereign identity, individuals could build up a profile that could be very useful to them, as well as to those organisations trying to help the individuals. It will save them a lot of time and effort, because they do not have to constantly provide their details and update them across multiple organisations.

Once multiple charities start collaborating and using the same shared database, it could make the entire process of helping poor people a lot more efficient, effective, and cheaper. This would improve the lives of poor people because it gives them an economic profile that could be used for various other activities, as discussed in Chapter 3.

4.11 The future of poverty

The future of poverty should be non-existent, meaning that, as per the UN goals, by 2030 poverty will be gone from the world. Big data analytics, artificial intelligence and Blockchain will enable us to achieve this audacious goal, but only if multiple organisations across the globe collaborate.

> The poor don't lack capital; it's that they can't monetize it. Fixing that, is the most important thing you could ever do to foster economic growth.
>
> (Hernando de Soto [172])

If they do, property rights on a blockchain could prove ownership of, for example, a house or a piece of land. A distributed ledger containing a tokenised and encrypted 360 degree economic profile of citizens using a self-sovereign identity, which is used by multiple organisations, could provide a (credit) history for poor people. The combination can be used to obtain a loan, instantly, through a blockchain-powered financial institution at very low cost, which will enable poor people to improve their lives and create or grow their business. With the right smart contracts, rule of law can be enforced automatically, thereby reducing the cost of doing business legally and reducing the number of informal economies. This could improve government regulation and increase tax received, which in turn could improve the stability and economy of a country. Blockchain can truly be a paradigm shift for poor people because it offers them the opportunity to improve their lives, monetise their (digital) capital and leave poverty behind.

Notes

1 A person is considered to live in extreme poverty if the person has less than 1.90 international dollars to spend every day.
2 In 2017, Walmart revealed plans to start using drones to deliver goods, benefiting from blockchain technology to ensure that the goods are dropped off securely.
3 In 2017, the company Zipline tested and launched drone delivery of medical supplies in Rwanda.

Chapter 5

Blockchain and corruption, tax evasion, and money laundering

Fraud /frɔ:d/: wrongful or criminal deception intended to result in financial or personal gain

The evils of corruption, tax evasion, and money laundering are driven by greed, perpetrators hiding legitimate but taxable income, the proceeds of crime, and the ill-gotten gains of fraud, bribes, and secret commissions. The direct victims of these crimes are employers, clients, legitimate businesses, and government, tax, and revenue agencies. The indirect victims are the communities or jurisdictions in which these acts are perpetrated and to which revenue is owed.

The cost of hiding money is significant. Estimates run to the billions of dollars worldwide. According to the Organisation for Economic Co-operation and Development (OECD), the cost of corruption is more than 5% of the global gross domestic product (GDP). Overall, corruption reduces efficiency and increases inequality [182, 183, p. 2]. Blockchain technology can help reduce the incidence of corruption, fraud, tax evasion, and money laundering by securely managing identity in permissionless networks.

There are two clear divisions in the ways in which blockchain technology can be used as discussed in Chapter 2: permissioned or permissionless. Bitcoin operates across a permissionless network, in which the users interact with each other pseudonymously. Users' identities are protected by private and public key access. The bitcoin blockchain and other permissionless cryptocurrency networks enable corruption, tax evasion, and money laundering. Meanwhile, a permissioned network is one where users have identified themselves or provided their identity to a central authority to create a user account. It is this latter type of blockchain network that appeals to business and governments for its capacity to report transactions seamlessly to regulators. We explore the potential use of permissioned blockchain networks to enable secure and authenticated exchanges. Together with digital identities, users on a permissioned network can securely conduct business online, while seamlessly reporting activity to regulators. With a lot of business and government records and transactions transitioning to online networks, the adoption of blockchain technology to manage permissions and ledgers, and to report to regulators is a next logical step in the evolution of the internet. This has been made possible by cloud-based applications and the increased processing power and interconnectivity of hand-held and portable devices.

Before the advent and adoption of computing technology in the mid- to late-20th Century, business and government records were maintained manually. Records and ledgers were kept in hardcopy format. This system was exposed to risk of error and destruction, and it was time-consuming and expensive for agencies to cross-check or share data. Failure to manage record retention policies and the administration of document access can result in significant running costs, and may have legal ramifications [184].

Businesses and governments all over the world started using computers to manage record-keeping from the late 1960s onwards. By the 1980s, networking computers within organisations enabled the sharing and transfer of data between nodes and departments. Users in these private networks did not need to hide their identity from each other because they were participating in the same joint endeavour. It was the advent of the internet and interconnectivity between competing or unknown nodes and users that gave rise to the need to create user identities and passwords.

Since the early 1990s, the misuse of computers and unauthorised access to or manipulation of data held on computers has posed a significant problem for society and for all economies [185, p. 23]. Most of these risks are difficult to contain, because the technology that enables them continues to develop [186].

Formal online relationships are created when banks, employers, businesses, and government ask participants in their online networks to create a user identity and password. In these relationships, it is not just financial security that is at risk. The collection of personal information and confidential data requires further levels of security to protect against privacy breaches and fraud. It is these formal online relationships that this chapter addresses. The sorts of activities that could benefit from blockchain technology are: verification, movement of assets, ownership, and identities.

If adopted by government, banks, and businesses, Blockchain can streamline online exchanges, and reduce corruption, mistakes, fraud, and tax evasion. This is achievable because blockchain technology is the most sophisticated tracking system yet to be developed [187, p. 589]. The first supply chain systems improved visibility and control on goods and products as they moved from point A to point B. The same methodology has applied to tracking movement of money and assets. Tracing money and its substitutes represents a significant element in any effort to identify and recover proceeds of crimes or undeclared income and profits. However, the old concepts and technologies no longer support today's complex global digitised assets and money.

The goal with Blockchain is to create networks for participants to set rules governing public ledger and smart contracts. If all users can see and verify transactions, the risk of any one player avoiding their private or civic obligations is removed. A key component of any strategy to address corruption, tax evasion, and money laundering is ensuring that no one player can hide from their obligations. With the removal of cash from our economies on the rise, it is important that online transactions be made visible and verifiable.

5.1 The trouble with cash

In January 2017, police in Boston found US$20 million dollars under the mattress of a Brazilian man suspected of laundering money. Prosecutors alleged that Cleber Rene Rizerio Rocha, age 28, was hiding the proceeds of a multi-billion-dollar fraud. For five years, Rocha and his associates had been promoting their company, TelexFree Inc., as a telecom company [188]. Initially, its main source of income was a US$20 per annum subscription fee for internet services. This business model looked innocent enough. However, TelexFree's first brush with infamy came soon after its inception, when it became apparent that its logo was exactly the same as the logo for the World Badminton Championships. TelexFree had plagiarised the design.

As the company grew, it moved to inviting investors to buy shares in the apparently successful business. Participants would buy shares for about US$1400 a piece, and were allegedly promised fast, double-digit returns. They received incentives for bringing in family and friends. According the Federal Bureau of Investigation TelexFree aggressively marketed its services by recruiting thousands of 'promoters' to post ads for the product on the internet. Each promoter was required to 'buy in' to TelexFree at a certain price, after which they were compensated by TelexFree, under a complex compensation structure, on a weekly basis so long as they posted ads for TelexFree's VoIP service on the internet.

The ad-posting requirements were a meaningless exercise, in which promoters cut and pasted ads into various classified ad sites provided by TelexFree, which were already saturated with ads posted by earlier participants. According to evidence filed by victims of the scam, TelexFree derived only a fraction of its revenue from sales of its services—less than 1% of TelexFree's hundreds of millions of dollars in revenue over the previous two years. The overwhelming majority of its revenue came from new investors buying into the scheme. TelexFree was able to pay the returns it had promised only to its existing promoters by bringing in money from newly recruited promoters. By 2014, it was clear that Rocha and his associates has been running an international Ponzi Scheme, using money taken from an ever-growing network of small investors to pay off earlier participants.

Ponzi Schemes are not new. Their history stretches back to the late 1800s. Named after Boston businessman Charles Ponzi [189, p. 871], the original operator of a 'robbing Peter to pay Paul' scam was a New York confidence trickster named William Miller. In 1899, Miller stole US$1 million from investors with a promise that he knew how companies operated and promising returns on investment of 520% [190].

At the heart of all Ponzi Schemes is a betrayal of trust. A client or investor gives their money to an investment manager. The fund manager is charged with investing their client's money in a certain way, for example, in exchange for bitcoin or stocks. The investment manager owes fiduciary duties to the client with respect to that money. Fiduciary duties are special obligations that not only ensure the health of the relationship between investor and trustee, but also are a significant cornerstone in our financial industry. Fiduciary law is not something that can be easily diluted or renegotiated. It is a complex social phenomenon with a rich history founded in law, psychology, anthropology, and religion. The fiduciary relationship underpins the morality of how we do business. Unfortunately, history has also taught us that many a fiduciary has turned predator.

What the case of Rocha's mattress reveals is that the fact and scale of his fraud were not the headline-grabbing part of the story—it was the cash hidden in his mattress. Most news services led with this feature. Hiding US$20 million in cash is not a simple proposition. The most popular denomination for money launderers is the US$100 bill. Smaller bills are too many in number to conceal and carry. If each of Rocha's bills were no bigger than US$100 in value, he had to hide at least 200,000 notes, removing them from circulation.

Despite the difficulty of concealing these numbers, cash remains very popular in criminal activity because it is one of the last remaining stores of value that is anonymous and untraceable. According to Australia's Minister for Revenue and Financial Services Kelly O'Dwyer, there are three times as many AU$100 notes in circulation in Australia as there are AU$5 notes. In the USA, studies have shown that the overwhelming majority of all US$100 notes are located either in Miami or on the border of Canada and Mexico [191, p. 2].

5.2 Shadow economies

Ponzi Schemes and corporate scams are not the only activities that rely on cash to hide ill-gotten gains from authorities. Shadow economies, such as Mexico's informal economy discussed in Chapter 4, (also known as 'black markets') take many forms. The activities of shadow economies generally fall within two broad classifications:

1. Trade in illicit goods or services, which is paid for in cash so that the business dealing itself remains undetected;
2. Otherwise legitimate business that deals in undeclared cash in order either to fraudulently claim welfare or to avoid paying either income or consumer tax.

Both of these types of activity are treated as criminal offences in most developed and many developing nations [192, p. 119].

Cash-in-hand economies cost nations billions of dollars in lost revenue every year. In 2015, the Australian Government put more than 21,000 small businesses on written notice that their accounts would be scrutinised in the ensuing year for evidence of undeclared cash transactions with customers and suppliers. Typically, owners of these businesses deal directly with their customers and can avoid taxes by under-reporting their income through understating cash receipts and/or overstating their business expenses. It is the first time in a decade that the bureau has updated its estimate of the 'non-observed economy'. The Australian Bureau of Statistics has estimated that the nation's 'underground production'—otherwise known as the cash economy—is worth 1.5% per cent of GDP or about US$24 billion a year [193].

5.3 Money laundering

Money laundering is the process of converting money received illegitimately by rendering its source undetectable to authorities. The most popular method is to gamble the money in a casino. The process is very simple. A criminal who needs to launder US$500,000 earned from selling illicit drugs will simply buy US$500,000 worth of betting chips at a casino. He or she places US$250,000 of the amount on a bet that has a 50% chance of success. The other US$250,000 is placed on the other side of the bet. Whichever side of the bet wins, the gambler will be placed in the pre-bet position. The chips are sold back to the casino and the funds are no longer the proceeds of crime, but have become casino winnings.

Reverse money laundering is a process that disguises a legitimate source of funds that are to be used for illegal purposes [194]. It is usually perpetrated for one of three purposes:

1 Financing illicit activity (for example, terrorism) [195];
2 Legitimate business conducted by criminal organisations that have invested which need to withdraw legitimate funds from official circulation;
3 Unaccounted cash received that is not included in official financial reporting which could be used to evade taxes and pay bribes or secret commissions [196].

5.4 Trade in illicit goods and counterfeiting

Trafficking in illicit goods is a generic term used to describe all types of illicit trade. It includes such practices as counterfeiting (trademark infringements), piracy (copyright infringements), smuggling of legitimate products, and tax evasion. Selling fake or counterfeit products as the real thing is one aspect of this crime; so is selling genuine goods on the black market to avoid paying taxes.

By avoiding regulatory controls, the criminals behind these activities typically peddle often-dangerous goods with a complete disregard for the health and safety of consumers. The phenomenon has grown to an unprecedented level, posing tremendous risks to society and the global economy [197].

All levels of society are impacted by trafficking in illicit goods. For example, counterfeiting harms businesses that produce and sell legitimate products, governments lose tax revenue from products manufactured or sold on the black market, and consumers are at risk from substandard products. As an example of the enormous costs involved in illicit goods, the annual trade in illegal drugs is worth 0.4% of the GDP or about US$6.5 billion a year, in Australia alone [193, 198].

5.5 Corruption

Corruption is the receipt of money, gifts, and opportunities in exchange for favourable rulings and treatment by government authorities. It presents itself in the abuse of public or private office for personal gain. It includes acts of bribery, embezzlement, nepotism, or state capture. It is often associated with and reinforced by other illegal practices, such as bid rigging, fraud, or money laundering.

It is a problem all over the world, and in many cases consists of generous cash and electronic payments to a decision-maker. Examples might include a multinational company that pays a bribe to win a public contract or tender to build a highway or bridge, despite its submission of a substandard proposal, or the appointment by an official of a friend or family member to a position of office, despite their lack of qualification or experience for the position [199, p. 1].

According to the OECD, the costs of corruption for economic, political, and social development are becoming increasingly evident. However, many of the most convincing arguments in support of the fight against corruption are little known to the public and remain unused in political debates [182]. The victims of corruption are the weak and vulnerable.

5.6 Tax evasion

Tax evasion is the illegal activity of avoiding tax payment to a government or a jurisdiction. It creates most of the 'shadow' economy that is hidden from official view. It occurs when people abuse tax and superannuation systems through intentional and dishonest behaviour, with the aim of obtaining a financial benefit. It encompasses a broad spectrum of non-compliant activity which can result in criminal sanctions, such as fines or imprisonment. This criminal behaviour ranges from deliberate offences, such as failing to report cash wages in order to avoid tax and receive welfare payments, to the use of complex offshore secrecy arrangements to evade tax. It is estimated that tax evasion in excess of 5.1% of the world's GDP occurs as a result of shadow economy activities in every state in the world [200].

Tax evasion can take many forms and, apart from offenders becoming increasingly innovative, law enforcements also become increasingly innovative, turning to technologies such as big data to stop tax evasion. In 2016, the Australian tax office decided to start cracking down on tax offenders by investing in data analysis of social media platforms such as Twitter or Facebook and combining that with other data sources to which they have access. The Australian Tax Office (ATO) collects data from a wide range of public and private services, including immigration, motor registries, stock exchange, banks, health insurers, and many more. By combining these with public data from social media, the ATO is capable of easily tracking tax offenders. As a result, in November 2016 the ATO discovered a family who reported a total income of AU$140,000. Although quite substantial, it was obviously not enough to send their three children to private schools at a cost of AU$75,000 and to book business class flights for the entire family three times a year and a holiday in the Canadian ski resort of Whistler. The ATO was able to link the data from their Facebook account, showing images of the family while skiing in Whistler, with immigration data as well as other data sources [201]. However, tax evasion is not the only way families or corporations are trying to avoid paying taxes.

5.7 Tax havens

A tax haven is a financial product or jurisdiction that offers more attractive tax rates specifically for the purposes of attracting business. The first tax havens offered competitive tax rates to attract not just the registration of the business into that jurisdiction, but also the means or operation of the business itself. For example, at the end of the 19th century, the State of Delaware sought to lure businesses away from New York and Chicago. In order to make Delaware a more attractive place to do business, the government imposed a much lower corporate tax rate than the other states in the USA. This strategy was very successful. However, in the past 30 years, the internet, telecommunications, and the changing nature of business have meant that many businesses have incorporated in Delaware without actually moving the business to the registration address. These businesses are using the address of registration merely as a 'booking centre' [202, p. 1013].

These booking centres are big business. It is estimated that more than a million American companies and trusts are registered in Delaware. More than 285,000 businesses are estimated to be registered at 1209 Orange St, Wilmington [203], one of Delaware's most popular registration addresses. Its customers include Apple, Google, Facebook, Berkshire Hathaway, Walmart, five of the Clinton foundations, and the Trump Hotels Partnership. Delaware's earnings from its attractive corporate tax rate account for a quarter of its income.

Although these Delaware company registrations are transparent, they are not without controversy. Neighbouring states—such as Pennsylvania—publicly complain that they are missing out on vital revenue from local businesses that extract minerals from Pennsylvania's soils, but avoid paying corporate tax in Pennsylvania by incorporating in Delaware.

Secret tax havens present a problem on a much bigger scale than their transparent counterparts. There are more than 30 countries in the world offering corporate and trust registration services. These include Switzerland, the Cayman Islands, the Bahamas, the Cook Islands, British Virgin Islands, and the Netherlands Antilles. Secret tax havens require the involvement of trusted third parties who are located in jurisdictions known to have low tax rates. These third parties are lawyers, accountants, trustees, nominees, and other agents. Central to the operation of these tax havens are the bank secrecy laws [204]. For example, income earned in Canada might be sent via a series of complicated transactions to the Cook Islands and then repatriated to Canada disguised as loans.

Most tax havens have the support of their legislature to ensure that very strict secrecy laws protect customers from international inquiry—including trustees in bankruptcy, subpoenas, court orders, and judgments. These rules do not necessarily mean that the parliaments of these countries intend to assist in the concealment of fraudulent activity [205, 206]. However, this is clearly an unfortunate by-product of the business culture. Those non-disclosure laws affect the booking centres and the banks where the funds are hidden in untraceable, numbered bank accounts. For this reason, it is difficult to estimate the extent of the wealth hidden in these locations. However, thanks to a leak by an anonymous employee to a German newspaper, one of the biggest tax haven operations in the world was exposed in 2016. The Panama Papers revealed that law firm Mossack Fonseca employed more than 600 employees in 45 countries assisting its clients to hide their wealth in Panama bank accounts. The sheer scale of their activities reveals a complex network of hidden wealth and shady practices to mask illegal activity and launder the ill-gotten gains of business people and criminals all over the world. Some commentators suggest that this revelation is just the tip of a tax haven iceberg [207, p. 131].

5.8 Welfare fraud

Welfare fraud is a controversial problem that has accompanied the growth of the welfare state. The modern welfare state was designed as a comprehensive system through which governments provide support for all citizens in need, with a view to eliminating poverty and enhancing health and well-being [208]. Welfare systems frequently entail a wide range of living allowances paid to elderly people, unemployed people, those with intellectual and physical disabilities, sole parents, and students. Support also normally includes a range of partial, indirect, or in-kind government-funded benefits, such as child support payments and free or discounted medical services and childcare. In recent years, entitlement to welfare has also been extended to refugees and asylum seekers.

The welfare state has been the target of numerous criticisms. One standard critique is that it attracts fraud. There can certainly be little doubt that early benefit systems were highly vulnerable to abuse [209, 210]. It was not without justification that the terms 'dole bludger' and 'welfare queen' became part of the social and political discourse in many countries in the 1970s and 1980s.

Anecdotes about people feigning illness or disability, living on welfare while avoiding work, or collecting benefits while working, became a standard part of social gossip [211]. The right to apply for welfare and the availability of money created intrinsic temptations for people to attempt to obtain benefits fraudulently [212].

Welfare is usually organised around two main criteria—universal eligibility or means testing. Under universal eligibility, all persons fitting general criteria receive a benefit. For example, anyone over a specified age receives an old age pension. Conversely, means testing involves a second set of criteria related to income and assets. Recipients must meet a criterion, such as age, and also have income and assets below a specified threshold. Means testing is the primary form of welfare provision in Australia. It appears to be less costly, by reducing the number of recipients, and appears to be fairer in providing income only to those in genuine need. Alleged disadvantages of means testing include the requirement for a more complex bureaucracy and the creation of temptations for some applicants to understate or hide income and assets [212].

Attempts to obtain benefits illegally used to be difficult to discover, if one looks at the statistics for Australia's federal welfare agency Centrelink (located in the Department of Human Services portfolio). In 2008–9, Centrelink distributed approximately AU$86.6 billion to 6.8 million customers, including AU$10.4 million in individual entitlements, across 140 benefit types on behalf of 27 government departments and agencies. It approved 2.7 million new claims, operated over 1000 service delivery centres, employed just under 28,000 staff and made over six billion transactions on customer records [213].

A major concern for these agencies is ensuring that the recipient is genuinely entitled to receive the payment they applied for and have received. With six billion transactions to monitor, this used to be difficult to control. However, with the advent of big data analytics, governments have been given a new tool to crack down on welfare fraud and to ensure 'payment integrity'. As a result, there are an increasing number of prosecutions brought each year against fraudulent recipients of welfare [210]. Indeed, many of these anti-fraud measures have been criticised as stigmatising welfare recipients and generating 'a punitive approach to income support' that is overly reliant on criminal prosecutions [211]. However, a particularly problematic type of welfare fraud occurs when recipients of cash income for gainful employment hide those payments in order to conceal the fact that they are working (and therefore not entitled to welfare).

5.9 Traditional approaches to closing the tax gap

The USA has an Annual Tax Gap that exceeds US$400 billion [214].[1] The tax gap is the difference between the amount of tax revenue that should be collected and the amount actually collected by the Internal Revenue Service. There are tax gaps in every developed country in the world. This gap exists in large part due to the bank secrecy laws of tax havens and the shadow activities of corrupt individuals and other money-launderers. In recent years, countries such as the USA which are losing out on much-needed revenue have entered into memoranda of understanding and treaties with a number of countries in an effort to address the shortfall. In addition to these measures, the US Department of Justice and the Federal Reserve targeted US branches of foreign banks to increase compliance with the USA [204].

In an attempt to protect the US securities market, US courts have begun to employ measures aimed at circumventing bank secrecy laws. The trend towards recognising the USA's interest in the integrity of its securities markets is reflected in US court orders requiring bank customers to waive bank secrecy laws. Courts justify these orders by reasoning that secrecy laws exist for the protection of customers, not for the protection of the foreign states' public interest [204].

The OECD has recommended three initiatives for a global approach to closing the tax gap: international tax rules, tax treaties, and transparency. There is the Model Tax Convention on Income and on Capital, which forms the basis for negotiation of the more than 3000 existing bilateral tax treaties in the world, and there are the Transfer Pricing Guidelines for Multinational Enterprises and Tax Administrations and providing regulators with sufficient information to conduct audits [215]. In recent years, the OECD has grown increasingly concerned with the effectiveness of current transfer pricing documentation guidance. In particular with the proliferation of diverse, local, transfer pricing, documentation rules, taxpayers have expressed concern that the compliance costs for transfer pricing to meet each jurisdiction's specific requirements are becoming oppressive. Tax authorities have, however, expressed the view that transfer-pricing documentation currently being prepared is insufficiently informative for their risk assessment and tax enforcement needs, and provides an incomplete picture of taxpayers' global operations. As such, the OECD has reiterated the core overarching objectives of encouraging taxpayers to make informed assessments of their obligations before they file their income tax returns.

Meanwhile, the OECD's Forum on Harmful Tax Practices has built support for fair competition and minimised tax-induced distortions, with more than 40 regimes identified over time as potentially harmful, all of which have been abolished or modified. The engine of harmful tax practices is a lack of transparency. Although blockchain is not the cure-all for the tax system, it could be applied in a number of areas to reduce the administrative burden and collect tax at a lower cost, helping to narrow the tax gap. Blockchain could cut costs and add value within a business, between businesses, between businesses and consumers, and between businesses and governments. There is a need for experimentation and courage to try different applications, and Blockchain can provide real-time and secure information about provenance, traceability, and transparency of transactions.

In order to address welfare fraud, the Australian government has a number of methods of detection. Anti-fraud measures adopted overseas and in Australia include: data-matching between government agencies; stepped-up identity verification checks; covert surveillance and video recording; stepped-up investigations, with greater use of forensic accounting and site visits; increased prosecutions; increased recoveries through debt collection strategies and asset forfeiture; and public tip-off lines [210]. Most of these measures can be automated by monitoring bank accounts as well as social media activities. However, when wages are received in cash it is easy to conceal those payments by using cash for day-to-day expenses (for example). If cash is removed from the economy generally, this sort of fraudulent activity becomes much harder.

5.10 Removing cash from circulation

In December 2016, the Australian Government announced its plan to establish a task force to explore the role of cash in black market economies. In particular, it will look at phasing out the circulation of AU$100 and AU$50 notes, in a bid to reclaim billions of dollars in lost revenue and to reduce welfare fraud. It has been suggested that large notes are being used to pay undeclared income, avoid goods and services tax (GST), and launder the ill-gotten gains of illicit activities. The Australian Government is also contemplating restrictions on the maximum size of cash purchases.

These ideas are not new. At least a dozen other countries are exploring similar measures, with Sweden introducing legislation requiring cash registers to transmit all transaction records directly to its Treasury.

Economists argue that most of the large denomination bills in countries all over the world are not in circulation because they are either being hoarded or hidden [216]. The hoarders fear economic or political collapse and the impact on currency. However, it is the facilitation of crime that wreaks the most havoc on the circulation of cash.

Paper currency, especially large notes such as the US$100 bill or the 500 euro bill, facilitate crime: racketeering, extortion, money laundering, drug and human trafficking, the corruption of public officials, and terrorism. There are substitutes for cash—cryptocurrencies, uncut diamonds, gold coins, prepaid cards—but, for many kinds of criminal transactions, cash is still king [217]. Nowhere in the world has the push to reduce cash as a means to tackle tax avoidance and corruption been received with so much enthusiasm as in India. Driving the push towards less cash is the amount of tax revenue lost each year to corruption, welfare fraud, counterfeiting, money laundering, and other black-market activities that are enabled by large denomination bills.

In November 2016, Prime Minister Narendra Modi dealt a blow to what has been described as India's endemic corruption with a surprise move to ban the country's largest currency bills. The ban was intended to curb the flow of counterfeit money and to target terrorist organisations that rely on unaccounted-for cash. It was also expected to help the government clean up a system that has relied on cash to pay bribes and avoid taxes [218]. But the announcement, made on national television in both Hindi and English, led to an immediate upheaval in the country. Abolishing the current version of the 500 and 1000 rupee notes, worth about US$8 and US$15, effectively removed 80% of the currency in circulation [219].

In addition, the European Central Bank announced that, from 2018, all large euro notes would be removed from circulation [220]. However, by September 2017 some individuals, most probably criminals, had already tried to get rid of these notes. A blocked sewer pipe beneath a UBS bank and nearby bistros in Switzerland revealed tens of thousands of high denomination euro notes that had been flushed down numerous toilets. A waiter in the Pizzeria du Molard told a local newspaper that the restaurant had called the police after the men's toilets became blocked up. On investigating the cause of the blockage, staff found dozens of shredded €500 in the bathroom's plumbing. Some of the notes had been shredded and investigators reported that they seemed to have originated from a safe deposit box in Geneva. Although destroying bank notes is not an offence in Switzerland, the local police confirmed that the case warranted further investigation. The disposal of these notes may be linked to illegal activities and money laundering, although at the time of writing the exact cause was still unclear.

All of these attempts to address the tax gaps in various jurisdictions suffer from one universal barrier to their implementation and success: there is no incentive for tax avoiders and their facilitators to cooperate. In the words of a Caribbean banking official [221], 'demand for disclosure is a call for extermination' [222, 223]. It is time for a new approach.

5.11 Using the blockchain to close the tax gap

The Blockchain's advantage over traditional online payment systems is its cash-like completeness and immutability. With permissioned access to payment networks and systems, it is possible to link transactions to tax obligations and ensure receipt of revenue by tax authorities. Similar to cash, the only way to return transfers conducted on a blockchain is to undertake a new transfer. The Blockchain's immutability means that there is no analogous danger of counterfeit. Although notes and coins can be replicated by sophisticated criminals, there is no equivalent process or deception available on Blockchain networks.

The Ukraine is exploring the use of the Blockchain to curtail corruption, particularly when selling government assets. Besides the immutable nature of the public asset ledger, the Ukraine Finance Minister, Oleksandr Danilyuk, has pointed out that a major advantage of the blockchain-based system is that it completely eliminates the possibility of administrative interference during bidding. He promised that, 'new online auctions will be fully transparent and open', with an eAuction that would not only fit into the existing infrastructure, but also reduce paper work [201].

By using blockchain technology, it is possible to monitor all electronic payments and transactions, including transfers to other jurisdictions. The technology underpinning and enabling the Blockchain can validate users and transactions, eliminate double spending, and improve the speed and security of transactions. One of the significant costs that can also be addressed on the blockchain is streamlining compliance with 'Know Your Customer' (KYC) and 'Anti-Money Laundering' (AML) obligations. In addition to identifying and verifying users, the blockchain can track the movement of assets. Each transaction is unique and cryptocurrencies themselves act in the same way as marked bills: from the moment of creation, it is possible to follow the trail of any single unit or file as it moves within the network. As such, it is important to understand that, despite what some people believe, Bitcoin is not anonymous; it is only pseudo-anonymous. This means that, with sufficient data at hand, something that is not too difficult to obtain in today's big data era, one could start to see patterns in the transactions and as such de-anonymise the data. By linking public keys to real identities, law enforcers could identify every link in the blockchain network. However, big data analytics does not solve the challenge created by so-called 'mixers', online platforms developed to conceal whose funds were sent to whom. These mixers enable situations where Alice and Bob both sends funds to Eve, and then Eve sends funds to Carl and Dennis; it's not obvious whether Alice's money flowed to Carl or to Dennis. If this is done at a scale of thousands of transactions simultaneously, it becomes even more confusing.

Nevertheless, to achieve these two apparently competing aims (de-identifying parties to legitimate transactions, while revealing the identities of parties to ones that are illegitimate or suspicious), smart contracts can be coded to monitor and report transactions on the network. Permissionless (public) blockchains allow users to control the degree of privacy with which they deal with others on the network. In the case of permissioned systems that include regulators, the system can still allow private transactions, with code that identifies certain types of conduct. This autonomy and control allow users to choose the level of privacy they want in their interactions, depending on the type of network [65, p. 42]. Parties to legitimate exchanges will have their privacy protected, whereas those who attempt to engage in illegal or suspicious transactions can be prevented from doing so until they defend what they are about to do. If that justification requires that they reveal their identity, this would be the cost of using the network for those types of transactions.

Although there remains a risk that some players will structure their transactions so as to mask or hide the total value or purpose of their payments, it is important to remember that this is a problem that already exists on a massive scale. The benefit of using an online system with built-in trust protocols is that more people can participate.

A 2013 study into the traceability of bitcoin transactions suggested that vulnerabilities in the blockchain network could be exploited to assist in the identification of specific transactions [224]. It is this potential for discovery that has led to innovations which add a secure transport layer on top of bitcoin (for example, ZCash). Providing confidentiality in a public blockchain brings distributed ledgers culturally into line with traditional financial privacy protocols enjoyed with physical cash. Financial privacy and even secrecy can be defensible. It is not always necessary for governments and regulators to know about all transactions. The types of transactions that need to be reported are already understood in current systems. What cryptocurrency can allow for is the trusted online exchange of value for things, absent or unsecured, expensive or slow third parties.

As long as there are legitimate users on the system, the passage and use of bitcoin can be revealed, particularly at the moment when the owner of the bitcoin wants to spend or convert it into goods or services [225]. A study by Small, and the possibilities offered by its author, are particularly important in light of bitcoin's growing popularity as a tax haven. Regulators need to apply resources to examining how this network can be exploited in a way that ensures that all participants on the network are using it for legitimate purposes.

How can blockchain technology achieve where other anti-corruption systems have failed? Very simply, through trust. As the bitcoin blockchain has proven, distributed trustless consensus is the Blockchain's major breakthrough. By deploying one of a number of zero knowledge proof mechanisms, the Blockchain can record and report to all users how participants are conducting themselves. To motivate users to behave well and to report on the good (or bad) behaviour of others, it is possible to give value to all transactions on a network. As such, many distributed networks apply game theory to incentivise good behaviour. Value could be represented by tokens or a crypto-coin. The tokens/coins could be converted to fiat money or fund data storage capacity or computational power on the blockchain (for example). In order to fund these rewards (or tokens), all or certain types of transactions on the network could be taxed. To ensure that there is no build-up of tokens or values in any one block or at any one time, the tokens created for tax purposes would be applied to the rewards within the same block. For every successful and trustworthy transaction, participants would receive a trustworthiness rating that increases with regular use.

It would be easy to include in this model a special rating that applies to users who have verified their identity with a regulator, thereby satisfying the KYC/AML requirements (as discussed in Chapter 3). Indeed, there could be a higher reward token for those who register with or identify themselves to the regulator. In this way, if any users have not received a KYC/AML proof, then all other users would be on notice about this and would restrict or completely preclude transactions with that participant. The idea that use of a blockchain network can be funded by participants, and that consensus mechanisms can be incentivised, is the reason why the bitcoin blockchain has been so successful. In addition to meeting regulatory requirements, the blockchain has the potential to monitor the financial sources of governments and politicians, and even the banks accounts run by committees to re-elect political leaders.

Underpinning this hypothetical solution to digital money laundering is the notion of trust. Trustless systems require that everyone can trust the network to behave as it should, regardless of the intentions of any particular party, which could be arbitrarily malicious. In the same way that coded messages can safely pass through enemy hands and an email can be encrypted and then safely sent through an untrusted channel, so too can the blockchain allow participants to rely on its consensus mechanisms. At any given time, every player on the ledger can observe all transactions, making it almost impossible to hide or manipulate transactions.

Similarly, cryptography answers the needs of *trust of safety*, because we can require transactions to have cryptographic signatures. If everyone in the system is able to verify cryptographic signatures and refuses to accept payment without one, the trust of safety is achieved [226].

5.12 Conclusion

Corruption corrodes public trust, undermines the rule of law, and ultimately delegitimises the state [182]. Rules and regulations are circumvented by bribes, public budget control is undermined by illicit money flows, and political critics and the media are silenced through bribes forcing out democratic systems of checks and balances. If basic public services are not delivered to citizens due to corruption, the state eventually loses its credibility and legitimacy. Removing large denomination bills from circulation is an essential step towards combatting shadow economies, corruption, and money laundering, and ultimately closing the tax gap. The challenge for regulators will be to harness the power of Blockchain to trace digital transactions. Permissioned blockchains can ensure that users are reporting income and meeting their tax obligations. These blockchains could also interact with other blockchains, so that agencies and departments can automate cross-checking of related transactions. Indeed, running discrete blockchains to manage different functions would ensure that the scale of each network remains manageable and would reduce the incidence of blockchain bloat.

Thinking back to the TelexFree scam and the US$20 million hidden inside Mr Rocha's mattress, one can see how a trust rating system would have quickly undone his Ponzi Scheme. Ponzi Schemes rely on new money to pay out previous investors. The fraud lies in the promise that payments are being made from profits generated by the business in which shareholders or customers have invested. With a transparent distributed ledger, it would be possible to see that new money into the scheme was being used to pay investors. This would indicate to other participants on the network that there is no successful business scheme generating profits and the payment of dividends. And with all cash removed from the economy, Mr Rocha's bed filled with US$100 bills would be worthless.

Note

1 According to the US Internal Revenue Service (IRS), the average Annual Tax Gap for 2008–2010 is estimated to be US$458 billion, compared with US$450 billion for tax year 2006. IRS enforcement activities and late payments resulted in an additional US$52 billion in tax paid, reducing the net tax gap for the 2008–2010 period to US$406 billion per year. The voluntary compliance rate is now estimated at 81.7% compared with the prior estimated rate of 83.1%. After accounting for enforcement and late payments, the net compliance rate is 83.7%.

Chapter 6

Blockchain and climate change

> **Climate change /ˈklʌɪmət tʃeɪn(d)ʒ/**: a change in global or regional climate patterns, in particular a change apparent from the mid to late 20th century onwards, and attributed largely to the increased levels of atmospheric carbon dioxide produced by the use of fossil fuels

On 7 January 2018, Sydney, Australia had its hottest day in almost 80 years. In most parts of the city, the temperatures topped 47°C. Less than a year before, on 11 February 2017, temperatures in Sydney also soared and reached a peak of 47.6°C. Half-way through February 2017, the maximum temperature for that month was 4° above average and the warm month followed Sydney's second-hottest December and hottest January since the start of the records, dating back to 1858 [227]. Meanwhile, the North Pole was experiencing its own version of a heat wave. With temperatures rising to melting point, 0°Celsius, for the third time in the winter of 2017 [228, 229]. Finally, the USA also experienced an unusual heat wave in the winter of 2017. In Oklahoma and Texas, temperatures went up to 37°Celsius, which was a new all-time record for February high temperatures [230].

Although Australia and the USA are developed countries, according to the Global Climate Risk Index 2017, the countries affected the most by the impacts of weather-related loss events (storms, floods, heat waves, etc.) were poorer developing countries, for example Mozambique, Dominica, and Malawi. The 12th edition of the report confirmed that developing countries are generally affected more by weather-related loss events than industrialised countries [231]. As a result, developing countries face a relatively bigger impact of climate change than developed countries, while having a smaller environmental footprint and therefore not being as responsible for climate change. Often these countries already face several other Wicked Problems as well.

Despite a lack of acceptance by some policy-makers, climate change is a very real Wicked Problem. In the past decades, the impact of climate change on the world has been well researched and documented. According to many scientists, climate change will have an impact on the world's food supply [232], human health [233], the world's marine ecosystems [234], our biodiversity [235], and our economic systems [236]. The objective of this book is not to argue that climate change is a real problem. We believe that there is overwhelming evidence provided by thousands of scientists from around the globe that climate change is real and that we need to act now. The Paris agreement, which was signed in 2015 within United Nations Framework Convention on Climate Change (UNFCCC), underlines and confirms the problem. The agreement was negotiated by representatives of 195 countries and has the objective of 'holding the increase in the global average temperature to well below 2 °C above pre-industrial levels and to pursue efforts to limit the temperature increase to 1.5 °C above pre-industrial levels' [237, p. 2]. Instead, this chapter is about how we can use the latest technology, specifically Blockchain, to contribute to combatting climate change and reducing the effects of rising temperatures.

Climate change is not caused by one activity, but by a combination of, among other things, burning fossil fuels, deforestation, and farming. Climate change is a problem that is not easy to solve. Thousands of scientists with different disciplines all argue for their version of the story, albeit with most of them agreeing that climate change is real. As such, we are dealing with a Wicked Problem, because it involves many different stakeholders, sometimes with conflicting views, where the information provided can be confusing [238], and where the actual problem consists of many interrelated 'smaller' problems.

Although climate change might not affect you at all personally or you might appreciate a warm summer or winter, or burning fossil fuels might be good for your business, we concur with the overwhelming idea that climate change has an impact on all of us and everything that is alive on our planet. As such, we have a moral obligation to our children to try to protect the Earth as well as possible and pass it on to the next generation in good order. In addition, protecting the Earth and combatting climate change actually make sense economically because climate change also adheres to some simple economics.

It works as follows. Whenever a new technology is introduced, be it the printing press in the 15th century, the steam engine in the 18th century, or the mainframe computer in the 20th century, the first version is always extremely expensive, and most of the time quite big as well. As technological progress is made, the technology becomes cheaper, easier to use, and gets more applications (whether for good or bad). The printing press significantly improved access to knowledge and made education cheaper. The steam engine created energy and made a wide variety of activities easier, cheaper, and more accessible. The mainframe computer significantly reduced the cost of communication and finding information. In this way, technological revolutions tend to involve certain important activities becoming cheaper and more accessible [239].

Climate change, and the resulting green energy revolution, is, in its essence, a production technology, so the economic shift will revolve around a drop in the cost of clean energy production. The impact of a reduction in price of clean energy production is that goods and services that rely on (clean) energy will become cheaper, whereas the value of products and services that complement clean energy will rise, such as the EnergyTech space. As long as the price of clean energy production drops and the value of related activities increases, the value of substitutes, such as fossil fuels, will eventually fall. So, economically it makes sense to start investing in clean energy or EnergyTech and reduce dependency on fossil fuels in your business models. Already, we see that, in some countries, the price of producing renewable energy is on a par with the price of producing fossil fuel energy. In 2016, solar and wind energy became even cheaper to produce than new fossil fuel energy in 30 countries [240], and it is expected that this 'grid parity' will be achieved by dozens more countries in the years to come. In fact, the average global cost of solar energy could fall below coal within the next decade. According to Michael Drexler, Head of Investors Industries and Member of the Executive Committee at the World Economic Forum: 'renewable energy has reached a tipping point—it now constitutes the best chance to reverse global warming. It is not only a commercially viable option, but an outright compelling investment opportunity with long-term, stable, inflation-protected returns' [241].

So, apart from the bare necessity of protecting the Earth from existential threats due to climate change, for the first time it makes sense economically to invest in renewable energy. As a result, we will probably see vast amounts of funding being invested in clean energy and energy-related technologies and companies or start-ups that develop the types of solutions from which we are likely to benefit. Apart from the 'traditional' clean energy solutions, emerging technologies such as big data analytics, Blockchain and artificial intelligence open whole new possibilities for organisations and governments to contribute to combatting climate change.

6.1 Life coming to a standstill

On 28 October 2012, life came to a standstill in New York. The governor of New York, Andrew Cuomo, had just declared a state of emergency and former President Obama had just issued a federal emergency declaration for the State of New York and New Jersey [242]. School was cancelled for the 1.1 million students living in the area, the New York Stock Exchange suspended floor trading and over 375,000 citizens were evacuated [243]. In addition, the New York transit system suspended service for several days and even the coffee-addicted New Yorkers couldn't get their daily caffeine shot because Starbucks closed all its outlets for several days [244]. New York was preparing itself for the monstrous hurricane Sandy.

A few days earlier, hurricane Sandy, or Superstorm Sandy, had battered several Caribbean islands including Jamaica, Haiti, the Dominican Republic, and Puerto Rico. The effects of the hurricane on these islands were dramatic, leaving many residents without electricity, causing food shortages, and making hundreds of thousands of people homeless. During the following days, the hurricane increased in strength and, when it arrived in New York, it had become the largest Atlantic hurricane ever recorded [245]. In the days that followed, New York was severely damaged, reaching almost US$42 billion in damages [246] and leaving vast parts of the city without electricity. In total, 2.2 million people lost power due to the hurricane, which took up to several weeks to restore for everyone, leaving Lower Manhattan and other parts of New York in the dark—a surreal experience for those being hit by the sudden power outages. In the weeks following, the power grid was fully restored, but it came at a cost.

Wide-area power outages such as the incident in New York are a problem for any country or city, and restoring power after an outage can often be very difficult and time-consuming. As a result, governments and organisations are looking for new solutions that can prevent wide-area outages and restore power more quickly in the case of an outage. One way to achieve this is through the use of a smart grid, ideally consisting of multiple micro-grids. A smart grid is a power network that is equipped with all kinds of sensors at different points in the supply chain of electricity. Sensors monitor the production of electricity, the transportation of electricity, and the demand for electricity. Using big data analytics, energy companies can predict supply and demand for different areas as well as any upcoming maintenance, reducing the likelihood of a power outage due to failed equipment. A smart grid will automatically match supply and demand and in the (not-too-distant) future it is probable that the smart grid will determine when you can charge your electric car (if everyone who drives an electric car and comes home from work would plug in their car and start charging it, this would result in a peak demand, which could cause the network to default). Smart grids offer a lot of advantages for governments, organisations, and consumers in terms of reliability and costs of electricity, but they are also very difficult to develop, due to the existing complexity within our existing energy networks. Therefore, a great way to start is by developing a micro-grid. A micro-grid is a small, independent, energy grid, which most of the time uses renewable energy. A micro-grid can be disconnected from the main energy grid, so that, in the event of a wide-area power outage, a micro-grid remains operational. Developing a smart micro-grid is a lot easier than developing a regional or national smart grid, because often only a few houses or buildings are involved within the smart micro-grid. Within a micro-grid, individuals will harness solar or wind energy and so become energy neutral, or even energy positive, meaning that they generate more energy than they use. In such events, energy can be sold back to the main grid, or to different participants in the micro-grid. As selling or buying energy is basically a transaction, it is perfectly suited to the Blockchain making these peer-to-peer transactions in a trustless environment that is immutable, verifiable, and traceable.

6.2 The world's first peer-to-peer energy transaction

On 11 April 2016, Lawrence Orsini went to work, knowing it would be a day unlike any other. The New York-based entrepreneur has a deep understanding of the energy sector and aims to apply the latest technologies to bring change in this traditional and often conservative industry. Lawrence Orsini is the founder of LO3 Energy, an energy- and technology-centric company that builds tools and develops projects to accelerate the proliferation of the emerging distributed energy and computation economy. On that sunny spring day in Brooklyn, Lawrence went to work, with the objective of creating a world first.

In the previous weeks, Orsini had built a micro-grid on President Street in Brooklyn, New York. Ten homes on President Street had been connected to each other, five on each side. One side of the street produced renewable energy, independently from the state grid, whereas the other side did not have solar panels but wanted to buy local solar energy. The objective of the pilot was to produce renewable energy using solar panels on rooftops of the homes and sell any excess to the houses on the other side of the street using Blockchain, without the involvement of national energy companies. As Lawrence explained, 'Blockchain technology is rapidly advancing across many sectors, but in the energy market, things are comparatively different. With our micro-grid solution in Brooklyn, we'll demonstrate just the beginning of what blockchain can do in the transactive energy world' [247]. As it happened, on 11 April 2016 the first paid energy transaction took place between two individuals: long-term local and social justice activist Eric Fruman traded his excess solar energy from his rooftop installation to ex-Energy Star National Director Bob Sauchelli [248]. The use of Blockchain technology enabled the participants in the micro-grid to see exactly who consumed or produced what amount of energy and exactly what transactions took place when. The micro-grid in Brooklyn was based on the Ethereum Blockchain to record the buying and selling of any electrons that were generated by the solar panels using trading energy certificates. As such, the blockchain enabled the residents of President Street to buy and sell renewable energy directly to and from their neighbours, without having to go through a centralised party such as a large energy company. However, rather than exchanging the actual electrons, the solution was developed to exchange energy certificates, that is the right to use a certain amount of energy. As Orsini explained during the launch of the project, there is no 'billing component around it, you don't have the infrastructure losses or the accounting losses in the system, while the energy and the money goes to benefit the community. When you buy energy from the community, the money goes back to the community' [249].

Since the pilot of the micro-grid on Presidential Street, Orsini has partnered with Siemens. They have combined the micro-grid solution developed by Siemens with the peer-to-peer trading platform based on the blockchain to develop micro-grids that enable locals to trade energy using Blockchain, and balance out local production and consumption. The benefits of a decentralised and distributed energy system is that it enables transparent, efficient, and effective trading between different, local stakeholders while taking grid-specific requirements into account [247]. As a result, these micro-grids may become more resistant than centralised energy grids when natural catastrophes happen, such as Superstorm Sandy, allowing people to keep their energy, during major infrastructural failure [249], and also making some extra money from the excess renewable energy.

The micro-grid developed in Brooklyn was just the start. Smart grids are the future of energy production and consumption, and offer tremendous advantages over the traditional energy grids. Smart grids will consist of billions of end-points such as solar systems, micro-grids, smart appliances, houses, etc. that are constantly interacting with each other over the internet. Apart from selling any excess energy, Blockchain can also help improve smart grids, and the management of those smart grids, by cryptographically ensuring trust among connected devices and actors in the smart grid. Quite a few start-ups are working hard to develop a decentralised solution. The UK start-up Electron wants to use smart contracts on the Ethereum Blockchain to develop a smart grid that will always deliver energy. In 2016, they were in the testing phase, using 53 million metering points and 60 energy supplier data to run experiments to test the platform.

The company Grid Singularity aims to develop a decentralised energy data management and exchange platform for the developing world. This platform will enable regulators, operators, investors, traders, and consumers to collaborate efficiently on smart grids. The Austrian company targets developing countries to offer them a pay-as-you-go solar energy system and they use Blockchain to authenticate energy transactions [250]. Samsung and IBM are also working on Blockchain solutions for smart grids. They developed a platform called ADEPT, which uses smart contracts on Ethereum to manage micro-transactions between smart appliances on a smart grid, because they autonomously react to changing grid conditions. The platform is a Blockchain–Internet of Things initiative and so very suitable for smart grids. These interactions will make a smart grid more stable, because peaks and lows in energy production and demand can be flattened out.

Smart, blockchain-enabled (micro) grids offer a lot of advantages for consumers and organisations. The possibility of selling surplus energy to other members directly in a (micro) grid, without the need for an intermediary taking a percentage of the revenue, creates a great incentive to move towards renewable energy and install solar panels or windmills because they offer an additional return on the initial investment. If more individuals and organisations move to renewable energy as part of a smart (micro) grid, it will have a positive effect on climate change. Having said that, this is a long-term solution, although Blockchain-enabled smart grids are not the only way that Blockchain technology can help reduce the effects of climate change.

6.3 Clean EnergyTech

Anything that becomes digitised will adhere to the exponential rules of information technology. Once something can be represented in ones and zeros, it becomes a data product, or service, which means that it opens up to the same exponential growth as we have seen with information-based technology [251]. Traditionally, energy production and distribution have been very centralised and analogue. Fossil fuel production requires large corporations to invest billions of dollars in equipment to retrieve oil from the depth of an ocean or to frack gas from deep underground. Apart from the analogue process, the distribution of that energy is done by centralised, often government-owned, grid companies. These companies move energy around the globe and determine the pricing, which has an impact on the world economy; if OPEC decides to reduce or increase oil production, it has an impact on everyone. However, energy production is moving away from a centralised approach to a decentralised one and is rapidly becoming digitised as well, thanks to new start-ups and new technological breakthroughs. Such breakthroughs include the smart micro-grids developed in Brooklyn or the solar energy roof tiles developed by Elon Musk. These solar roof tiles eliminate the need for expensive solar panels to be installed on a rooftop and Musk aims to make them as expensive as traditional roof tiles [252]. As a result, the energy world is opening to the exponential rules of information technology and consequently (Clean) EnergyTech is rapidly changing the way we produce, store, consume, or trade energy.

Clean energy technology offers a lot of opportunities for reducing climate change, and it appears that Blockchain could play an important role as well. Apart from blockchain-enabled smart grids, there are multiple other ways that Blockchain can help reduce carbon emissions, affect carbon pricing, enable energy data analysis, improve energy distribution, or enable, as we have seen, distributed and decentralised smart micro-grids. Already, there are multiple start-ups and research initiatives that try to understand how Blockchain enables custom, distributed, and decentralised value flows and which, if successful, will benefit each of these energy-related aspects and so positively contribute to reducing the effects of climate change.

6.4 Carbon emission, pricing, and energy trading

The Industrial Revolution, which started with the invention of the steam engine, completely changed how people lived and worked. The transition, which involved moving from hand production to machine production, offered citizens energy to improve their daily lives and resulted in a new organisation design that ensured more efficient and better production of goods. The Industrial Revolution propelled humankind into a new, more prosperous era. Unfortunately, it also resulted in a massive increase in greenhouse gases because human activities have resulted in a 40% increase in the atmospheric concentration of carbon dioxide, from 280 parts per million (ppm) in 1750 to 400 ppm in 2015 [253]. The emission of carbon dioxide affects everyone. CO_2 released in India will affect the people in the USA and coal factories operating in Beijing will have an impact on the climate in South Africa. It has been estimated that, if the emission of greenhouse gases continues at the same rate in the coming decades, the Earth's average surface temperature could exceed historical values by 2047 [254] and the limit of a rise of 2°C could be reached as early as 2036 [255]. This highlights the importance of the Paris agreement. We are dealing with a global problem that requires a global solution and Blockchain can enable the achievement of some of the key global solutions.

Carbon emissions are a significant contributing cause of climate change; the carbon footprint is defined as the total set of greenhouse gas emissions caused by an event, organisation, or country. In the past years, governments around the globe have worked hard to try to limit the emission of greenhouse gases. As such, carbon pricing was invented, which is a certain amount of money that must be paid for the right to emit one tonne of CO_2 into the atmosphere. These rights can be traded if an organisation has any left or if an organisation or country is emitting more carbon dioxide than allowed. However, there are significant challenges with the system because they take place in international markets. As a consequence, taxation arrangements, fraud, crime or currency fluctuations, and transaction settlement costs affect the success of carbon credit transactions [256]. The global carbon market continues to grow and, in 2015, the total value rose by 9% to US$52.6 billion [257]. Next to that, voluntary buyers traded a total of 84.1 million tonnes of carbon dioxide equivalent ($MtCO_2e$) in 2015, representing a 10% increase over 2014 [258]. This continued growth, as well as the associated challenges of a global carbon marketplace, require a new approach to carbon credits trading. Blockchain is the perfect technology for improving the system. It enables reduced transaction settlement times (because anyone with access to the Blockchain instantly has an updated record), increases efficiency and transparency (currently carbon trading is notoriously not transparent) because all transactions are verifiable and traceable on the blockchain, and significantly reduces the costs of carbon trading, virtually eliminating fraud in carbon credits trading, because transactions are immutable and governed by smart contracts. The use of smart contracts could automate a large part of the trading process, while at the same time removing any taxation or juridical uncertainties, because the code of the smart contracts is universally readable and understandable.

Various initiatives around the globe are exploring the possibilities of a blockchain-based carbon credits trading platform. In Russia, collaboration between AiraLab and Microsoft Russia resulted in the development of an Ethereum-based trading platform. The objective of the distributed trading platform is to enable private companies to buy and sell carbon credits. Those transactions are then recorded on the blockchain. In 2016, the first test carbon credit transaction was carried out on the platform, and valued at US$120,000 [259].

In 2016, a partnership between IBM and the Beijing Energy-Blockchain Labs resulted in the first Blockchain platform for carbon trading in China. It is no surprise that China is experimenting with Blockchain technology for carbon trading. It is expected that the global market for carbon trading will grow to US$3.5 trillion by 2020 and China will become the world's largest carbon trading market [260]. The objective is to make it more efficient to develop and manage carbon assets, and so reduce carbon emissions. In addition, recording carbon assets on a blockchain will offer transparency and ensure that transactions are valid and settled in minutes.

However, carbon credits are not the only things that can be traded on the blockchain. As we have seen in the example of the micro-grid in Brooklyn, any energy-related transaction can be recorded on the blockchain and become immutable, verifiable, and traceable. Multiple start-ups are developing peer-to-peer renewable energy trading platforms to increase the usage of renewable energy. The Australian company, Perth-based Power Ledger, is developing a peer-to-peer renewable energy-trading platform, using the blockchain. The platform enables consumers to buy, sell, or exchange excess renewable electricity, directly with each other. This works via crypto-tokens, which are tradable digital assets representing a certain energy production. These can be sold to others via the Blockchain to prevent double spending and ensure valid transactions. As a result, Blockchain enables Power Ledger to offer a transparent, auditable, and automated marketplace that settles and clears transactions between consumers in minutes, without the need for a trusted centralised third party such as an energy company which charges a fee for its services. The objective of the platform is to empower consumers in relation to their energy consumption and production.

Jemma Green, the co-founder and chairman of Power Ledger, as well as a prominent Western Australian CleanTech evangelist, believes that 'consumers want to become "prosumers" and become citizen utilities and that this is a technology that will enable them to do that' [261]. The blockchain-enabled, energy-trading platform removes the need for trust between individual energy traders, and energy transactions can be carried out frictionless among people unknown to each other. For consumers to participate in the energy-trading platform, they would need to install a piece of hardware, which must be connected to a standard digital energy meter. This sensor will track the amount of energy created, bought, or sold, and convert this into tokens that can be monetised into any fiat or digital currency. However, peer-to-peer energy trading still has some legal challenges. Many incumbent energy companies do not favour empowering their customers and decentralising energy creation and distribution. Despite these challenges, Power Ledger is steadily expanding its pilot projects for peer-to-peer energy trading, with a new pilot project starting in Auckland, New Zealand as well as Fremantle, Australia to take part in peer-to-peer energy trading. Fortunately, there is a tendency towards opening up government regulations around peer-to-peer energy trading.

The New South Wales government, for example, is pushing for a renewable energy, rooftop, trading scheme, which will enable individuals to trade energy that they generated on their rooftops with other individuals or businesses within their local community [262]. When households can be turned into mini-generators and electricity retailers, it could result in reduced costs for everyone and an increase in available renewable energy—a win–win situation for the people and for the Earth.

6.5 The Internet of Things and energy distribution

One aspect of peer-to-peer trading platforms is the generation of big data. In order to trade energy, smart meters are required to monitor any energy creation, storage, or trading. The data is stored on a blockchain and can then be analysed to improve the energy distribution in the (micro-) grid. A more efficient energy distribution network, with a reduced energy loss, can help reduce energy consumption. The reduction of (traditional) energy consumption will have a positive effect on carbon dioxide emissions, especially given that it will take at least a few decades before we will have moved completely to renewable energy. Therefore, in order to gain insights into energy consumption, we need to turn to the Internet of Things. The Internet of Things is a distributed network of devices that are connected to each other over the internet. As a result, these connected devices can communicate with each other, understand their needs, and adopt their behaviour accordingly. Before we dive into the advantages of energy data analytics, let's first, briefly, discuss the Internet of Things and the impact it will have on energy consumption.

In the coming years, the number of smart devices in our households could grow drastically and Gartner predicts that a typical home could contain more than 500 smart devices by 2022 [263]. The falling costs of sensors and the upcoming domotica platforms, such as Apple's Homekit, will contribute to this growth. However, this is just the beginning. IDC expects the market for the Internet of Things to grow to US$3 trillion by 2020 [264], whereas Cisco believes that the Internet of Things is a US$19 trillion opportunity [265]. The reason why the Internet of Things has become such a buzzword with such inflated expectations is because the required infrastructure, cloud computing, is easily available, scalable, and relatively cheap. The required sensors are becoming smaller, better, and cheaper every year, and all Internet of Things manufacturers, of course, claim that it will make everything in our lives 'smart' and our lives easier. In the coming years, the Internet of Things will experience enormous growth, because of (among other reasons) the expanded internet connectivity [266]. With the 4G roll out completed in most developed countries and experimentation with 5G already begun, the Internet of Things will get the network required to transmit trillions of messages in real-time.

We can therefore say that we are at the brink of a completely new, connected world—a connected world where billions or even trillions of devices are connected to the internet and to each other, in real-time. This connected world will change how organisations should be managed. It will change how organisations should approach innovation. And it will change how organisations should connect with their customers. The Internet of Everything will change innovation as we know it which will drastically impact energy consumption. Once there are dozens, or hundreds, of smart devices in your home, it becomes possible to optimise their energy consumption through smart meters. A smart meter is an electrical meter that monitors the energy consumption every 15 minutes or every hour. In the (near) future, smart meters will, however, be able to monitor the energy consumption of each individual product in a house in real-time and suggest, for example, a better timing to do your laundry based on real-time demand, forecasts, and pricing.

Of course, the Internet of Things will not create only smart homes, but also smart offices, smart manufacturers, or even smart cities. The new Deloitte Head Office in Amsterdam, the Netherlands, was certified as the most sustainable office building in the world in 2016 [267]. The building, called the Edge, is packed with 28,000 sensors that monitor everything in real-time, while generating gigabytes of data daily. As a result, the building optimises itself based on the number of employees in the building or the weather, significantly reducing the energy consumption in the office [268]. The South Korean city Songdo takes smartness a step further. The city has been built from the ground up and is completely connected to a smart grid. Songdo is located 40 miles from Seoul and will become a completely connected city, where almost any device, building, or road will be equipped with wireless sensors or microchips that generate massive amounts of data, which help reduce the energy consumption of the city [269].

As a result of the Internet of Things, we will see more smart homes, offices, and cities in the future, and this will enable us to drastically reduce energy consumption. Once hundreds of smart devices have been connected to smart meters, which in turn are linked to a smart grid, it becomes possible to optimise the energy consumption, demand, and distribution in real-time. The analysis of massive amounts of energy data will help organisations such as universities, meteorological organisations, and financial institutions to gain insights from energy consumption. This information can help create new applications and reduce energy consumption. It will become possible to link a smart grid to a blockchain platform and when tokens or crypto-coins are used, it becomes possible to have connected devices perform transactions among each other automatically through smart contracts. Imagine a connected device that automatically pays for a little bit of energy consumption when it performs a certain activity using a cryptocurrency. In the future, the analysis performed by the connected device can be sold automatically using micro-transactions to anyone interested and, with the revenue made, it can pay for the energy consumed. Everything will work automatically and instantly using smart contracts and all transactions will be recorded on a blockchain.

Price differentiation can be used to incentivise connected devices to use renewable energy instead of traditional energy. The Internet of Things in combination with Clean EnergyTech and the Blockchain will drastically change how we, and connected devices, consume and pay for electricity.

The Finnish energy company Fortrum has developed a blockchain solution to empower consumers to control their connected devices over the internet. Consumers living in connected homes can use Fortrum to optimise heating inside their houses and get insights into their electricity consumption. A dashboard offers real-time insights into their energy consumption and, by connecting to weather forecasts and real-time electricity pricing, it automatically optimises the heating of their homes, increasing the heating when prices are low, or limiting heating when prices are high. Blockchain and smart contracts are used as a push for renewable energy and to be better able to respond to small loads required by connected devices [270, 271], enabling micro-transactions using a cryptocurrency, which would not be viable with fiat money.

The South African company Bankymoon has developed a typical African solution for an African problem. In South Africa, many individuals pay for the electricity after they have consumed it, as happens in many countries in the world. However, in South Africa, many middlemen are involved in the billing of energy, thereby significantly raising the price. As a result, many South Africans have difficulties paying their utility bills, resulting in large losses for the energy companies. Therefore, Bankymoon has developed a pre-paid solution that enables citizens to pre-pay for their energy. However, as most of the Africans don't have a bank account, and paying in cash is too expensive, Bankymoon reverted to pre-paid blockchain smart meters. Individuals send bitcoin to the bitcoin wallet attached to their smart meter, and in exchange the user receives credits for energy consumption. In the end, such a solution will empower Africans, making them more aware of their energy consumption, which, in the long run, could reduce their energy consumption [272]. Although this solution is only carried out on very small scale (after all, more people still have bank accounts and use cash money than use bitcoin), it shows the potential of blockchain and energy for the developed world.

Another EnergyTech start-up working on using Blockchain in combination with the Internet of Things and renewable energy is the company ElectriCCHain. ElectriCChain is an open solar energy generation data project with an initial focus on verifying and publishing data from seven million solar energy generators globally and on an open Blockchain. ElectriCChain uses a crypto-coin, SolarCoin, to incentivise solar electricity generation. In February 2017, SolarCoin had a market cap of US$9 billion and was the world's largest community solar electricity reward programme. SolarCoins are rewarded to anyone generating solar electricity and 1 MWh of solar energy represents 1 SolarCoin. Any verified solar energy producer can get SolarCoins for free and 99% of the SolarCoins will be distributed to 97,500 TWh over the next 40 years. The data provided by the connected solar installations enables ElectriCChain to empower its users to deliver cheap and clean energy. The objective of ElectriCChain is to gather non-confidential energy data related to solar energy and build a network of millions of solar installations worldwide. In 2017, they had 7 million solar installations connected to the blockchain, which they aim to increase to 200 million in 15–25 years.

6.6 A future for decentralised energy

The energy sector has tremendous opportunities for change and improvement using Blockchain technology. Clean energy tech start-ups are developing new solutions and applications that focus on renewable energy, reducing carbon emissions, and developing smart grids. Blockchain can assist these start-ups in offering a decentralised solution that is reliable and effective thanks to the usage of cryptography to ensure trust and crypto-tokens to trade value. As such, Blockchain has a significant chance to help combat climate change because it enables the creation, usage, and exchange of renewable energy in a trustworthy and reliable manner. However, it should be noted that blockchain also costs a lot of energy, especially the bitcoin blockchain that uses a Proof of Work consensus mechanism. The computational power required to calculate the mathematics of Proof of Work needs a tremendous amount of energy. Different consensus mechanisms, such as Proof of Stake, require significantly less computational power and energy, and many start-ups are working on more environmentally friendly consensus mechanisms. Eventually, the application of Blockchain in the energy sector could result in Virtual Power Plants (VPPs). VPPs are independent energy-generating resources that are connected using the Internet of Things across a smart grid. These renewable energy installations are geographically distributed and not concentrated at one central location as is the case with traditional power plants [273]. VPPs bring together different technologies such as the Internet of Things, big data analytics, and Blockchain to develop the power plant of the future.

A decentralised and distributed power plant offers significant advantages over a traditional power plant, for example it will be a lot more resilient in the case of a natural disaster. If one node is taken out of the distributed network due to a hurricane, the other micro-grids can remain operational and even take over energy distribution to the affected area. In addition to this, smart contracts will enable fair and immediate payment for any creation, distribution, or usage of energy across the grid using crypto-tokens, and enable individuals or organisations to trade any surplus energy that they generate, thereby creating an additional revenue stream. Furthermore, Blockchain will prevent fraudulent actions, while at the same time offering transparency in energy usage across different stakeholders because any energy transaction data will be recorded on a (private) Blockchain and become immutable, verifiable, and traceable. Insights into how renewable energy is created, distributed, and used will enable the VPP to flatten out energy demand and prevent peak demands, when at the end of day everyone connects his or her electric car to the grid. In addition, smart homes, offices, or cities can optimise their energy consumption based on real-time energy pricing, thereby reducing energy consumption as well as the energy bill.

The future of energy is a decentralised and distributed one. Once individuals and organisations can generate, use, and distribute their own renewable energy it will significantly reduce the need for fossil fuels. Governments should, therefore, stimulate the development of VPPs, as long as they generate only renewable energy. The pilot projects of the different micro-grids are a great start, but there is still a long way to go.

6.7 Conclusion

Climate change is a real Wicked Problem that has the potential to significantly impact our lives, anywhere on Earth. We have a moral obligation to solve climate change, regardless of some of the disbelievers who have risen to power in the past years. Thanks to the uncontrolled use of fossil fuel in the past decade and the initial reluctance of many governments to tackle this problem, we are now left with a mess that urgently needs to be cleaned up. We are obligated to our children to do so and hand on the planet in good order. We have one Earth and it is our obligation to protect it, no matter how different we are, the different viewpoints we have, or whether we personally are affected by climate change. We can, and should, all play our part in solving climate change.

A distributed and decentralised solution, based on the Blockchain, smart contracts, Internet of Things, and big data analytics offers a chance at winning this game, but it will require significant investments to move to 100% renewable energy and create smart (micro-) grids. Fortunately, thanks to technological advancements, clean energy technology adheres to standard economic principles. As a result, it is now more interesting to invest in clean energy than in traditional, polluting, energy. Once the potential to make a lot of money becomes visible, the first step towards success will have been made.

Therefore, how can you help? What can you do? Join the smart grid movement, become energy neutral or even energy positive, so that you can give back. Join start-ups such as SolarCoin and start generating a real income by doing the right thing. Exchange your petrol-guzzling car for an electric car, use smart, secure, devices to create a smart home that is more energy efficient, and trade your surplus renewable energy on the Blockchain to make an extra buck. We can, and should, all play our part. Even for those disbelievers in climate change, let's give you one reason why you should take part in this: it will make you money! Climate change is good for business.

Chapter 7

Blockchain and Fair Trade

Fair Trade /ˌfɛəˈtreɪd/: trade between companies in developed countries and producers in developing countries in which fair prices are paid to the producers

7.1 Introduction

Blockchain can make trade fairer. In this context, 'Fair Trade' means ensuring that producers are paid fairly, and work in conditions that are safe and humane, and that consumers can be guaranteed the origins and quality of the products they consume. These requirements imply notions of social responsibility. For the purposes of this discussion, this chapter focuses on trade in agricultural produce and extracted minerals. Issues around how Blockchain might solve Wicked Problems in other areas of trade are either dealt with directly elsewhere in this book or may be applied by analogy.

7.2 What is Fair Trade?

Fair Trade is a way of buying and selling products that ensures that the people who produce the goods receive a fair price. Fair Trade brings a better standard of living to poor farmers in developing countries.

Fair Trade is about stable prices, decent working conditions, and the empowerment of farmers and workers around the world. For consumers of food and other goods produced in developing countries and vulnerable communities, Fairtrade is a label that is attached to products to ensure the quality of the product and the claims made on its label.

There is a strong relationship between Fair Trade and ethics. In this discussion of Fair Trade, the authors adopt the United Nations' definition of ethics as understood in the human rights context. The UN's *Principles on Business and Human Rights* are the product of six years of research conducted by Harvard Professor John Ruggie [274]. They are based on 47 consultations and site visits in more than 20 countries, and involve governments, companies, business associations, civil society, and investors. According to Oxfam, they are an authoritative global reference point for business and human rights, and they implement ethical trade by ensuring that governments and companies have a collective responsibility to protect human rights in business enterprises. Most of the work done by the UN to ensure that these rights are recognised and upheld around the world is conducted by the International Labour Organization (ILO).

Established in 1919, the ILO is dedicated to improving the standards of living of workers throughout the world. Its focus for the past 100 years has been to address issues such as excessive working hours, unemployment, minimum age, and work for women. Fair Trade seeks to ensure that the ethical standards for employment conditions articulated by the UN and the ILO are the minimum working conditions of all participants in the production of food and consumer goods. It is in this frame that the term 'ethical' is used in this book.

7.3 Empire, colonialism and capitalism: a toxic soup for Fair Trade

The power imbalance between developed and developing countries is not easily explained, but can be readily classified along economic lines. When a country has been ravaged by war, famine, or drought, or its resources exploited and depleted without the fruits of those resources benefiting the country's citizens, then hardship and insecurity will set in. These vulnerable populations are easy to exploit: their needs are basic and immediate. Meanwhile, the business models of corporate companies and large organisations in developed countries reward those who can make a profit. Profits are needed to satisfy shareholders and the rewards to senior executives of multinationals who return large annual profits for the organisations run to the millions. This business model incentivises the pressure that companies put on producers and service providers to agree to rock-bottom prices. Whether they are buying coffee beans from Nigeria or having their shoes manufactured in Vietnam, businesses are often focused on delivering higher returns to wealthy owners, top executives, and shareholders, while failing to ensure equitable distribution of profits along the supply chain. Indeed, the relationship between suppliers and the businesses that manage distribution and marketing is a tenuous one. Fair Trade is sometimes criticised for unjustly serving the rich [275], whereas others argue that fair markets can benefit everyone [276].

In January 2017, it was reported by the World Economic Forum (WEF) that rising inequality and social polarisation pose two of the biggest risks to the global economy in 2017 [277]. Oxfam said the world's poorest 50% owned the same in assets as the US$426 billion owned by the eight wealthiest people [278]. This group of eight is headed by Bill Gates, Amancio Ortega (the founder of the Spanish fashion chain Zara), and Warren Buffett, the renowned investor and chief executive of Berkshire Hathaway. The others are Carlos Slim Helú (the Mexican telecoms tycoon), Jeff Bezos (the founder of Amazon), Mark Zuckerberg (the founder of Facebook), Larry Ellison (chief executive of US tech firm Oracle), and Michael Bloomberg (a former mayor of New York and founder and owner of the Bloomberg news and financial information service).

In 2015, Oxfam said that the world's 62 richest billionaires were as wealthy as half the world's population. However, the number dropped to eight in 2017 because new information shows that poverty in China and India is worse than previously thought, making the bottom 50% even worse-off and widening the gap between rich and poor. Meanwhile, the WEF reported that, according to its research, median income fell by an average of 2.4% between 2008 and 2013 across 26 advanced nations. The vast majority of people in the bottom half of the world's population were facing a daily struggle to survive, with 70% of them living in low-income countries [279]. This yawning gap between rich and poor people is a cause of disharmony within and between nation states and economies [280].

7.4 Where does Fair Trade fit into this picture?

In a freer market, all markets would be driven by supply and demand. Every producer of any commodity would be rewarded equally for their skill and labour, no matter where they are based in the world. However, this is not the case. There are a number of forces at play that prevent open and free markets of this type. The controllers of these forces are nation states. Typically protectionist, they can control production, supply, demand, and consumption price by operating at both ends of the process, by directly taxing or subsidising goods and services, by regulating the use of goods and services, and by structuring domestic markets [281]. However, there is a tension between the notion of a 'freer' market and that of 'fairer' markets. Economic fairness may not necessarily be achieved by removing all the protectionist behaviour that dominates the world marketplace.

Coffee, sugar, cocoa, and other food products dominate the Fair Trade market. Fair Trade coffee, the largest selling certified product, accounts for over 3% of the total retail market for coffee and for close to 20% of the market for specialty coffees, the fastest growing segment of the US coffee market [282].

However, it is Fair Trade in the diamond market that has a special grip on the imagination of consumers. This is probably because the consumption of coffee, sugar, and chocolate is not quite as decadent as the west's attachment to diamonds.

Every day in a number of African countries, diggers and other workers in diamond mines face dangerous and harsh working conditions. Many of the world's diamonds are mined using practices that exploit workers, children, and communities. A million diamond diggers in Africa earn less than a dollar a day. Miners are dying in accidents, child labour is widespread, and corrupt leaders are depriving diamond mining communities of funds badly needed for economic development. Too often, the world's diamond mines produce not only diamonds, but also civil wars, violence, worker exploitation, environmental degradation, and suffering. The Central African Republic, Zimbabwe, Angola, and the Côte d'Ivoire all produce diamonds that are precious, beautiful, and lucrative. However, the market for these highly sought-after stones fuels civil war and violence, which is why diamonds from these regions are often called blood (or conflict) diamonds.

Amnesty International reports that 3.7 million people have lost their lives in the exploitation of and conflict over diamonds [283]. The industry is worth billions of dollars and yet most diamond production and trade is in the hands of warlords and rebels, who profit from the sale of diamonds, at the expense of the impoverished communities supporting the mining process.

7.5 Fair Trade as an expression of social conscience

Fair Trade is a key tool in the development of sustainable economies, businesses, and communities. It is a way of doing business that enables long-term partnerships and equitable relationships [284].

The Fair Trade movement has been gaining momentum over the past few years and there is now an expectation among consumers (particularly in developed countries) that there should be a choice of products produced under Fair Trade conditions. The driver for consumers is that they do care about ethics and are prepared to pay extra for a cup of coffee in order to support these ideals. It is an expression of social conscience. In a survey of 808 Belgian respondents, the actual willingness to pay for Fair Trade coffee was measured. It was found that the average price premium that the consumers were willing to pay for a Fairtrade label was 10%. Of the sample 10% were prepared to pay the current price premium of 27% in Belgium [285].

In general, the ethical consumer feels responsible towards society and expresses these feelings by means of his or her purchasing behaviour. Ethical consumption falls into two broad types of behaviour: the choice of certain products because they are produced ethically; and the boycotting of products that are produced unethically. The ethical issues that are taken into consideration when making these choices include: human rights, labour conditions, animal well-being, environment, and distribution of wealth (particularly in war zones and in times of conflict, including those related to blood diamonds). For example, consumers might refuse to buy any products that they know are made by children [286]. Boycott campaigns against companies that exploit child labour or distribute their substandard products to poor people are among the most-cited examples of this type of expression of ethical consumption [287].

There are three main problems arising in trade that can lead to inequity and financial distress. First, it is important to ensure that producers of all types of goods are paid a fair price for their skills, resources, and time, in a timely manner. Second, the conditions of all workers in the production process need to meet the ILO's minimum standards. Third, consumers need to be able to trust that the products they purchase meet these standards and that the money they pay to purchase the product is going to reward or benefit those who contributed to its production or creation.

7.6 Paying a fair price

In the commodities market, Fair Trade price is the minimum price that importers must pay to producers of some agricultural products such as coffee and bananas. It is the 'floor' price that must be paid irrespective of the market price.

When the market price of a commodity is higher than this minimum price, the buyer must pay the former. But if the market price falls below the Fair Trade price, the producer must be paid at least a price equal to the Fair Trade price.

Fair Trade price acts as a security net that reduces the market risks of farmers and attempts to improve their living conditions. The Fair Trade price policy comes under the Fair Trade standards, which stipulate that it is unfair to pay the market price to the producers in developing countries if the price is too low to survive and does not provide them at least the cost of production.

As long as the trade price is above the Fair Trade price, it allows traders and producers to negotiate higher prices depending on the quality and other attributes. Fair Trade price focuses, in particular, on goods or products that are normally imported from developing countries, including products such as coffee, handicrafts, cocoa, bananas, sugar, tea, wine, fresh fruit, chocolates, and flowers [288].

7.7 Setting standards and certification

So far, the main tools for supporting Fair Trade are setting standards and certification. Fair Trade benefits small-scale farmers and workers by facilitating links to international markets through the development of supply chains. Small-scale farmers and workers are among the most marginalised groups globally and through Fair Trade they can lift themselves out of poverty to maintain their successful livelihoods. Some products, such as coffee, cocoa, and cotton, can be certified by Fair Trade only if they come from small-scale farmer organisations. By working through democratic organisations of small-scale farmers, it can offer rural communities the stability of income, which enables them to plan for the future and invest in developing their organisation.

For some products such as bananas and tea Fair Trade can certify plantations (companies that employ large numbers of workers on large areas of land called estates). Standards for large-scale production differ from those for small-scale farmer organisations by focusing on the protection of workers' basic rights: keeping them safe and healthy, allowing them freedom of association and collective bargaining, preventing discrimination, and ensuring no bonded or illegal child labour is present. Fair Trade standards also require employers to pay wages that progress towards living wage benchmarks.

A number of organisations have established themselves for the sole purpose of supporting and promoting fair trade. FINE is a consortium of four Fair Trade networks: FLO (Fairtrade Labelling Organisation); International Fair Trade Association (which is now the World Fair Trade Organisation); the Network of European Worldshops; and the European Fair Trade Association. The aim of FINE is to enable these networks and their members to cooperate on:

- the development of harmonised core standards and guidelines for fair trade;
- harmonisation, and increase in the quality and efficiency of Fair Trade monitoring systems; and
- advocacy and campaigning work, harmonisation of their information and communication systems.

FINE members have agreed on a strategic intent that stipulates their aims:

- Deliberately to work with marginalised producers and workers in order to help them move from a position of vulnerability to security and economic self-sufficiency;
- To empower producers and workers as stakeholders in their own organisations;
- Actively to play a wider role in the global arena to achieve greater equity in international trade.

The Fairtrade Labelling Organisation International (FLO) monitors the Fair Trade floor price and changes it from time to time in light of the average cost of production, working conditions, and other economic factors. Products sold at Fair Trade prices must follow the standards outlined by the FLO certification process and are generally sold at higher prices. They also contain Fairtrade labels, indicating that the products were produced and traded in agreement with these standards.

Despite its best intentions and many supporters, Fair Trade saw UK consumption of its certified products drop 4% in 2014 [289]. This was its first fall in sales since inception in 2004. So, what is going on? Analysts point to two reasons for this decline: the increasing popularity of cheap supermarkets, which do not participate in the Fair Trade market; and the rise of ethical labelling. The ethical labelling movement is directly in competition with Fair Trade and it has caused some damage to the Fair Trade brand. Ethical labelling aims to create more choice in the market for consumers about the way that produce is grown and shipped to the marketplace. With Fair Trade labels, the most recognised in the ethical consumer market, it is hard to imagine a movement that would attempt to undermine its foothold. However, there is criticism of Fair Trade that is fuelling a new ethical labelling movement. Some recent audits of 'Fair Trade' certified producers conducted by third parties have revealed instances of uneven distribution of higher wages and better working conditions. Some argue the Fair Trade products are not always the best quality, which suggests that certification is not being awarded on merit [289].

7.8 What's so unfair about Fair Trade?

The effect of the disparity between rich and poor nations is that, although most developed countries have ended their colonial control over developing countries, they continue to exert economic pressure on and influence the domestic policies of the poorer countries with which they trade. Herein lies the rub. Fair Trade is regarded as another controlling mechanism (albeit well intentioned) and has been described as a kind of neo-imperialism [290]. The counterpoint to the terms and conditions imposed by Fair Trade advocates and certifiers is the notion that there needs to be more transparency, to ensure that the intended beneficiaries of the Fair Trade arrangement are being rewarded for their role in production or delivery of goods and services from developing and poor countries to the wealthy consumers in the west.

To address the concerns that Fair Trade is failing to deliver on its promises, individual traders, retailers, and consumers are finding ways to connect with their producers so as to ensure that they are rewarded and to control the quality of the products being produced [289]. Consumers want to create a closer link with the producer. They want proof that what the label promises is being delivered. This calls for transparency and proof.

In addition to these strains on the Fair Trade brand, sceptics dismiss Fair Trade and other ethically labelled products as cheap public relations ploys by companies, and highlight the fact that such products currently account for a tiny share of retail sales [291].

7.9 How can the blockchain solve the problem?

Blockchains can transfer title and record permissions and activity logs in order to track the flow of goods and services between businesses and across borders. A fundamental advantage of this distributed system is that it resolves problems of disclosure and accountability between individuals and institutions whose interests are not necessarily aligned. Mutually important data can be updated in real time, removing the need for laborious, error-prone reconciliation with each other's internal records. It gives each member of the network far greater and timelier visibility of the total activity.

Blockchains can gather information from the supply chain to share it with consumers at the point of sale. It can substantiate product claims with secure, real-time data about the origins of food and ingredients, as well as the time that perishables spend in transit or refrigeration. By digitising this information and making it available on machine-readable labels, consumers can discover more about the food they purchase.

In the USA, Walmart is exploring the use of blockchain technology to provide the retailer with a way to indelibly record a list of transactions indicating how meat has flowed through a commercial network, from producers to processors to distributors to grocers—and finally, to consumers. In October 2016, the Commonwealth Bank of Australia announced that it, Wells Fargo, and Brighann Cotton had successfully undertaken the first global trade transaction between two independent banks combining blockchain and smart contract technologies. The transaction involved a shipment of cotton from Texas, USA to Qingdao, China [292, 293]. The announcement concluded that, after the successful completion of this transaction, Commonwealth Bank and Wells Fargo would continue collaborating with trade finance clients, financial institutions, fintech companies, and other fintech consortia, as well as players in the insurance and shipping industries, to ensure that their clients benefit from the changes in technology across the global trade ecosystem.

7.10 Authenticating provenance

Provenance refers to the origins and earliest known history of something. It is important in the context of Fair Trade because some agricultural products and natural resources have particular inherent qualities or sensitivities based on where and how they were grown or extracted. Blockchain technology provides traceability for materials and products by recording key data about provenance in real time, and reporting it in a way that is transparent and auditable. Online tracking of ham, diamonds, wine, coffee beans, and fabric assures customers that claims made on packaging and in advertising can be substantiated and looked up, ideally via an App, in real time while the consumer buys the product.

The current method by which assertions of Fair Trade production are communicated to purchasers is labelling and certification. The problems associated with certification of Fair Trade are complex, and create a level of expense and audit that is time-consuming and susceptible to manipulation. However, blockchain can track these elements transparently and in real time.

In addition to big banks, credit card companies, and payments providers looking to bitcoin-like systems to exploit the possibilities presented by blockchain technology, governments and regulators have also noticed its potential to monitor transactions [294].

Despite the potential risks that accompany any innovation of code and expansion of the utility of blockchain technology, Lawrence Lessig, the Roy L. Furman Professor of Law at Harvard Law School, asserts that the technology is 'the most important innovation in fundamental architecture since the tubes of the internets were first developed' to potentially 'bypass corruption, to bypass fraud, to improve efficiency, and to enhance freedom' [295].

7.11 Smart contracts

The use of smart contracts can play a significant role in achieving financial fairness in trade. Research indicates that farmers in developing countries often accept low prices and delayed payments for their goods [296, p. 155]. They can ensure the prompt payment of suppliers and distributors at the time of supply and distribution. The internal complex and conditional logic of a smart contract can manage the variable data as agreed by all users with respect to how much to pay, when, and to whom.

For example, in December 2016, Australian tech start-up AgriDigital successfully managed the world's first settlement of an agricultural commodity on a blockchain. The cloud-based transaction platform allows grain growers, buyers, and bulk handlers to manage contracts, deliveries, invoices, payments, and inventory all in one place. The landmark transaction occurred after David Whillock, a grower from Whillock Pastoral, near Geurie, in New South Wales, delivered 23 metric tonnes of wheat to Dubbo-based Fletcher International Exports, which is run by meat industry disrupter Roger Fletcher.

To make the experiment work, AgriDigital played every role in the transaction—acting as operator, buyer, and regulator to create an example of the ecosystem that will occur in the future. The pilot system captured real-time data of a 23.46-metric tonne grain sale between grower Whillock Pastoral Co. Pty Ltd and buyer Fletcher International Exports. In this case, the blockchain system provided fast and secure payment for the grain on delivery. The AgriDigital smart contract autoexecuted the settlement by:

- valuing the delivery;
- verifying that the buyer had sufficient funds to pay the grower;
- securing the funds in the grower's name;
- verifying the delivery; and
- transferring the title and, at the same time, creating a payment for the grower from the reserved funds.

Farmer and director of Whillock Pastoral Co. Pty Ltd, David Whillock, said the smart contract that managed this transaction would help him to maintain cash flow and manage his business more confidently. According to the team at AgriDigital, current payment terms for Australian grain growers range from two weeks to five weeks, so real-time payment will make a significant impact on a farmer's financial stability and certainty. AgriDigital is now exploring the use of blockchain technology in Australian livestock, the Canadian grains industry, and ownership and provenance in Europe.

A key feature of blockchain is its auditability by all participants in a transaction, including counterparties, authorities, and regulators. In any deterministic system, it is possible to verify and audit the actions within the system as correct; indeed, the inputs and outputs of the system serve as a record of the various interactions (for example, automated bank transfers or ordering additional components in a stock control system). In traditional systems, the maintenance of all relevant data is expensive, impractical, or impossible. The inputs to a business system typically include various types of data coming from a wide variety of sources, and the auditing itself is technically challenging. Furthermore, auditing may require strong knowledge and assurance of operator identity, which can often be compromised or flawed in a system with many actors.

By design, a public blockchain is perfectly transparent to all members of that network. Each individual operation or interaction, such as the provision of a new employee or the recording of outgoing stock, is perfectly recorded and archived, while privacy is ensured due to the usage of tokenisation. Auditing becomes as simple as joining the blockchain network, because this allows users to see all past operations in order to build a correct model of the present.

7.12 Conclusion

The blockchain can work much like any data system. It takes inputs and carries out actions based on these inputs, changing the database in a manner perfectly determined according to its program. These steps are crucial in supply chains and for certification of Fair Trade.

Fair Trade is not just about farmers or producers. It is about making sure that the entire supply chain is sustainable. Frontline producers need to be paid enough to create a sustainable business. To deliver traceability, Fair Trade provides independent third-party certification to give a robust and transparent audit of the supply chain process from farmer to exporter or trader, through to manufacturer, and on to the consumer. Blockchain technology can ensure that tracking and payments are transparent, secure, and timely.

With so many components and players making up the supply chain between growers and consumers, it is important to ensure both fair distribution of wealth along this line and timely payment along the way. Until now, this has been very difficult because a price is often set at the end of the process, whereas the most financially vulnerable have done the hardest work and laid out the most risk at the start of the production line. Blockchain technology can improve the experience for all participants, including the end-consumer. It allows buyers and receivers to track the movement of goods and the exchanges made along the way. Meanwhile, information, including history, transport, events, and ownership, can be used to verify authenticity.

Fair Trade is not just about ensuring that consumers can trust the origins and quality of produce and products, and the back story of the human interaction with their production and supply; it is also about ensuring equal pay for equal work. Smart contracts can ensure the integrity of payment systems by reporting to the network that payment has been made and how much of the price paid went to the grower or worker responsible for its production. Equal pay for equal work is regarded by the UN as a human right. Fair Trade is one of the UN's 17 Sustainable Development Goals. The blockchain's capacity to audit and automate transactions can play a significant part in the achievement of this particular goal.

Chapter 8

Blockchain and voting fraud

Vote /vəʊt/: a formal indication of a choice between two or more candidates or courses of action, expressed typically through a ballot or a show of hands

The year 2017 was a year of major elections and political shifts around the globe. Donald Trump was, after being elected President of the USA in 2016, inaugurated as President on 20 January 2017. Two months later, the Netherlands was the first of four countries in Europe to go to the ballot box, a few months later followed by France, Germany, and unexpectedly the United Kingdom. That's not all—in total 69 countries[1] held elections in 2017, ranging from national elections, to regional or local elections. Most these countries still use a pen and paper to have citizens cast their votes and the votes are counted manually afterwards by a group of volunteers. Although various security measures are in place to prevent fraudulent activities during elections, it is not that difficult to manipulate votes (often referred to as vote rigging) and interfere with the process of an election, and either add or remove vote share for candidates. It happens in many countries, although no one who won an election would of course ever admit to electoral fraud, and it will continue to happen if we stick to pencil and paper to cast our votes.

In the past decades, many countries have been experimenting with electronic voting. The first-known use of electronic voting happened in 1991, when Belgium experimented with two types of electronic voting in two locations for the general election of 1991. Approximately 25 countries have followed since and have experimented with electronic voting, all with different rates of success. For example, the Netherlands followed Belgium after a few years, but stopped electronic voting in 2007, when it was revealed that there were significant security problems with the voting machines (namely, they could easily be hacked). Belgium, on the other hand, still allows electronic voting using magnetic cards. Other countries that have experimented with electronic voting are Australia, Brazil, Canada, France, India, Switzerland, and of course Estonia. Estonia is by far the most advanced country in terms of electronic voting, which is made possible by the Estonian Digital ID card, a mandatory smart card for government services based on Public Key Infrastructure. Estonia started with electronic voting in 2005 and, in 2007, it was the first country in the world to allow online voting. In the 2015 parliamentary elections, 30.5% of the Estonians eligible to vote did so over the internet [297].

Despite these experiments with electronic voting, in many countries voting is still done with a pencil and a paper. Apart from being very traditional, voting with a pencil and paper is a slow process that is prone to errors and fraud. But there are more problems with our current voting system. Voting, nowadays, has low utility, meaning that, although all votes are counted, not all votes count. Making votes count is the basis of democracy in many countries. As a result, when the majority wins, minorities are often neglected. In addition, voting fraud is still very common and the list of controversial elections is long and still growing.

8.1 Electoral fraud

Electoral fraud comes in many flavours, ranging from manipulation of demographics (artificial control of electorates in order to ensure an outcome), disenfranchisement (preventing some classes of people from voting), intimidation (putting pressure on voters to vote in a certain direction), vote buying (compensating voters with cash for voting in a certain direction), misleading ballot papers (making it difficult for people to understand the ballot paper), ballot stuffing (submission of multiple ballots by one person), misrecording of votes (either accidently or on purpose), tampering with electronic machines (hacking the machines to change the voting results), and disinformation (also known as fake news since the 2016 USA election). Although voting is such a fundamental part of democracy, it is not perfect, which could have contributed to how democracy has, or has not, evolved in the world. Democracy has not changed for hundreds of years, despite different tests with new forms of democracy. Give or take, there are two main forms of democracy: direct (or pure) democracy and represented (or indirect) democracy, and each has its advantages and disadvantages.

In a direct democracy, every citizen decides on initiatives or proposals directly. Each vote counts and the outcome is determined by the majority of the votes. It originated in the fifth century BC, when the Athenian democracy allowed its male citizens to control the entire political process [298]. Currently, the only known direct democracy exists in two Swiss Cantons [299] and this is because direct democracies pose multiple problems for today's society. First of all, there are so many topics that require a decision that it is impossible for all citizens to be informed about all topics, because it would require too much time. In addition, we do not have the technological capabilities, or the funds, to vote on every topic, because, as mentioned, voting is a slow and manual process. These two problems make a direct democracy impractical on a daily basis.

Represented democracy is the other and most accepted form of democracy. Within a represented democracy, citizens will vote for a delegate who represents their constituents. The system of elected officials is adopted by almost all western-style democracies, including Australia, the Netherlands, and the USA. It has become so popular because it is seen as the most efficient form of democracy. However, a represented democracy presents its own problems. First of all, in many countries there is a disconnection between citizens and politicians, and citizens no longer trust the traditional parties of elected officials representing the citizens. Representatives are only loosely held accountable for their actions [300] and promises are not necessarily kept. In addition, the problem with having elected delegates is that corruption becomes possible. Power corrupts and, in some countries, delegates listen to money rather than the people who elected them. Finally, countries that use a two-party system, such as the USA, significantly limit the choices that citizens have, whereas in multi-party systems, such as in the Netherlands, coalitions need to be formed, often taking months. In both systems, progress is slow.

Democratic systems do not exist only in countries—of course, organisations also have democratic systems. Direct democracies are more common in smaller organisations, where shareholders can still vote on all decisions to be made and as such determine the company's strategy. However, as soon as an organisation becomes bigger with multiple shareholders, or even goes public with thousands of shareholders, direct democracy no longer works. Such organisations opt for a represented democracy, where the shareholders appoint a board to make decisions for them and the annual shareholders' meeting can hold the board accountable for their actions.

Although represented democracy has worked very well for the past hundreds of years, the causal link between democracy and economic performance is controversial. Both democratic countries and non-democratic countries, have grown at approximately 1.5% of the gross domestic product (GDP) per capita per year for the past 40 years [301], although autocracies such as North Korea, Iraq, Afghanistan, and Cuba are not included in this figure. However, democracies have been performing better in terms of consistency of growth as well as social welfare dimensions such as life expectancy or child mortality [301]. This does not mean that the current form of democracy is the best form. As Winston Churchill famously said in the House of Commons in 1947 [302]:

> Many forms of Government have been tried, and will be tried in this world of sin and woe. No one pretends that democracy is perfect or all-wise. Indeed, it has been said that democracy is the worst form of Government except for all those other forms that have been tried from time to time . . . .

Nevertheless, democratic systems have their merits as well as their challenges, but with today's Blockchain technology we can solve these challenges and develop a better system, known as 'liquid democracy', which combines the advantages of both direct democracy and represented democracy.

8.2 Voting characteristics

Before we dive into what liquid democracy entails, let's first discuss three characteristics of voting that are vital for a democratic process. First, if you vote, you need to know that you will be *able* to submit your vote for it to be counted. This is called censorship resistance and it refers to the electoral fraud of disenfranchisement. The second characteristic is that, after casting, you need to *know,* and be certain, that your vote was included in the result. This is called consensus protocol and refers to the electoral fraud of misrecording votes. Finally, you need to know, and be certain, that your vote, and others, will *not be changed* after they have been cast. This is called immutability of votes and refers also to the electoral fraud of misrecording [303]. Without these three key aspects of voting, the democratic process is deemed to fail. Until today we have trusted electoral committees to ensure that these key characteristics were in place, at least in western democratic countries, and this is why it works. However, it is impossible for individuals to check to be 100% sure that their vote was included, counted, and not changed afterwards. Blockchain, however, being an immutable, verifiable, and traceable record of data, can change this and the combination of Blockchain and liquid democracy offers a chance to solve many, if not all, problems currently related to voting.

8.3 Democracy 2.0

Technology can bring the power back to the people, rather than giving it to politicians who are elected once every four to six years. Technology will enable people to vote for the right decision instead for voting for the right representative. At the core of Democracy 2.0 is the Blockchain and it revolves around the concept of liquid democracy.

Liquid democracy combines the best of both worlds from a direct democracy and a represented democracy. It is also known as 'delegative democracy', 'proxy voting', or 'voluntary direct democracy' and is a fairly new concept. Liquid democracy (see Figure 8.1) enables citizens to choose which role they want to take in the political process (or strategy process in the case of organisations). Either they choose to vote directly on individual policy issues or they can choose to delegate their vote to competent delegates who vote on their behalf.

Delegation of votes is policy specific, meaning that you can delegate your voting power to multiple experts in different domains and any vote can be retracted instantly.

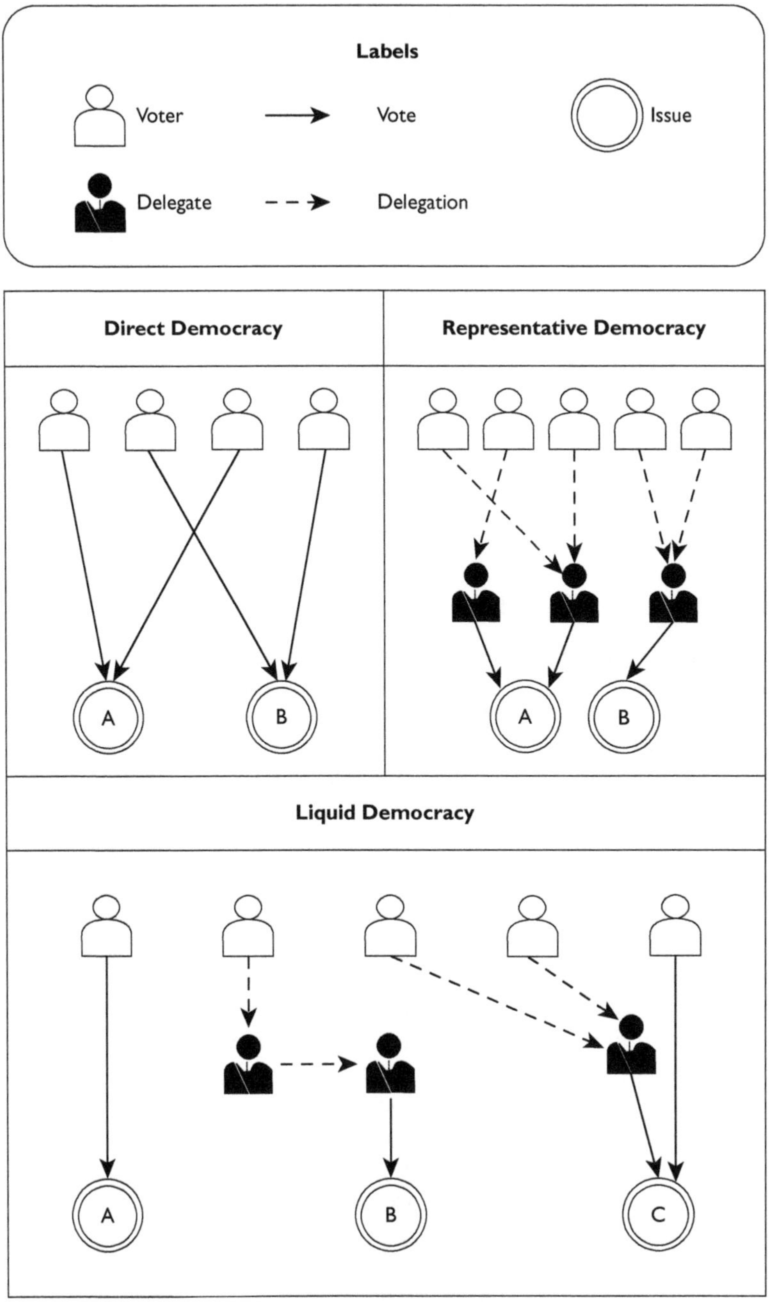

Figure 8.1 Liquid democracy (© Dominik Schiener)

As a result, delegates who have attracted many votes, and so have gained a lot of power, can lose that power at any given moment [304]. Delegates are people with domain-specific knowledge that can influence decision-making if they manage to attract sufficient votes, resulting in better governance, because no, or fewer, politicians with more generic knowledge are involved in policy-making [300]. Different delegates can exercise different levels of decision-making power and the delegates involved in the political process depend on the topic up for a decision. In addition, delegates can re-delegate their voting authority on certain topics with which they feel less comfortable. In this way, experts can accumulate large amounts of voting authority relatively quickly [305], which is why a fluid democracy naturally evolves into a meritocracy.

Voting by individuals is done completely privately and known only to the voter. This entails the votes cast on individual policy decisions as well as the votes delegated to experts. The delegates do not know who delegated their vote to them. In contrast, the votes made by the delegates are completely public, so that those individuals who delegated their vote can check whether their vote was cast correctly, ensuring accountability. This prevents delegates from saying one thing and doing another—a common trait in existing politics [305].

8.4 Advantages of liquid democracy

There are multiple advantages of liquid democracy [300], above all it being truly democratic, while solving the problems of a represented democracy. Individuals have complete freedom to decide how they want to vote—whether they want to remain passive and delegate all their votes to one person, or multiple representatives, whether they want to vote on each topic themselves, or even whether they do not want to vote at all. In addition, anyone can become a delegate and start collecting voting authority and as a consequence decision-making power. Political parties are no longer required to win votes and because individuals select delegates based on expertise and not political colour, everyone can tailor make 'their own political party' by selecting those experts, or friends, whom they trust most for the different topics. However, any delegate can just as easily lose any voting authority if they mislead the individuals who have entrusted their votes to them, work with lobbyists, or take money for their vote from organisations. As such, lobbyists will no longer be needed, corruption in politics will cease to exist, and delegates will be held directly accountable for their actions, saving billions of dollars annually. As a result, democracy evolves in a network of experts, making well-informed decisions that are not based on political grounds, resulting in better governance and strategy making.

Liquid democracy empowers voters and brings people closer to decision-making, reduces voter apathy, and, by being a direct representation of a society's structure, ensures that minorities and ethnic groups will be able to have a say as well. The advantages of liquid democracy are numerous, but until recently the technology was not available to make it work. Now, with the availability of Blockchain technology, liquid democracy can become a reality.

8.5 Liquid democracy and Blockchain

Liquid democracy solves all issues currently linked to direct or represented democracy, but by itself it does not stop electoral fraud. To ensure individuals that they can submit or delegate their vote, to ensure that their vote, or delegated vote, is included in the result and that it will not be changed afterwards, an immutable, traceable, and verifiable data record is required, that is the Blockchain.

Already, there are multiple start-ups working on Blockchain solutions for voting, whether for societies or for organisations, and there are various political parties using open-source software to obtain input from interested citizens, but more on that later. First, let's see how a liquid democracy using Blockchain technology works. As the underlying technical infrastructure, Blockchain is important because it enables the casting and delegation of votes. It also prevents participants from voting multiple times on the same topic or creating pseudonymous identities to increase influence (the problem of 'double spending', as discussed in Chapter 2).

Many of the concepts discussed earlier come together with a liquid democracy: smart contracts, Public Key Infrastructure, cryptography, tokenisation, self-sovereign identity, verification, and reputation, in addition to algorithmic up/down voting of proposals. It would work as follows: anyone can propose legislation and the best, most popular, or best articulated proposals will receive the most votes and therefore have the greatest reach. The cream will rise to the top, similar to the voting systems that manage comments and articles on Reddit. The most popular proposals can be discussed and improved using consensus on the exact wording by those interested in the topic and with expert knowledge. Of course, any action related to creating a proposal will be recorded on the blockchain, so that it will always be possible to trace back how the proposal was developed and who was involved. Once one or more proposals are deemed ready for voting, a popular vote could be organised instantly and participants can vote, or they can delegate their vote, using their smartphone, tablet, or computer. Smart contracts will monitor any delegation of votes. In order to vote, your self-sovereign identity will be verified using the Public Key Infrastructure and biometrics information, so it is known who is voting as well as to prevent voting under duress because voting will no longer be required in a secure and private space (a scan of your face using your smartphone's camera and your fingerprints, for example, could reveal if that would be the case). Your vote will be tokenised, time stamped, and added to the blockchain. At any time before the closing date you can change, withdraw, or (re-)delegate your vote. The blockchain will record all 'transactions', ensuring that the public can at any time inspect that their own vote has been submitted, has been included in the results, and has not been changed. Users can also see the number of votes each proposal has received. Results will be available instantly once the 'e-ballot box' closes. Of course, such a complex system requires significant administration and governance. Although the basic administration can be taken care of by artificial intelligence, humans would still need to be involved, similar to moderators on online platforms. These moderators can be selected based on their reputation, and possible shadow reputation, and can be held accountable at any time.

Of course, such a system will take time to implement and a natural first step would be to enable online voting using blockchain technology in a representative democracy. As mentioned earlier, Estonia had already implemented this technology a few years ago and it enables voters to submit their vote, and ensure that the vote is included in the result and not changed afterwards. It would work by using the Public Key Infrastructure, cryptography, tokenisation of votes, and, although Estonia already enables voting online, initially it could require citizens to still go to a polling station where they can use a secure computer.

Although liquid democracy offers clear advantages over representative democracy and blockchain technology enables proxy voting, it is unlikely that we will achieve this at governmental level any time soon. Moving from a representative democracy to a liquid democracy requires the representatives to vote on such legislation, which would mean a significant change to the constitution. It would also mean that, by voting for such constitutional change, representatives and parties would put themselves out of a job, which would mean loss of influence, power, and money. It is likely, therefore, that many elected representatives would not even start to think about implementation of a new democratic system and everything will remain as it is. For now, only progressive and digitally advanced governments such as that in Estonia are likely to move in this direction.

8.6 How to move to liquid democracy

In order to move to a liquid democratic system, a more gradual approach is needed, starting at a very small and local level and over time moving to a regional, national, and perhaps someday even a transnational level. The first step would be for organisations to move to a new approach in voting, for popular television shows such as *The Voice*, *Idols* [306], or the *Eurovision Song Contest*, which could enable blockchain voting. It would be relatively simple to implement and would familiarise a large group of people with blockchain and the possibilities of online voting. Television shows would benefit from increased transparency in their voting system. At the same time, organisations could start to look at developing new approaches to governance and shareholder or boardroom voting. ConsenSys, a developer of products based on Ethereum, was, in 2017, developing BoardRoom, a decision-making platform for organisations to simplify board member elections, budget allocation, shareholder voting, and more. Subsequently, larger organisations can start to experiment with blockchain voting.

In 2015, Google performed a liquid democracy experiment on their corporate social network Google+ [307]. *Google Votes* was a decision-making system using social-networking technology and the experiment lasted for three years. The users of the social network became the voter base in the experiment, the system used the identity verification system of Google+ to verify users, and Google Votes was a web application integrated into Google's internal Google+ network. Anyone in the network could create *issues*, which, once created, were opened up for voting to all, or a select group of, users. Users could discuss the issues and vote or delegate their votes. The system enabled delegation advertisements, which enabled people to convince others why they should delegate their vote to them. This enabled group leaders and potential leaders to build and reinforce their reputation [307]. In the three years of operation, the employees at Google created 370 issues and 20,000 involved employees cast over 87,000 votes, of which 3.6% were delegated votes. The development of the liquid democracy system in Google using a social network shows how organisations could experiment with new decision-making systems, which in turn could familiarise more people with liquid democracy and its processes.

Apart from commercial organisations experimenting with liquid democracy, various political parties across the world have been experimenting with it. The best known are the Pirate Parties active across Europe and Italy's 5 Star Movement. They use Liquid Feedback, an open-source software for policy making and political discussion, certain decisions, and even elections, which was created to facilitate liquid democracy. The software can be used to enable anyone to propose policy, edit other people's proposals, propose alternatives, and vote on these issues themselves or delegate their vote [308]. Although this would fulfil the needs of a liquid democracy, the technology is suitable only for organisations, or parties, and cannot replace a legislative body's core function. At this moment in time, the system is not suitable for elections (of persons) and it does not use Blockchain to verify, trace, and make immutable the votes cast. Nevertheless, it can enable small(er) organisations to test the workings of a liquid democracy, which in the long run could result in a more fundamental shift in democratic systems. The software delivers results on what the members of an organisation or party want and empowers them to make democratic decisions independent of physical assemblies [309].

Another party is the Flux movement from Australia which participated in the 2016 election. The objective of this political movement is to promote, according to Max Kaye, founder of the movement and founder of XO.1, the most prosperous form of democracy we can identify, which is currently Issue Based Direct Democracy (IBDD). IBDD goes a step further than liquid democracy because, apart from offering direct voting on proposals and delegating votes, it also enables vote trading, which means the redistribution of political power. IBDD offers participants the ability to reorganise political power by trading votes. They can forgo their vote on certain topics and in return they receive tokens that can be used to acquire voting power on other topics [293]. As a result, they can gain political power with topics on which they have expertise and, with topics that they know less about, they can empower other experts. With this idea, Flux participated in the Australian elections of 2016. The objective was to convince the people of Australia of the new system, but he had no luck; Flux received 0.15% of the votes. Since then, Flux's idea has been turned into a start-up, XO1, to develop a secure and scalable online voting system.

A third example is Partido de la Red, which developed an open-source platform called DemocracyOS. This was started in 2013 with the objective of hacking the democracy in Buenos Aires. The representatives from the local political party promised always to vote on political issues according to the will of the citizens [310]. They built a digital platform that enabled citizens to tell the representative how to vote on the different issues. It is not a full liquid democratic system, more a hybrid form of liquid and representative democracy. DemocracyOS achieved just 1.2% of the vote so their representative was not elected to the city council. However, the initiative did garner the attention of organisations and governments around the world, and eventually the government in Buenos Aires tried to use the system to get feedback from citizens. When DemocracyOS tried to run a candidate for the second time, they were told that they had to bribe a federal judge to participate [310], which shows the resistance that can be expected when moving to a new democratic system. Eventually, the idea moved into a not-for-profit organisation called Democracy Earth Foundation. This foundation uses an incorruptible identity platform to record votes and the platform was piloted during the 2017 Colombian Peace Referendum. The pilot enabled 7 million Colombians who fled the country during the war to vote, together with those aged under 18 years. Although these results were not binding for the government, it offered a glimpse of how liquid democracy can become a reality in the future.

Follow My Vote is another start-up working in the space of blockchain and liquid democracy. It develops a secure, open-source, online-voting software based on blockchain technology that enables elections to be verified from start to finish using blockchain, by giving everyone access to the ballet box without compromising privacy or security.

8.7 How to get to a liquid democracy

So, what is required for a liquid democracy to become possible?

First, we would need to have better understanding of how blockchain would work for voting. Yes, the first start-ups and political parties are experimenting with secure online voting using blockchain, but the technology is still very new, so more research will be needed. Once the technology has become readily available for organisations, and potentially governments, to use, it will be necessary to educate the people. Liquid democracy will mean a radical shift in voting for citizens and it will require them to trust technology with which they might not be very familiar. Educating the public about how liquid democracy works could be achieved by using liquid democracy systems in popular TV shows, small organisations, or local governments. In particular, in commercial applications, such as the Google Votes experiment, blockchain technology is not, at first, required. The next step would be to have a new identity system in place, as explained in Chapter 3. Self-sovereign identity is key to liquid democracy, because, once citizens can prove their identity through cryptography, it becomes possible to build a variety of new services on top of it, which is currently not even imaginable. From there on, more organisations and citizens can become aware of the possibilities of liquid democracy, leading eventually to a possible shift in democratic systems. However, it is highly unlikely that this will happen any time soon, because a shift in democratic systems will put all those politicians who voted in favour out of a job.

The most likely scenario is that liquid democratic systems will be adopted commercially first, either with or without blockchain technology. The next step would be to build Decentralised (fully or semi-) Autonomous Organisations (DAOs) that apply a liquid democratic system and combine it with smart contracts and artificial intelligence. Customers, shareholders, or board members could use such a system to make decisions and, when combined with smart contracts, this could trigger automatic implementation of those decisions or investment choices. This does not have to be in the far future. Already, the Hong Kong-based venture capital firm Deep Knowledge Ventures has given an algorithm a seat on the board of directors [311]. The algorithm has an actual vote on where the company will invest. Fast forward this a few years and the board of directors could consist completely of algorithms that execute investment decisions based on the voting results of the shareholders of the company. Combining blockchain-based voting systems with smart contracts enables the automatic execution of a certain decision or policy based on the results of the election, which could significantly speed up the decision-making/democratic processes.

Although liquid democratic systems for DAOs are still quite far away, blockchain is already used for proxy voting during annual general meetings (AGMs). These meetings tend to be high-cost events, with low shareholder participation. In an increasingly global world, where investments are made across the globe, investor engagement becomes important, but participating in person becomes more difficult. Therefore, a new solution is required that enables shareholders to exercise their rights in a secure and transparent way, which at the same time could foster cross-border investments. As a consequence, in 2016, Russia's central securities depository, National Settlements Depository, a member of the Moscow exchange, developed and tested a blockchain prototype for proxy voting [312]. The open-source, e-proxy voting system prototype was developed to securely process electronic interaction between security holders and issuers when exchanging information during the meetings of the holders of the annual securities. The voting instructions are stored on a private blockchain, accessible to all nodes in the network. If a regulator needs to get access to these instructions, they can simply do so by joining the private blockchain network. All records are distributed among participating members, making the voting instructions immutable, verifiable, and traceable.

Blockchain-enabled e-proxy voting also improves corporate governance. In 2017, Broadridge Financial Solutions, JPMorgan, Northern Trust, and Banco Santander successfully accomplished a blockchain pilot developed to improve transparency in the proxy voting process [313] during an AGM. The pilot acted as a 'shadow' digital copy of votes cast by the shareholders. The objective of the pilot was to increase transparency during proxy voting as part of the AGM, and as a result to improve corporate governance. Blockchain-enabled voting during AGMs will remove the complexity of proxy voting during traditional AGMs, while increasing the quality and efficiency of proxy voting.

8.8 Conclusion

Using blockchain in our democratic processes could significantly improve the democratic system and eliminate electoral fraud. At first, it could be used to simply improve the existing system of representative democracy. Bringing voting online using Blockchain, as seen in Estonia, makes votes immutable, verifiable, and traceable, which is a significant improvement to the existing system. It will reduce or eliminate electoral fraud, and will make results instantly available, as soon as the election closes. When votes are recorded on a blockchain, it will enable citizens to be 100% sure that their vote has been submitted, counted, and not been changed, while ensuring complete privacy for the voter. Although voting over the internet, as done in Estonia, might still be far away for many countries, improving and linking existing, albeit insecure, voting computers to the blockchain could already significantly improve the electoral processes. A natural next step would be to enable voting over the internet, so that voters could participate in the election without having to go to the ballot box, which will probably increase voter participation if citizens can vote anywhere by simply using their smartphone. In 2016, in the Australian state Victoria, Australia Post started developing a blockchain-based e-voting system. It is building an independent e-voting application, linked to its existing identity platform, which offers anonymous voting and prevents electoral fraud by allowing only one vote per identity and monitoring misuse. The localised solution for corporate, civic, and community organisations will help governments and the public become familiar with a new system, while offering insights into voter behaviour and preparing the traditional voting process for the 21st century [38].

However, before governments move to blockchain-enabled voting, it is likely that the first organisations to start with this will be publicly listed companies, which want to improve corporate governance. Blockchain-enabled e-proxy voting will offer corporations a secure and immutable digital copy of voting instructions cast by shareholders during an AGM. In 2016, Nasdaq experimented with using blockchain to record ownership of securities and offer voting right assets based on those assets to shareholders [314]. The company worked with the Tallinn Stock Exchange and it benefited from the already developed digital identification solutions. Consequently, shareholders with the right voting right asset could view relevant information, transfer voting rights to a proxy, monitor the proxy, and recall if necessary and review previous meetings and votes [315].

Once organisations and (local) governments have become familiar with online e-voting and e-proxy voting using Blockchain, perhaps there is a chance of slowly changing democratic systems as well. This will give policy-making processes back to the people, while creating an efficient, trustworthy, immutable, and verifiable electoral system that minimises fraud. It is a lot to ask of existing leaders in power and time will tell if there are governments who dare to take the leap forward.

Note

1 https://en.wikipedia.org/wiki/List_of_elections_in_2017

Chapter 9

Blockchain and censorship

Censorship /ˈsɛnsəʃɪp/: the suppression or prohibition of any parts of books, films, news, etc. that are considered obscene, politically unacceptable, or a threat to security

9.1 Introduction

Article 57 of the Venezuelan Constitution states that 'Everyone has the right to freely express his or her thoughts, ideas or opinions orally, in writing or by any other form of expression, and to use for such purpose any means of communication and diffusion, and no censorship shall be established'. It also states that 'Censorship restricting the ability of public officials to report on matters for which they are responsible is prohibited'. Despite these entrenched protections and formal assurances, Venezuela is censoring the internet and increasing surveillance of its citizens.

Anger at President Nicolás Maduro's use of emergency powers to pass laws without congressional approval has created a sense of general unease in Venezuela that is finding expression in physical and online protests. Maduro claims to be using his powers to fight an 'economic war' with unseen enemies, but taxes on alcohol and tobacco, alongside a collapsing economy, have turned people against him. As that anger has translated into protests, the government has responded by trying to shut it down.

Bloomberg reports that Venezuela has the highest misery rating in the world. The cause of this crisis is falling oil prices, astronomical inflation, and empty supermarket shelves. In 2017, civil unrest broke out with increasingly hostile anti-government sentiment. Violent confrontations between citizens and police led to a state of emergency. Anger spilled into the streets, resulting in violent public protests. Dozens were killed during this crisis. The government responded by trying to shut it down. Although mobile phone ownership has increased significantly in recent years, more than a third of Venezuelans do not have mobile coverage or access to the internet. They rely on broadcast television to receive their news.

The power of the internet is that it gives a Venezulean blogger the same power to speak to the world as CNN [315a].

The Venezuelan Government took control of the country's news services by threatening to revoke the licences of any television stations that broadcast news reports depicting anti-government protests. Journalists have been harassed, threatened, and arrested for filming or recording these events. A large section of the media in Venezuela is now under government control. As the government ramps up its surveillance and censorship, the country is slowly slipping into anarchy.

Although Venezuelans have taken to sharing news via text messaging, President Maduro personally ordered an investigation into the telephone company Movistar for its alleged role in assisting the opposition. In response, Venezuelans have taken to social media using Instagram, SnapChat, WhatsApp, Twitter, and Facebook to inform each other and the world of what is happening in their country. In response, the government flooded social media with positive images of happy people and peaceful government. The juxtaposition of images of bloodied protesters and smiling football supporters has been described as surreal.

The government has justified its control of news, restriction on social media, and increasing surveillance of its citizens on the basis that hate speech and fake news are damaging the economy. The result is that Venezuela's government is broadcasting an alternate reality to its citizens' mobile phones. The interrelationship of censorship, democracy, and human rights has a long and tortuous history. Censorship of the internet by government and corporations is a mechanism to silence dissent, suppress free speech, or prevent whistle-blowers from revealing corruption and misuse of power [316].[1]

9.2 A brief history of internet censorship

Censorship has followed the free expressions of men and women like a shadow throughout history. Censorship of content and services delivered via the internet is incompatible with democracy [317, p. 43]. In its infancy, the internet became a great ally of democracy. It enabled quick and inexpensive communication between like-minded activists. It gave the downtrodden a medium for sharing stories and for speaking with one voice. It was a scourge of anyone who abused their power.

The prospect that a government could take control of the internet or its content stabs at the very heart of its democratic ambitions. It is therefore not surprising that most of the governments that (overtly) censor the internet are authoritarian regimes.

9.3 Types of censorship

Censorship comes in many forms.

Moral censorship is the removal of materials that are obscene or otherwise considered morally questionable. Pornography, for example, is often censored under this rationale, especially child pornography, which is illegal and censored in most jurisdictions in the world. Military censorship is the process of keeping military intelligence and tactics confidential and away from the enemy. This is used to counter espionage, which is the process of gleaning military information. The justification for military censorship is that state secrets protect national security.

The tension between national security and freedom of speech was at the heart of the government's complaint in the wake of WikiLeaks. The US Government condemned the leak of 90,000 classified military records as 'irresponsible', saying that their publication could threaten national security. The documents released by the WikiLeaks' website include details (for example) of previously unreported killings of Afghan civilians, and records showing that NATO had concerns that Pakistan's intelligence agency was helping the Taliban in Afghanistan—an accusation Islamabad had denied. WikiLeaks was founded in 2006 by Julian Assange. It describes itself as a multi-national media organisation and associated library. WikiLeaks specialises in the analysis and publication of large datasets of censored or otherwise restricted official materials involving war, spying, and corruption. It has so far published more than 10 million documents and associated analyses.

Religious censorship is the means by which any material considered objectionable by a certain religion is removed. This often involves a dominant religion forcing limitations on less prevalent ones. Alternatively, one religion may shun the works of another when they believe the content is not appropriate for their religion.

Corporate censorship is the process by which editors in corporate media outlets intervene to disrupt the publishing of information that portrays their business or business partners in a negative light, or intervene to prevent alternative offers from reaching public exposure.

Political censorship occurs when governments hold back information from their citizens. This is often done to exert control over the populace and prevent free expression that might foment rebellion. Experts say Chinese media outlets usually employ their own monitors to ensure political acceptability of their content. Censorship guidelines are circulated weekly from the Communist Party's propaganda department and the government's Bureau of Internet Affairs to prominent editors and media providers.

In general, there is an east/west division on the types of censorship practised by governments. The west seeks to protect children and prevent terrorism, whereas in the east there is a desire for cultural preservation, the maintenance of harmony, and the prevention of unflattering portrayals of the government. Meanwhile, propaganda and fake news seem to be equally an issue on both sides of this ideological divide. In many poor countries or those with autocratic regimes, government actions are more important than the internet in defining how information is produced and consumed, and by whom [318].

9.4 Censorship's relationship with free speech rights

'The remedy is more speech, not enforced silence', wrote US Supreme Court justice Louis Brandeis in 1927 in his defence of freedom of speech. Ninety years on, his position is often taken as read: in the marketplace of ideas, eventually the truth will out. Allowing government any control over the processes by which speech is produced and opinions are published poses obvious dangers [319, p. 75]. It is the province of the courts—not the government—to respond to victims of those who abuse the right to free speech and who use this process to defame, offend, bully, harass, mislead, or deceive.

Censorship and free speech are often seen as being two sides of the same thing, censorship often being defined as 'the suppression of free speech'. Free speech is the right to express any opinion in public without censorship or restraint by the government. Of course, this suggests that the government is within earshot of what is being said. For this reason, private communications are not usually the subject of censorship. It is the public expression of speech that is being protected by the right. The advent of the internet, email, text messaging, and social media has made it easier than ever to self-publish and reach a wide audience. It is these platforms that post the greatest threat to authoritarian governments.

The desire for the right to speak as we wish is universal, but it is also accepted that it is mandatory that society control certain articulations. The classic case, with which even strict libertarians would concur, is that it is not permissible to shout 'fire' in a public setting when there is no real threat and where a rush of humans towards a few exits would probably result in many unnecessary injuries and deaths. Other instances include threats aimed at a head of state, hate speech, child pornography, violence against women, and other barbaric manifestations, all of which seduce sensitive people into thinking that perhaps this case does warrant censoring [320]. Notwithstanding these examples, care is still warranted or we will soon control every articulation, every action, and every thought. Taking away these reasonable justifications for censorship, the suppression of free speech is not taken lightly in most societies.

9.5 The battle against censorship on the internet

With the advent and increasing popularity of the internet in the 1990s, the fight against censorship took a new turn. A digital underground has emerged in the face of new threats to freedom of speech and freedom of association—both of which are given new and enhanced processes and forums, particularly across time and space.

The role that Twitter, Facebook, YouTube, CNN's iReport, and many other websites and blogs played in 2010 in Iran is a great example of this. Known as the Twitter Revolution, it was an early example of social unrest being broadcast to the world by those directly involved in real time. It is likely that social media did not play as strong a role as word of mouth and text messages in organising people to rise up against the authorities, but Twitter was the preferred medium for sharing what was happening with external news agencies and governments. The critical role of Twitter as a lightning rod for international attention established it as a tool for political communication rather than outright organisation. Iran's post-election unrest was the micro-blogging service's baptism by fire as a means to observe, report, and record, real time, the unfolding of a crisis.

Barack Obama's use of Twitter and Facebook in his 2008 presidential campaign was an early testing ground for new media as a means of political communication and organisation. The practices pioneered there quickly spread to other political movements around the globe. President Obama's immediate successor, Donald Trump, has adopted Twitter as his preferred platform to share his policies and his late-night presidential musings. Indeed, Trump's failure to self-censor has brought him under fire. However, Twitter is now providing a powerful bulwark against a slide in his poll numbers, by allowing millions of supporters to make his case for him and deflect the controversies he delights in touching off. It was probably his single most effective tool in his defeat of Hillary Clinton in the 2016 presidential race.

Now let's imagine that the owners or majority shareholders of Twitter decided to take control of its content for their own political ends. Twitter was created in March 2006 by Jack Dorsey, Evan Williams, Biz Stone, and Noah Glass, and launched in July the same year. In August 2008, the first hashtags entered the Twittersphere. On 15 January 2009, a US Airways flight crashed on New York city's Hudson River. A photo posted to Twitter broke the news before traditional media outlets, highlighting its emerging role as a news breaker.

In 2017, the key investors in the business of Twitter are Ev Williams, Saudi Prince Al-Waleed bin Talal, Jack Dorsey, and former Microsoft CEO Steve Ballmer. These investors expect financial returns for their investment; this begs the question how best to wield the power that comes from controlling a major player in the speech platforms provided by social media. With more than 300 million monthly active users, it is a platform for views rather than content creators. It was only in 2015 that it finally turned a profit for the first time.

In 2017, Twitter introduced a hate speech filter for the first time. The company has refused the opportunity to provide details on specifically how the new system works, but, using a combination of behavioural and keyword indicators, the filter flags posts it deems to be violations of Twitter's acceptable speech policy and issues users with suspensions of half a day, during which they can post only to their followers. From the platform that once called itself the 'the free speech wing of the free speech party', these new tools mark an incredible turn of events. It is indicative of the general public's distaste for certain types of speech. Before the introduction of the filter, Twitter took a more reactive role, shutting out users or imposing blackouts in certain countries only when asked. This responsive approach can be slow and one senior judge described Twitter as 'out of control' [321].

What caused Twitter to change its policy in the free speech versus hate speech debate? The answer is business. In 2016, the company attempted to sell itself and suitor after suitor walked away, with several since apparently suggesting that their decision was at least in part due to concerns about Twitter's role as a centrepiece of the online hate speech movement. Suddenly hate speech was a big deal to the company, and it announced plans to invest heavily and swiftly in curtailing abusive posts and behaviour. Censorship in this case has been self-imposed and the driver for this decision was capitalism. The market has spoken and free speech was the victim.

Should free speech be curtailed to limit the distribution of hate speech? Should racist activity be monitored, even if this impinges on civil liberties? It is extraordinarily difficult to draw a meaningful line separating constitutionally protected hate speech and hate speech that should be the subject of criminal prosecution. Hate speech is also subjective and contextual. What is hateful often lies in the eye of the beholder [322].

Studies have shown that authoritarian regimes tend to censor the media to limit potential threats to the status quo. In 2014, Vladimir Putin shut down the state-controlled news agency RIA Novosti, replacing it with RT—the state's propaganda arm. Officially, the Kremlin described the change as a way to 'provide information on Russian state policy and Russian life and society for audiences abroad'.[2] But it is easy to see through this thinly disguised veil to the truth that this is the Kremlin's latest effort to reassert control over its domestic mass media. RIA Novosti had a growing reputation for pursuing independent and analytical reporting. Putin's patience wore out [323]. And Putin's Russia is only one of an increasing number of authoritarian regimes that has effectively retooled its strategy of controlling the media.

Despite the rapid rise of the internet and social media, governments in China, Azerbaijan, Vietnam, Iran, Zimbabwe, and elsewhere are finding ways to use state-controlled media to help themselves stay in power. China's central government has cracked down on press freedom as the country expands its international influence, but, in the internet age, many of its citizens hunger for a free flow of information. The Chinese government has long kept tight reins on both traditional and new media to avoid potential subversion of its authority. Its tactics often entail strict media controls using monitoring systems and firewalls, shuttering publications or websites, and jailing dissident journalists, bloggers, and activists [324]. They achieve this through selective censorship of political expression and by using state media to influence crucial audiences. Although such censorship practices were traditionally aimed at broadcast and print media, the emergence of the internet and social media, in particular, prompted some authoritarian regimes, such as the Assad regime in Syria, to try to exert a similar level of censorship on the internet as well. During the Arab Spring, the Syrian regime blocked hundreds of websites that provided social networking, news, and other services. Taking Syria as a case study, media research indicates that internet censorship succeeded in preventing internet users from reaching censored online content during the Arab Spring of 2010–12. Syrians fought back by using technology that circumvents website-blocking tools [325].

In Zimbabwe, censorship is squarely aimed at poetry, songs, satire, and film. In 1967, the Rhodesian government crafted the Censorship and Entertainment Act to stifle dissenting black voices. This Act contains some very controversial sections which would make life difficult for all Zimbabweans. The Act also states that all radio stations and DJs in bars are supposed to send their music for approval 24 hours before they play it, something that is practically impossible. In 1967, there was only one radio station and a few bars, but now, with more than eight radio stations directly linked to the state and more than a thousand bars in Harare alone, it is nightmarish to implement. As an instrument to suppress entertainment, the Act is outdated. It is out of sync with technological advancements. However, since independence, the Act has been used to control political plays and human rights artistic productions that may empower opposition and dissenters. In an act of blatant nepotism and cynical control, President Robert Mugabe's daughter Bona Mugabe-Chikore was appointed in May 2017 to the Zimbabwean censorship board. The Board has been mandated to regulate the media, particularly to gag social media platforms ahead of next year's general elections [326]. The appointment of a younger generation of Mugabes to enforce heavy censorship and smooth the way for 'democratic process' is a clumsy approach to managing opposition when technology is being used elsewhere to pseudonymise voices and hide content.

For several years over various jurisdictions, censorship circumvention tools constituted a threat to the information control systems of authoritarian regimes, highlighting the potential of such tools to promote online freedom of expression in countries where internet censorship is prevalent [325].

9.6 Fake news and reputation

The term 'fake news' has become so commonplace that it is hard to believe it was barely in use before November 2016.

With powerful social media organisations controlling their users' newsfeeds, there is a danger that this bastion of democratised free speech is actually controlled by middlemen and brokers who are mediating and manipulating the reputation of our news feed. This phenomenon has significant implications for the way that information is shared.

For the first time since the start of the 20th century, the generation of news and publications was in the hands of individuals. However, the internet has also created a hierarchy of websites that have grown in dominance and worth, not by winning exclusive broadcasting licences, but by feeding users with the content they want [317]. And how do these websites and platforms know what the users want? The users tell them: every time they react to or like a post, they communicate their political, social, and personal preferences about every aspect of their lives.

The withholding of news or the context and timing of its distribution can shape the way it is received, if at all. The role that 'fake news' can play in choosing leaders and deciding national interests played out in 2016, a year of counterintuitive elections shaped by rampant misinformation.

The term 'fake news' exploded in popularity during the 2016 US election, when commentators pointed to fabricated and inflammatory clickbait distributed through social media as both cause and evidence of the country's polarisation. The news media elites, from Facebook, to Twitter and Reddit, far from championing freedom have instead engaged in overt censorship [327].

One of the most profound and successful attempts to avoid internet surveillance and censorship is the Tor browser. Often associated with 'the dark web', Tor software protects internet users from detection by bouncing their communications around a distributed network of relays run by volunteers all around the world: it prevents somebody watching your internet connection from learning what sites you visit, it prevents the sites you visit from learning your physical location, and it lets you access sites that are blocked. Tor defends against traffic analysis, a form of network surveillance that threatens personal freedom and privacy, confidential business activities and relationships, and state security. It is an effective censorship circumvention tool. In addition to Tor, the Tor2web project is software that allows users to access the services provided in Tor via their usual, more conventional internet browsers.

Developed by Aaron Swartz and Virgil Griffith in 2008, Tor2web supports whistle-blowing and anonymous publishing through Tor, allowing materials to remain hidden while making them accessible to a broader audience. Meanwhile, Griffith is the mastermind behind WikiScanner, which was a publically searchable database that allowed users to detect the organisations behind edits in Wikipedia. Griffith asserted that WikiScanner could help make the content that is regarded as factual in Wikipedia more reliable. This style of internet activism has been lauded by some human rights agencies, most notably with humanitarian awards conferred on Julian Assange and Edward Snowden for their work revealing secret government and military documents and video footage via WikiLeaks.[3]

However, these internet applications and their developers have a major flaw: they do not protect the identity of the whistle-blowers and developers.

Assange and Snowden have both sought asylum in London and Moscow, respectively [328]. Tor also has its weaknesses. For example, Tor cannot and does not attempt to protect against monitoring of traffic at the boundaries of the Tor network (that is, the traffic entering and exiting the network). Detection of this activity is akin to seeing someone enter and leave a bank, although activity and transactions inside the bank are not detectable.

9.7 What part can the blockchain play in the war against internet censorship?

Censorship and fake news can contribute equally to the manipulation and degradation of information in all societies. Blockchain has the potential to address both of these Wicked Problems.

The pursuit of truth—of facts—is the necessary foundation for human decision-making and human progress, in the policies of governments, in the discoveries of science, and in the lives of individuals, societies, and nations [329].

In the early days of the internet, users who wanted to circumvent authorities would use proxies or anonymisers to avoid detection. The obvious difficulty with this approach is that, once the address of a proxy or an anonymiser has been announced for use to the public, the authorities can easily filter all traffic to that address. This poses a challenge as to how proxy addresses can be announced to users without leaking too much information to the censorship authorities. This model is also relatively weak when it comes to protecting information, as opposed to individuals. It accepts that content will be detected by government agencies. Rather than disguising the content, this approach disguises the user. Not only is this problematic once the user's identity has been revealed, also the content itself is not safe from detection.

With the internet playing an ever-increasing role in social and political movements around the globe, it is important for the foot-soldiers in the movements to find ways to elude authoritarian regimes and communicate their plans and activities. Activists also need to connect with, organise, and communicate to ordinary citizens (and the rest of the world) the news of arrests and crackdowns that the political powers do not want to be known to the wider local and global community. Importantly, they need to protect their identities. This is where the blockchain comes in.

Blockchain-based social networks can operate without surveillance and censorship. Veritas, for example, is a Swiss-based decentralised platform for journalists. Harnessing blockchain's revolutionary features, this community-based forum confers the validation process on the community of users. By voting on content, the community rates it as valid, spam, or unwanted. Once an article reaches 1000 votes, it is treated as validated. Those who vote are rewarded with tokens or 'trusted' points, and their votes increase in value compared with the rest of the community. To incentivise voting, an initial coin offering released 100 million coins for a crowd sale, to ensure sufficient value in the system to support the technologists and development cost of the platform. Later coin releases paid for the validators and writers.

The popular social commentary website, Reddit, is also looking to migrate on to a blockchain network so that it can no longer be censored. Reddit's registered members can contribute content and then the platform's algorithms aggregate the metrics about its articles and posts. Organised into categories known as 'subreddits' the position of the content is curated by the community it serves. Users vote for the best articles and the name of the platform is a play on the words 'I read it'. However, Reddit's commitment to free speech is not necessarily a happy path. Policing abusive, offensive, and illegal content is slow, expensive, and time-consuming. Users do not appreciate being confronted by Nazi symbols and hate speech against 'fat people', but monitoring and deleting content is not consistent with Reddit's business model.

As modern Venezuelans know, the key to a government's efforts to censor their citizens is surveillance. Finding ways to preserve public communication in the face of government disapproval and control is very difficult, particularly for those who aim to avoid detection. Promoting freedom of speech, Alexandria is a web-based project that detects and then automatically encodes controversial Twitter posts on to a blockchain network, before authorities have had a chance to censor or take down the post. Detection is achieved with a keyword search, based on a bank of politically sensitive topics [44]. Alexandria monetises media and ensures that content creators can distribute the same artefact in countless ways [330].

A peer-to-peer decentralised system could combat the growing problem posed by both government censorship and 'fake news'. The key to any success in combating fake news will be the use of reputation systems to provide a clear and reliable indication to readers that the content they are reading is not fabricated or manipulated. This is not easy. The decentralisation of information poses one of the blockchain's biggest challenges. How does one decide which source is reputable?

Wikipedia is a very good example of how useful and yet at the same time unreliable online information can be. Validating volunteered information is not easy. Even though Wikipedia is filled with interesting information and its popularity drove the final nail in the coffin of hard copy encyclopaedias, it is impossible to fully validate its contents. Indeed, in March 2016, an anonymous user accessed the editing function in Wikipedia to alter the definition of blockchain to remove the words 'bitcoin' and 'permissionless' [331]. Although it is accepted that blockchain networks are not necessarily permissionless and do not have to tokenise value or assets like bitcoin, this tampering with definitions was regarded as vexatious enough to see the revocation of the culprit's Wikipedia editing rights. Bitcoin and blockchain enthusiasts took to Twitter in response, expressing their concern that this was a deliberate effort to use the forum as a vehicle to push an agenda. Keeping Wikipedia free of political or commercial interests is key to ensuring its reputation as a reliable source of objective facts and information. Wikipedia is just one (albeit significant) website of 'facts'.

There are many who need protection from 'fake news' and manipulation by interest groups. There is a groundswell of interest in the protection of the integrity of online information, particularly when facts and analysis are intended to inform democratic processes. The blockchain can do for news and other social media what it has done for bitcoin and Veritas—allow the community to curate, police, and censor its content [332].

9.8 How Blockchain will disrupt the content industry

Ever since the first online article or video was published, there have been a plethora of problems that content creators face, no matter how secure or professional the sites may be. Almost any content creator has experienced their content being copied or ripped by others, without their consent. In addition, since the start of Trump's presidency, fake news is, unfortunately, the new normal. According to *Bloomberg Businessweek*, even medical journals are now experiencing problems with fake news [333]. The open-access system of allowing the internet to distribute high-quality research to a wider audience has allowed unreliable content into the mix.

Spam also remains a problem, because people keep falling for it. In addition, spam is extremely cheap to send out, which means only a few individuals out of millions have to be taken in to make it worth sending. For the last few years, the best methods to fight spam have been to attempt to legally shut down spammers and create better spam filters. However, now there is a new solution that could dramatically limit the possibility of sending spam.

Blockchain can limit or prevent spam by creating email networks with individual nodes rather than centralised servers. A system will be guarded against attacks by using blockchain when receiving or sending emails. The system is protected and not open to spam on any individual node. There are even methods available for nodes to receive tokens in the network, similar to how Bitcoin operates. Users can ultimately get fair compensation for receiving only legitimate content. Another option to prevent spam is the application of a reputation mechanism when creating content. Users who send spam will need to pay a very small amount for each email sent, but when you are sending millions of emails it can become expensive very quickly.

Losing control of your content online is not just limited to other individuals using it without giving you credit. 'Proof of Existence' is an online service that incorporates blockchain. It involves content being certified and time stamped into the blockchain, providing a cryptographic record. It is a public record proving that you own the content without actually revealing the information or yourself. When you add the metadata of the content on the blockchain as well, it becomes possible to prove at any time that you were the original creator. These aspects of blockchain will lead to increased accuracy and overall confidence in online content.

Although blockchain is still in the beginning stages of practical implementation, there are several companies that are already using the technology. The following are examples of how different blockchain start-ups are incorporating blockchain into their business model.

1 **Theta Labs**: Theta Labs is starting a decentralised network that provides blockchain video streaming. They have taken on the challenge of featuring videos all over the world at lower costs. Theta is accomplishing this by offering a peer-to-peer video delivery system. Theta will also offer a cryptocurrency. Using blockchain, this network will provide quality streaming without the usual high cost of content delivery infrastructure;
2 **Mine Labs**: Mine Labs is a New York-based company that has created Mediachain which will protect the creator's rights to a variety of digital work. Mediachain allows content providers to store data with time stamps. This means that the digital content can be found in a decentralised system, thereby safeguarding a content creator's work;
3 **Chimaera**: using blockchain, Chimaera has provided a way to manage complicated game worlds while also securing the sharing and ownership of virtual assets. Chimaera is providing a platform for almost an unlimited number of players to play a variety of games;
4 **Civil**: Civil, a journalism company, is providing a news platform with the help of blockchain. Using Civil, creators of news content can publish news, collaborate with colleagues, and directly receive compensation for their content;
5 **Veredictum**: this Australian start-up is in the process of creating applications that will register content on blockchain. The company is working to reduce the amount of video and film theft. This process will make it easier to recognise illegal content. Users can load their content, certify ownership, and set the terms of distribution;
6 **Blocktech**: Blocktech is also working on a concept that creates an unalterable ledger. They have found a way to preserve tweets cryptographically to make sure that they are not edited;
7 **LBRY**: this is a digital marketplace that provides a platform for you to upload your own content to a variety of hosts and ultimately for you to own your own data. LBRY features a digital library where you can find everything from music to e-books;
8 **Imagjn**: this is a decentralised collaboration platform enabling individuals, organisations, and things to collaborate and create high-quality content, governed by reputation.

Without any one individual maintaining or controlling a database, blockchain will ultimately change the way content is created and maintained. Literally thousands of people will have their own copy of a particular database.

Further down the road, even Facebook and Google may lose the power they currently possess, with privacy and autonomy restored to the individual.

Providers such as Amazon and YouTube currently take a fairly high percentage of artists' and authors' products. Blockchain will hopefully disrupt the status quo and provide an easier and more effective way for creators of content to keep more of their earnings, which is one of the objectives of the company Imagjn.

The days of centralised, commercially owned data may eventually go the way of the horse and buggy. The beginning of the revolution may include improving commerce, saving money, and changing the content industry as we know it. As blockchain technology continues to improve and advance, content creators will finally recover control over their content and be able to make a fair living with it.

9.9 Conclusion

Free speech plays an important role in democracy, freedom of association, and freedom of expression. It is a fundamental human right. Without freedom of press and support for information integrity, development in countries that struggle to house, educate, and feed vulnerable people cannot happen. Freedom of expression and access to information play a crucial role in good governance, transparency, and accountability—and these in turn are pillars of sustainable development [334].

Human rights and fundamental freedoms are essential for equitable and sustainable development, and good governance (specifically rule of law, democracy, access to justice and information, transparency, and accountability) enables sustainable development. The UN's Sustainable Development Goals include education, equality, innovation, and climate action. To achieve these aims, it is important to allow democratic institutions to operate free of constraint on truth and information. Decentralising control and allowing consensus to curate truth and journalism using blockchain technology may be a valuable tool in this campaign. For Venezuelans, blockchain-based innovation cannot come soon enough.

Truth, famously, is the first casualty of war and this is experienced daily in the troubled streets of Caracas. In Venezuela, the media have been under immense pressure for years, first under Hugo Chávez and now from the Maduro administration [329, 335]. Venezuelans describe their daily lives as confused and exhausted. A recent alleged attempted coup by a lone helicopter pilot dropping grenades was reported by some to be a government conspiracy—manipulated by Maduro to justify government oppression [336]. Conspiracy theories were fuelled by conflicting reports that the perpetrator was either ex-special forces or an aspiring actor, or both. Revelations of fake news about threats to the government and deaths of activists, and rumours that the first family is fleeing the country [337], and the military is mobilising against Maduro [338], only make a bad situation worse. As it is difficult to distinguish fact from fiction, Venezuelans say they are unable to make decisions [339].

While Maduro promises a prosperous post-oil future and a strong agricultural economy, the outlook seems unlikely to brighten soon. Venezuela is expected to remain deep in recession unless the structural problems afflicting the country are addressed soon [340]. In this context, separating fact from fiction has never been so important for decision-making. The fake news in Venezuela comes from a variety of sources, many of them unidentified, most of them with vested interests in the current conflict [335]. However, blockchain technology can offer secure social networks and verified journalism, protecting not just content, but also its creators.

Notes

1 The most widely censored content on the internet is pornography. Although some may regard pornography as harmless and defend its publication on the grounds of free speech and freedom of expression, the suppression of such content is not generally regarded as impinging on the freedoms associated with democratic free speech and journalistic integrity. It is this latter type of censorship that is the subject of this chapter.

2 https://thebarentsobserver.com/en/security/2017/10/kommersant-russia-lists-norways-svalbard-policy-potential-risk-war

3 Julian Assange has been awarded media, journalism, peace and freedom prizes, and medals by more than a dozen organisations including *The Economist*, Amnesty International, the Sydney Peace Foundation, and the Union of Journalists in Kazakhstan. Meanwhile, in 2013 and 2014, Edward Snowden was awarded the Sam Adams Award for Integrity in Intelligence, the Right Livelihood Award (an international award to 'honour and support those offering practical and exemplary answers to the most urgent challenges'), and the Stuttgart Peace Prize.

Chapter 10

The convergence of exponential technologies

Solution /səˈluːʃ(ə)n/: a means of solving a problem or dealing with a difficult situation

We live in exponential times. As might be clear by now, Blockchain is a disruptive technology and it will have a massive impact on how we live, work, and build our societies. Distributed ledgers facilitate trustless peer-to-peer transactions, removing the need for intermediaries and making data immutable, verifiable, and traceable. It has been said that blockchain will do for transactions what the advent of the internet did for the sharing of information. Leaders, organisations, and societies that want to innovate and lead the pack should be aware of Blockchain and how it will change—well everything. In writing this book, it was our objective to offer you some insights into how Blockchain could be used to create a better world and not just focus on the commercial benefits of Blockchain. Of course, Distributed Ledger Technology provides ample opportunities for organisations to create better products and services, reduce their costs, and improve their bottom line significantly. However, as may be clear by now, the technology can also be used for the social good and create a better, fairer, and more equal world. Of course, if you look at the statistics as discussed in Chapter 4, you can argue that we have never had it better, but that does not mean that we can sit back and relax. Climate change is a severe threat to humanity, over 700 million people still live in extreme poverty [147], corruption, fraud, money laundering activities, and censorship continue to take place on a wide scale across the globe, and Fair Trade often is not really fair at all. In addition, our current identity system is long overdue for a replacement, which in itself would help solve many of the Wicked Problems discussed in this book.

Blockchain is not, however, the only disruptive technology coming our way. Currently, the world experiences an accelerated change and many disruptive technologies are coming to fruition. Big data analytics, artificial intelligence, the Internet of Things, Virtual and Augmented Reality, 3D printing, robotics, and quantum computing are just a few of the technologies that will increasingly have an impact on our lives. When these technologies converge, a radical shift, or a 'gestalt shift', will occur, which means that the character of the experience will drastically change. All of a sudden, we can see the world through a different, more technologically advanced, lens and this opens up a completely new perspective. The convergence of multiple disruptive technologies will offer us new possibilities and solutions to improve our lives and create better organisations and societies, as well as build a better world all together. Let's briefly discuss three of them, which we believe are also key to solving the Wicked Problems that have been discussed. We do not go into too much depth, because there are plenty of other books that cover these topics in great detail.

10.1 Big data analytics

First of all, big data analytics. Big data refers to the creation, storage, and usage of data in high velocity, volume, variety, and variability. In recent years, we have been generating large amounts of data, which is expected to grow exponentially in the coming years [341]. Big data changes organisations, and their culture and identity, as well as decision-making [342, 343]. For many organisations, the most likely path to competitive advantage is via big data analytics [344]. Hence, it is not only start-ups such as Uber or AirBnB that can profit from a data-driven approach [345]—any company has become a data business where big data analytics is now a prerequisite to understand the environment and remain competitive. Big data analytics offers organisations competitive advantage and can help not-for-profit organisations and governments create better products and services.

There are three stages of big data analytics of which it is important to be aware: descriptive analytics, predictive analytics, and prescriptive analytics, where each stage offers more and better insights into creating a better organisation. Each phase also growths in complexity as does the value it can offer the organisation. [345a]

Descriptive analytics enables organisations to understand their environment and it is similar to looking into the rear-view mirror of your car—using a variety of structured datasets and statistical methods to achieve insights about what has happened from a second ago to decades ago. Predictive analytics improves decision-making across an organisation [346], in order to understand how to respond to the changing environment. It is your car's navigation system that tells you the fastest route despite a traffic jam. [345a] Predictive analytics uses artificial intelligence to find patterns and relationships in multiple (un)structured data sources to create recommendations [347]. Organisations that use predictive analytics gain a competitive advantage, because they can anticipate the future [348]. Finally, prescriptive analytics transforms an organisation and is the final stage in understanding a business. It allows a permanent and real-time (re)alignment of (in)tangible assets based on recommendations obtained from analysing unstructured and structured data sources. It uses a variety of algorithms and data-modelling techniques to offer recommendations on how to take advantage of predictions provided. Continuing with the car metaphor, it is like a self-driving car bringing you autonomously to your destination. [345a]

Organisations that make data and insights from widely available data experience a shift in the power structure within the business; decision-making power moves from those leaders with the most experience to anyone who has access to data and the analytic tools to derive insights from it. In a data-driven business, the real decision-makers within an organisation are not senior managers or C-level executives, but those employees who face the customer or are directly involved in creating the product or service. Some leaders might be reluctant to accept this shift in power, but, only when all leaders accept such a power shift, can the organisation truly benefit from big data analytics. Empowered employees are more likely to collaborate with different stakeholders to create the best result for the business, because they feel more involved and more responsible for the success of the organisation. In this way, those organisations that want to remain competitive in a constantly changing and increasingly data-driven world should foster employee collaboration and promote the use of (advanced) analytics across the business, and network organisations in particular are in the right position to do so. However, big data analytics does not only offer benefits for commercial organisations. In fact, big data analytics is a key aspect of solving the Wicked Problems discussed in this book.

Data has become a fundamental factor in every part of our lives, businesses, and societies. Almost any new technology generates data nowadays and every business has become a data business that happens to make product X or Y. The same goes for any not-for-profit or government institution—all have become data organisations that happen to offer service X or Y. For example, a car company is a data company that helps people move from A to B, whereas a bank is a data company that happens to help customers with their financial needs. Viewing your organisation from this new perspective will enable you to find new solutions, develop better products, and offer improved services. The same goes for the Wicked Problems discussed in this book. If we see them as a data problem, it will become a little bit easier to solve them.

The United Nations also saw the potential of big data analytics. In 2009, they launched the Global Pulse initiative, which serves as an innovation lab to raise awareness of the opportunities that big data brings. The objective is to be a catalyst for big data adoption and bring together different stakeholders, such as big data scientists, data providers, governments, and development sector practitioners [269]. Climate change is one of the areas that can benefit from big data analytics by monitoring processes that previously could not be monitored. The UN's Global Pulse data analytics initiative launched the Big Data Climate Challenge in 2014. This programme funded, among others, programmes to monitor deforestation by combining satellite data, crowd-sourced witness accounts, and public data. These insights help policy-makers and organisations, such as Nestlé or Unilever, ensure that their activities do not worsen deforestation [349, 350]. On the other hand, poverty can be reduced by providing the right medicines to the right people at the right moment [351], as we have already shown in the fictional business in Chapter 4. A programme called SMS for Life significantly improved the distribution of malaria drugs in Tanzania, by predicting demand more accurately [352]. A big data study by the World Bank revealed that, in many countries, people are not literally starving of hunger, because they have enough food, but that they are dying because the food was not nutritious enough. As a result, governments could change their aid by focusing on more nutritious food rather than subsidising rice or noodles [353]. Fraud, corruption, or money laundering, in any industry, can also of course be reduced using big data analytics. With an estimated US$3.5 trillion in revenue lost every year due to fraudulent activities [354], there is a huge incentive for organisations to look into the details. Pattern recognition and anomaly detection will offer insights into cases that are out of the ordinary and require additional attention. The more such analytics can be automated using artificial intelligence, the better we will be able to find solutions to the Wicked Problems. It is for these reasons that the advances in artificial intelligence are so promising.

10.2 Artificial intelligence

In 2017, AlphaGo Zero, the new and improved version of the AlphaGo algorithm developed by Google's DeepMind, was released. Although previous versions of AlphaGo had been trained using human data, this version of the algorithm is completely self-trained, with no human intervention or historical data. This is a mind-blowing feature, especially given that, within three days of teaching itself how to play the game, it beat the version that beat Lee Sedol in 2016. It did so using a new form of reinforcement learning where the algorithm became its own teacher. It played against itself, which meant that it always had a component of equal strength, and learned from every move it made. Although the previous version that beat Lee Sedol already surprised the world champion with moves he had never seen or thought about, the new version applies completely unknown strategies that it had taught itself. As a result, after 40 days it surpassed all previous versions of AlphaGo and, arguably, became the best AlphaGo player in the world. This was a significant event in the world of artificial intelligence, because it represented a new form of artificial intelligence—intuitive artificial intelligence, something that is remarkably more challenging than standard artificial intelligence.

The disruption happening thanks to algorithms is taking place all around us. The largest taxi company in the world, Uber, owns no taxis, but uses smart algorithms to connect drivers and passengers. The largest telephone company in the world, WhatsApp, has no telecom infrastructure, but sends over 35 billion messages per day. Finally, the world's second most valuable retailer,

Alibaba, owns no inventory but uses algorithms to help others sell products. Companies such as Uber, WhatsApp, and Alibaba clearly show that artificial intelligence can disrupt an entire industry [345]. However, we are just at the start of this disruption and the coming decade will probably see all industries being disrupted thanks to artificial intelligence. Gartner calls this trend the 'Algorithmic Business' and it will fundamentally change how we do business and run our governments [355, 356].

The algorithmic organisation is an organisation built around smart algorithms—algorithms that define company processes, deliver customer services, take action when necessary, and as such define the way the world works. In order to understand all the data coming our way, artificial intelligence will be required. Thanks to machine learning and deep learning, these algorithms will be able to understand customer behaviour, learn from devices, and perform the right action accordingly. Algorithms will optimise your supply chain, drive your cars, monitor your robots, determine the right marketing message, and even become your boss.

Thanks to technological advances, companies and consumers are generating more and more data. Some organisations, such as Walmart, create and store dozens of petabytes of data every day [357]. Collecting and storing massive amounts of data is not, however, enough to solve some of the Wicked Problems. For this to happen, organisations must do more than simply analyse the data. It is about what actions you can derive from your data in order to add value. Algorithms define actions and they are pieces of software that are extremely good at very specific actions, much better than humans are. As a result, the more algorithms used within organisations, the more people will be out of a job in the future. In fact, 2013 research from Oxford University and Deloitte estimated that in the UK alone, more than 35% of current jobs are at high risk due to computerisation [358]. And the UK is not alone. The same research estimated that almost 47% of US jobs could be lost due to algorithmic business within one or two decades. A society with almost half the workforce without a job does sound frightening and is another Wicked Problem to be dealt with. However, if we prepare ourselves today it also offers great possibilities to drastically improve our societies.

Artificial intelligence is already applied in a variety of ways. Organisations such as Associated Press use algorithms to write financial reports at a rate of 2000 stories per minute. Of course, these are not in-depth, award-winning articles, but business-related stories, such as quarterly earnings, involving stock market performance and corporate profits—stories, however, these used to be written by humans. Does this mean robot journalists are putting journalists out of business? No, at least not yet, although the developments in artificial intelligence that can write a readable novel are progressing rapidly. Also worth mentioning is Lapetus, a start-up that promises to use artificial intelligence to analyse your selfies and determine whether or not you will be accepted for life insurance, within 2 minutes.

The algorithmic organisation has the potential to change society and recent developments are bringing us closer to the holy grail of artificial intelligence: artificial general intelligence (AGI), which means artificial intelligence as smart as humankind. AGI is becoming possible because of deep learning, which is a subfield of machine learning and inspired by the neural networks in our brain. The objective is to create artificial neural networks that can find patterns in vast amounts of data. Deep learning is becoming widely available now, because of the increased computing power and large datasets that are available to scientists around the globe. New deep learning applications could have a significant impact on our lives and help solve some of the Wicked Problems.

Deep learning algorithms are not trained by humans. Rather, they are exposed to massive datasets, millions of videos/images/articles, etc. and the algorithms must figure out for themselves how to recognise different objects, sentences, images, etc. As a result, they can come up with solutions no humans could have thought of, so without big data this would not have been possible. For example, in 2016 a set of algorithms developed an encryption algorithm that humans could not decipher, because it was using patterns humans would never use [359]. Naturally, artificial intelligence is particularly well suited to solving Wicked Problems, because they can easily process large amounts of data and confusing information, link it back to any stakeholders involved, and propose solutions that could point us in the right direction. The more intelligent artificial intelligence becomes, the more useful it becomes in solving our Wicked Problems. In fact, already artificial intelligence can no longer be ignored when trying to solve Wicked Problems. For every Wicked Problem discussed in this book, it is vital to have vast amounts of data, and artificial intelligence can then be used to recognise patterns, discover (inter)dependencies, understand differences and similarities, classify data automatically, make predictions, and take action accordingly. Demis Hassabis, CEO of Google DeepMind, the division within Google responsible for AlphaGo and doing ground-breaking research on artificial intelligence, said 'the goal is to harness artificial intelligence for grand challenges. If we can solve intelligence in a general enough way, then we can apply it to all sorts of things to make the world a better place' [360]. The more data available to artificial intelligence, the better it will become, because deep learning feeds on big data. This is why the Internet of Things is so important, because it has the potential to increase the amount of data exponentially.

10.3 The Internet of Things

The Internet of Things, Industrial Internet, or the Internet of Everything, no matter how you name it, will change everything and create massive amounts of sensor data. According to Cisco, it is going to be a US$19 trillion market within the coming decade [361]. This includes a projected US$2.9 trillion for the Industrial Internet. Gartner predicts that, by 2020, 150 new devices will be connected to the internet, every second, resulting in approximately 50 billion sensors in the coming decade to around 100 trillion connected sensors by 2030 [355]. When you have billions and billions of devices connected to the internet, it changes your perspective, especially when these connected devices are becoming truly smart. Robots, autonomous vehicles or boats, drones, and any other Internet of Things product will become increasingly intelligent. These devices will become a lot better at understanding the user and adapting the product or service to its needs and context. Software updates will be done over the air, reducing the need to constantly buy a new product.

The Internet of Things is all about actions taken by artificial intelligence based on the data that is generated by the connected devices, resulting in massive amounts of data that need to be analysed to understand what's going on. For example, you have a connected thermostat and your car knows that you are driving home; your car knows that the temperature is low in your house and tells the thermostat to turn up the heating. When you arrive home, it is nice, warm, and cosy inside.

Artificial intelligence will significantly influence the Internet of Things. Without artificial intelligence, the Internet of Things would not be possible, because analysing the vast amounts of raw sensor data can be achieved only with algorithms that can take automatic action at the right moment. Of course, what an algorithm can do for your home can also be done on a large scale in your organisation or within a government. As Senior VP at Gartner, Peter Sondergaard explained: 'algorithms define action' and 'by 2020, smart agents will facilitate 40% of interactions' [355].

Algorithms will also be able to take into account the context—context that is so important, and necessary, to truly understand what is going on within a particular process, individual, business, or connected device. With sufficient data sources from connected devices that each tell their side of the story, algorithms will be able to determine the right action based on a myriad of data points. In essence, artificial intelligence combined with the Internet of Things will be able to find the right business moments, make meaningful connections, predict all kinds of behaviour, help solve Wicked Problems, and so improve organisations, governments, and our society.

The contribution of the Internet of Things to solving Wicked Problems is by enabling new data sources that can be analysed. For example, smart grids, as discussed in Chapter 6, offer all sorts of new possibilities thanks to smart meters.

These connected devices monitor what is going on, for example in your home or office building, and artificial intelligence will then take action accordingly, make secure transactions that are recorded on a blockchain, and save or make you money. The more devices connected to the internet, the better we will be able to analyse a variety of processes, and insights from these analyses will help us solve multiple Wicked Problems.

10.4 The convergence of technology

The convergence of technologies such as big data analytics, artificial intelligence, and the Internet of Things with Distributed Ledger Technologies such as blockchain will mark a paradigm shift in our world. In fact, you cannot see these technologies as separate, and combined they will strengthen each other. Once these technologies have been brought together, we have a real chance of solving all the Wicked Problems that discussed in this book, and possibly many more. Connected devices and online services will increase the amount of data available, which can then be analysed by smart algorithms. Blockchain will ensure that data transferred between different actors will be immutable, verifiable, and traceable. In addition, any smart contract recorded on a blockchain will enable intelligent automation, where the output of one smart contract can become the input of another, thereby creating smart, decentralised, autonomous organisations.

However, all this technology will also have a downside and create new Wicked Problems. One of these is the jobless future, where robots and artificial intelligence have taken over most of the jobs available. Many jobs that we believe, or used to believe, were immune to automation are also being affected by artificial intelligence. There are already restaurants without staff, where the burgers are made by a robot or the sushi is delivered by a robot. The company Momentum Machines, for example, has made a robot that produces burgers, which replaces two or three fast food cooks. As Momentum Machines cofounder Alexandros Vardakostas said in 2012: 'our device isn't meant to make employees more efficient, it's meant to completely obviate them.' However, the redundancy does not stop there—the more complicated jobs such as accountants, truck drivers, or customer service agents will be taken over by algorithms and robots. If you believe that software development would be safe, forget it. In 2017, Google worked on developing an algorithm that was more capable of creating new code than the programmers who created the algorithm in the first place. In 2017, they unveiled a new approach using neural networks to train artificial intelligence to build better neural networks. The technology, called AutoML, uses reinforcement learning and is capable of creating networks that are more powerful, more efficient, and better to use than what developers can build. The more advanced artificial intelligence becomes in the next decade, the more jobs will disappear as a result. Therefore, a future in which robots and algorithms have taken over 50% or more of our jobs, is, according to us, a very realistic scenario. The questions that remain are when will this happen and how we should approach this Wicked Problem.

Fortunately, the technology that will put many of us out of a job can also be used to find a solution. Already, some governments are experimenting with Blockchain for welfare payments. The UK collaborates with Barclays, the UK arm of German energy firm RWE, fintech start-up GovCoin, and University College London to send welfare payments using the blockchain and record any payments sent or received by welfare recipients [362]. Finland takes it to the next level—they are the first country in the world to have started a large experiment with an unconditional basic income for a group of 2000 unemployed Finns, aged 25–58 years, in order to prepare for a jobless future. According to several Finnish experts, the blockchain technology offers significant benefits for an unconditional basic income scheme, including transparency, while ensuring privacy, automating government tasks, reducing any bureaucracies, and as such significantly reducing costs associated with government services [363]. An unconditional basic income is one solution to solving the issue of a jobless future and it will enable humans to focus on other aspects of life such as creativity and self-actualisation. Of course, a basic income for all citizens does not come cheap, so governments should streamline any tax systems currently in place, remove any social and tax benefits, and therefore opt for a simplified tax system. Blockchain would enable this, especially when a country uses an existing, or its own future, cryptocurrency such as the crypto-dollar, crypto-euro or crypto-yuan. It would make any tax payment or social benefit immutable, verifiable, and traceable, while ensuring anonymity. Added benefit is that doing your annual taxes will be automated as well.

The convergence of emerging technologies is rapidly changing how we live, work, and run our societies, and it is important for governments to investigate how these technologies can be used to create a better, more inclusive, fairer, and transparent society, while respecting citizens' privacy and security. Starting with moving basic government services to the blockchain, such as is currently happening in Estonia and Dubai, is very promising and gives these countries a competitive advantage over other countries, and a possibility of contributing to reaching the UN Sustainable Development Goals.

10.5 The UN's Sustainable Development Goals

The blockchain revolution has given rise to billions of dollars in investment in potential applications. Some of those projects have revealed other uses for distributed ledgers and similar non-blockchain programmes. A number of the Sustainable Development Goals developed by the UN may be more achievable with blockchain capacity. The creation of verifiable digital identities authenticates supply chains, and immutable records and transactions can all contribute to ensuring that trade is fair, tax is paid, votes are counted, provenance is respected, and displaced populations have an enduring identity and qualifications, despite a lack of documentation. The benefits of digitising identities become more apparent as populations are displaced by war or environmental catastrophe. In the future, climate change has the potential to create a new generation of displacement. With digital identities, human movement does not have to result in the loss of those attributes that we need to prove in order to make a new life in a new place. It is possible for entire nations to be recorded along with their digitised archives and history. Whether it is Kiribati losing land to rising water levels or Estonia's fear of the return of a Soviet-like regime, the blockchain can securely record sufficient information to identify individuals and their personal attributes. It can manage permissions and provenance so that the use of sensitive and private information is controlled by the technology, and not by a third party in a fixed location that has been destroyed or dissipated.

10.6 A Blockchain roadmap for your business

Knowledge of what blockchain is and how it can contribute to solving some of the world's biggest challenges is one thing; knowledge of how to develop a blockchain strategy is another thing altogether. Meanwhile, understanding how to implement a blockchain strategy within your business is even more difficult.

Blockchain, particularly when used in concert with emerging technologies, such as big data analytics, artificial intelligence, or the Internet of Things, offers organisations an opportunity to re-think their internal processes, remove inefficiencies, and build a better organisation. However, within large process-oriented organisations, transforming a centralised business to a decentralised organisation, in which cryptography is used to create trust, smart contracts automate decision-making, and governance is embedded in code, can be a daunting task. In fact, the steps that are needed to transform your business into a decentralised organisation are clear and straightforward. Therefore, we wish to provide you with a roadmap as to how your business could start with and benefit from blockchain. Because, although blockchain can help solve the Wicked Problems discussed and improve our world, it can also transform your business.

Step 1: understanding blockchain

Hopefully, this book has offered you a clear understanding of what Blockchain is and what its different components are. At its core, Blockchain is nothing more than a database technology, but the implications of the technology are transformative and can be far reaching. Therefore, it is crucial that the organisation has a shared understanding of what Blockchain is and what it can do for your organisation or industry. As the wide range of Blockchain start-ups discussed in this book shows, Blockchain can be applied to any industry and any business objective. For each industry, Blockchain offers different opportunities, ranging from data or product provenance, improved identity, and verification systems, to increased payment efficiencies. Therefore, creating a shared understanding, at the board level, of what Blockchain can do for your business is a vital first step.

Knowing what Blockchain is and what it can do for your business will help to win management support and buy in from the rest of the organisation. With the enormous potential of Blockchain, it is more a strategy matter than an IT one. This is particularly because, if you wish to take Blockchain seriously, it will take time and in the beginning the return on investments may be unclear and could even be negative. Possession of a shared understanding of the decentralised future of your business will help in achieving your long-term vision.

Step 2: identify the problem that you want to solve

This is a crucial step towards the strategic adoption of blockchain technology. Many problems can be solved with a database or even a spreadsheet. As blockchain technology is a financial investment, it is crucial to establish that it is the best solution for the problem at hand.

To assist in this analysis, it is useful to summarise the types of business problems that lend themselves to a blockchain-based solution. These include: roadblocks in supply chain and trade facilitation, where multiple parties need access to common data while needing to protect their commercial interests; protection of markets that rely on provenance; registration of title and rights; recording permissions for the use of digital assets and creative works; preservation of digital works in perpetuity; and recording transactions where it is important to make those transactions transparent to a network. Blockchain offers neutral territory for sharing information across organisational boundaries. In addition to these business service examples, blockchain technology can facilitate sharing information about trends, voting patterns, data analysis, and record keeping.

Importantly, all of these scenarios assume that the information being shared is not private or confidential. In a world of heightened data and privacy protection, this issue must be borne in mind before advertising information to participants on a public or permissioned network.

Not all problems require a decentralised solution, a cryptocurrency, or smart contracts. Blockchain should be a means to an end, not the other way around. When deciding to require a token, understand clearly why you need a token and what sort of token, because there are plenty of decentralised solutions that do not require one.

Step 3: define a minimum viable product

As is with any new technology that you wish to implement within your organisation, it is wise to start small and develop a minimum viable product (MVP). The best way to learn a new, disruptive technology is to start small and grow from there, and slowly implement it throughout the organisation. In addition, Blockchain differs from any other emerging technology because it often requires organisations to collaborate with industry partners, customers, or even competitors as, only through decentralised collaboration with your stakeholders, do the benefits of Blockchain become truly visible. Whether the product needs to serve a vertical organisational structure or a horizontal supply chain scenario (or both), all participants need to understand why certain information is being shared and to trust that personal, commercial-in-confidence, and industry-sensitive information is secure. Blockchain's transparency can make all of these functions explicit (as outputs or nullities).

In addition to this, the Blockchain ecosystem is still being developed. At the time of publication, the adoption journey of this new technology has travelled to the same point that the internet had reached in 1994 or 1995. Obviously, it will not take another 20 years for this new ecosystem to develop fully, but many of the technologies required for your decentralised organisation are still in their beta or even alpha stage of testing. This is why developing an MVP with your stakeholders is the best way to get started and ensure that the technology works as it should, before further expansion into your organisation.

Step 4: start hiring new talent

Blockchain technology requires new specialists, including developers, business and technical architects, solidity developers, and cryptographers, but also data scientists, mathematicians, and security specialists. If you also want to do an Initial Coin Offering (ICO) at some stage, you also require ICO specialists, a new type of job that is rapidly becoming more important. Unfortunately, the market for Blockchain developers (a general term to include all of the above) is still very small, simply because the technology is still so new. Hence, it is important for your organisation to start hiring (or partnering with) the right Blockchain developers as soon as possible. Make sure that they have the right industry experience because Blockchain technology does differ per industry.

Of course, you can also turn to one of the many consultancy businesses helping organisations to implement blockchain solutions. These include traditional consultancy firms such as Accenture, IBM, KPMG or Microsoft, or you can turn to new more specialised firms such as Consensys or Chainsmiths.

Step 5: start scaling your efforts

Once you have a shared understanding of Blockchain, developed your hypotheses and an MVP, and lined up new resources, it is time to start expanding your efforts. With luck, your steps into the world of Blockchain result in tangible improvements to your business and your bottom line, which you can then use to start focusing on the impact of Blockchain on your core business. The MVP that you develop will help you create a long-term Blockchain strategy and roadmap, including your intended objectives such as increased efficiencies, reduced risks, better governance, or quality improvements.

When developing your long-term Blockchain strategy, you will start to understand whether it will stay on the periphery of your organisation, only slightly affecting your business, or moves into the mainstream of your business, thereby radically changing your business. Whichever it is, by investing in one or more MVPs, you are prepared for the future ahead, because you have learned the capabilities needed to develop a decentralised business. This, in itself, it very valuable and will help you gain a competitive advantage in an increasingly decentralised society.

10.7 A distributed and decentralised future

The future is distributed and decentralised, and in the coming decade we are returning the web to its decentralised and distributed nature. Today, the three biggest online companies, Google, Facebook, and Amazon, have enormous power, which they apply to increase shareholder return using their customers' data. As Jonathan Taplin revealed in his 2017 book *Move Fast and Break Things*, this 'surveillance capital' actually increases inequality, does very little for the social good, and can actually be very bad for democracy [364]. It is time for change and to apply emerging technologies to improve our world rather than just increasing shareholders' returns. Of course, this does not mean that you cannot make money. In fact, the drive to make a good profit offers tremendous opportunities. The few billion people who are currently excluded are a great target market, if done in a fair and honest way. As we wrote in Chapter 6, reducing climate change is a good business opportunity that can make millions while improving our world.

Solving the Wicked Problems discussed in this book requires a collaborative effort of individuals, organisations, and governments. Governments should start applying Blockchain to improve government services, making it easier to do business and comply with the law. Blockchain offers so many opportunities for governments to reduce bureaucracy, remove inefficiencies, and help organisations do what they can do best: run a business and, hopefully, create a better world. On the other hand, organisations can apply Blockchain, as well as other emerging technologies, to develop better products and services, create a better customer experience, and return control of personal data to the customer. The immutability, verifiability, and traceability of data on a blockchain will result in more transparency and security, and bring a new level of privacy, currently lost in many countries. Finally, individuals will be able to directly transact with their peers, across time and space, in a secure manner. It will foster collaboration on a global scale unseen before, enabling individuals to help each other and make money along the way in new and innovative ways. Cryptography and encryption will ensure that individuals can trust each other without knowing each other, opening up new connections and trade across the globe.

Solving the identity crisis will be a catalyst for solving the other Wicked Problems. Offering every citizen a digital and secure self-sovereign identity enables them to interact with other individuals, organisations, and governments in a secure, transparent and private manner. This would require governments to embrace blockchain and other emerging technologies, similar to the Estonian model, and create a digital-first strategy. Governments should no longer focus only on attracting companies with tax benefits, but also on those with efficiency benefits. Governments should remove any bureaucratic inefficiencies for organisations and individuals. After all, a government is a data organisation as well, which happens to enable a free, safe, equal, prosperous, clean environment in their citizens' best interests. Once self-sovereign identities are commonplace, it will become a lot easier to solve the other Wicked Problems and create a fair, transparent, and secure world for all. Of course, this does not mean that solving the other Wicked Problems can wait until we have a self-sovereign identity system in place. Existing organisations and start-ups, as well as governments and individuals, should embrace Blockchain technologies today to create a better world for tomorrow, by reducing climate change, ending poverty/corruption/fraud/money laundering and improving our democracies and Fair Trade. The technology is here and there is not a moment to lose.

Glossary of terms

Algorithm: a process or set of rules to be followed in calculations or other problem-solving operations, especially by a computer.

Annual Tax Gap: an estimate of the difference between the amounts a tax regulator collects and what it would have collected if every taxpayer were fully compliant.

Artificial intelligence (AI): the process of constructing an intelligent artefact. Using computers to amplify our human intelligence with AI has the potential to help civilisation flourish like never before—as long as we manage to keep the technology beneficial and prevent AI from inflicting any damage.

Augmented Reality (AR): sometimes also referred to as 'mixed reality', AR is the technique of adding computer graphics to a user's view of the physical world.

Big data: a term that describes the large volume of data—both structured and unstructured—that inundates a business on a day-to-day basis. These datasets are so voluminous and complex that traditional data-processing application software is inadequate to deal with them.

Bitcoin: an innovative payment network and a new kind of money. It is a type of cryptocurrency. It is the first decentralised digital currency, because the system works without a central bank or single administrator.

Blockchain: a digital ledger in which transactions made in bitcoin or another cryptocurrency are recorded chronologically. The cryptography underlying blockchain ensures a 'trustless' system, thereby removing the need for intermediaries to manage risk, making data on a blockchain immutable, traceable, and verifiable.

Consensus mechanism: a feature in decentralised networks to determine the preferences of the individual users (or nodes) and to manage decision-making of the whole network. The key to any blockchain: with a consensus algorithm, there is no longer the need for a trusted third party and, as a result, decisions can be created, implemented, and evaluated, without the need for a central authority.

Cryptocurrency: a digital asset designed to work as a medium of exchange that uses cryptography to secure its transactions, control the creation of additional units, and verify the transfer of assets.

Cryptocurrency mining: a race that rewards computer nodes for being first to solve cryptographic puzzles on public blockchain networks. By solving the puzzle, the miner verifies the block and creates a hash pointer to the next block. Once verified, each block in the chain becomes immutable.

Cryptography: protects data from theft or alteration, and can also be used for user authentication. Earlier cryptography was effectively synonymous with encryption but nowadays cryptography is mainly based on mathematical theory and computer science practice.

Decentralised Autonomous Organisation (DAO): an organisation that is run through rules encoded as computer programs called smart contracts. A DAO's financial transaction record and program rules are maintained on a blockchain. It is an organisation without management or employees, run completely by autonomous code.

Decentralised networks: a computing environment in which multiple parties (or nodes) make their own independent decisions. In such a system, there is no single centralised authority that makes decisions on behalf of all the parties.

Digital signatures: a digital code (generated and authenticated by public key encryption) that is attached to an electronically transmitted document to verify its contents and the sender's identity. Digital signatures are based on public key cryptography, also known as asymmetric cryptography.

Distributed application (DApp): blockchain-enabled products and services are commonly referred to as decentralised applications, or DApps. A DApp has at least two distinctive features: (1) any changes to the protocol of the DApp have to be approved by consensus; and (2) the application has to use a cryptographic token, or cryptocurrency, which is generated according to a set algorithm. Bitcoin is probably the best-known DApp.

Distributed Ledger Technology (DLT): a digital system for recording the transaction of assets in which the transactions and their details are recorded in multiple places at the same time. A blockchain is a distributed ledger.

Distributed networks: distributed networking is a distributed computing network system, said to be distributed when the computer programming and the data to be worked on are spread out across more than one computer. Usually, this is implemented over a computer network. Participants in a distributed network are able to verify and authenticate other users' transactions and exchanges. For this reason, the community values its own worth and reputation.

Double-spending problem: this arises when a given set of crypto-tokens is spent in more than one transaction. By solving the double-spending problem, digital or cryptocurrency has now become viable.

Fair Trade Ensuring that producers are paid fairly, work in conditions that are safe and humane, and that consumers can be guaranteed of the origins and quality of the products they consume.

Hash Algorithm: each block of data on a blockchain receives a hash ID, as a database key, calculated by a Secure Hash Algorithm. This block hash is fixed. In other words, the hash ID allocated to the block never changes. Hash Algorithms are used in a variety of components of blockchain technology, one of them being the hash ID, which is a unique string of 64 numbers and letters linked to data in each block.

Hash Function: this is any function that can be used to map data of arbitrary size to data of fixed size. The values returned by a Hash Function are called hash values, hash codes, digests, or simply hashes.

Human insecurity: people's fear of want (of food, water, land, and other resources), fear of conflict, fear of loss of freedom, fear of climate change, or fear of health or economic crisis.

Immutability: unchanging over time; and impossible to change.

Initial Coin Offering (ICO): crowd funding by issuing crypto-tokens in exchange for fiat money. Also known as a Token Generation Event (TGE).

Machine learning: a method of data analysis that automates analytical model building. It is a branch of artificial intelligence based on the idea that systems can learn from data, identify patterns, and make decisions with minimal human intervention.

Nanotechnology: science, engineering, and technology conducted at the molecular or nanoscale (which is about 1–100 nanometres).

Nodes: computers confirming transactions occurring on the network and maintaining a decentralised consensus across the system.

Peer-to-peer transactions: also referred to as person-to-person transactions (P2P transactions or P2P payments), electronic money transfers made from one person to another through an app.

Practical Byzantine Fault Tolerance (PBFT): a process that relies on the sheer number of nodes in order to confirm trust. Assuming that a malicious attach on the network will occur, the PBFT provides a level of assurance and trust that would not otherwise be achievable.

Private Key Infrastructure (PKI): a set of roles, policies, and procedures needed to create, manage, distribute, use, store, and revoke digital certificates and manage public-key encryption.

Proof of Stake (PoS): a way of validating transactions and achieving a distributed consensus. It is an algorithm and its purpose is to incentivise nodes to confirm transactions. PoS uses someone's stake in a cryptocurrency to ensure good behaviour.

Proof of Work (PoW): a requirement to define an expensive computer calculation, also called mining, that must be performed in order to create a new group of trustless transactions (the so-called block) on a distributed ledger or blockchain.

Quantum computing: incredibly powerful machines that take a new approach to processing information. Built on the principles of quantum mechanics, they exploit complex laws of nature that are always there, but usually remain hidden from view.

Self-sovereign identity: the concept that people and businesses can store their own identity data on their own devices, and provide it efficiently on request. The key benefits of self-sovereign identity are the user only provides the information that is needed by the provider and the provider only receives and stores essential information (and with the identity-owner's express permission).

Smart contracts: programmable applications that can be automated to initiate on satisfaction of certain conditions. These conditions can include complex conditional logic. The smart contract verifies that parties to a transaction can meet their promises, and then the technology manages the exchange so that each promise is satisfied simultaneously, almost certainly eliminating risk for all parties to the transaction.

Timestamp: a sequence of characters or encoded information identifying when a certain event occurred, usually giving date and time of day, sometimes accurate to a small fraction of a second.

Trust protocol: a mechanism whereby trust is managed by technology in a decentralised network. Trust is established through verification or Proof of Work, and is supported by immutability of that work and the consensus of all participants.

UN Sustainable Development Goals (SDGs): in 2015, the United Nations set an ambitious agenda for the developing world. They aim to achieve discernible change by 2030, including the eradication of poverty, zero hunger, decent work, and economic growth, climate action, reduced inequalities, peace and justice, and strong institutions. There are 17 SDGs.

Virtual Reality (VR): a computer-generated scenario that simulates a realistic experience.

Wicked Problem: a particular type of problem that is difficult or impossible to solve due to the incomplete, contradictory, and changing requirements that are often difficult to recognise. It refers to problems wherein many stakeholders with conflicting values are involved and information is confusing.

References

All of the definitions used as epigraphs in this book come from Oxford Dictionaries Online, https://en.oxforddictionaries.com/ [accessed 13 July 2017].

1 The World Bank Data. *Poverty*. 2014. Available from: http://data.worldbank.org/topic/poverty.

2 The World Bank Data. *Account at a financial institution, female*. 2015. Available from: http://data.worldbank.org/indicator/WP_time_01.3.

3 The World Bank Data. *Climate Change: CO_2 Emissions*. 2015. Available from: http://data.worldbank.org/topic/climate-change.

4 Nye, J. Corruption and political development: a cost-benefit analysis. *American Political Science Review* 1967;**61**(2):417–427.

5 Gupta, S., Alonso-Terme, R. International Monetary Fund Fiscal Affairs Department. *Does corruption affect income inequality and poverty?* IMF Working Paper WP/98/76, 1998.

6 Mauro, P. Corruption and growth. *Quarterly Journal of Economics* 1995;**110**(3):81.

7 De Mendonca, H.F., Da Fonseca, A.O. Corruption, income, and rule of law: empirical evidence from developing and developed economies. *Brazilian Journal of Political Economy* 2012;**32**(2): 305.

8 Qassim, H.H.A. *Promoting Sustainable Population Growth, Key to Raising Human Rights Standards*. Inter Press Service News Agency—North America, 11 July 2017.

9 Australian Government, Productivity Commission. Economic impacts of migration and population growth. *Productivity Commission Research Report*, 24 April 2006.

10 United Nations. *UN Demographic Yearbook (1949–50)*. 2015.

11 United Nations. *The World at Six Billion*. 1999.

12 Kevane, M. Darfur: rainfall and conflict. *Environmental Research Letter* 2008: p. 3.

13 Salehyan, I. From climate change to conflict? No consensus yet. *Journal of Peace Research* 2008;**45**(3):315.

14 Schipper, L., Pelling, M. Disaster risk, climate change and international development: scope for, and challenges to, integration. *Disasters* 2006;**30**(1):19.

15 Watson, R. Poverty and climate change. *Environment Matters* 2000;**6**:22.

16 Walker, G. *The Rule of Law: Foundation of constitutional democracy*. Melbourne: Melbourne University Press, 1988.

17 The Hon. Lex Lasry AM. Sentencing, politics & the media. *Criminal Congress Laws* 14 October 2016.

18 Ghosh, D., Scott, B. #DIGITALDECEIT—The Technologies Behind Precision Propaganda on the Internet. *New America* 2018:42. Available from: www.newamerica.org/public-interest-technology/policy-papers/digitaldeceit/.
19 Munoz, C. Turning their backs on the world: The integration of the world economy is in retreat on almost every front. *The Economist*, 19 February 2009.
20 Bean, C.R. Globalisation and inflation. *Bank of England Quarterly Bulletin*, 13 December 2006.
21 Inland Revenue Service. *The Tax Gap—Tax Gap Estimates for the years 2008–2010*. IRS, 2017.
22 ATO. *Australian Taxation Office Annual Report 2015–2016*. Australian Taxation Office, 2016.
23 Secretariat, Global Partnership for Education. *17 ways education influences the new 17 global goals*. Global Partnership for Education, 2015.
24 Simonsen, S. *5 Reasons the UN is Jumping on the Blockchain Bandwagon*. Singularity Hub, 2017.
25 Staff Reporter. *Blockchain Technology Can Boost Climate Action—UNFCCC Recognizes Potential*. United Nations Framework Convention on Climate Change, 2017.
26 United Nations, Department of Economic and Social Affairs. *United Nations urges commitment to fight humiliation and exclusion to end poverty*. Department of Economic and Social Affairs, 2016.
27 United Nations News Centre. Eleven global banks partner with UN to make financial markets more climate transparent, 12 July 2017.
28 United Nations. *Goal 9: Build resilient infrastructure, promote sustainable industrialization and foster innovation*. United Nations, 2015.
29 Shiller, R.J. *The Subprime Solution: How today's global financial crisis happened, and what to do about it*. Princeton, NJ: Princeton University Press, 2012.
30 Reid, F., Harrigan, M. *An analysis of anonymity in the bitcoin system*, in *Security and privacy in social networks*. New York: Springer, 2013: 197–223.
31 Nakamoto, S. Bitcoin: A peer-to-peer electronic cash system, 2008. Available from: https://bitcoin.org/bitcoin.pdf [cited 2016 December 22]
32 Chaum, D. Blind signatures for untraceable payments. In: *Advances in Cryptology*. New York: Springer, 1983.
33 Mattila, J. *The Blockchain Phenomenon—The Disruptive Potential of Distributed Consensus Architectures*. Berkeley , CA: University of California, 2016.
34 Palychata, J. Bitcoin: what you didn't know but always wanted to ask. 2015 Available from: http://securities.bnpparibas.com/insights/bitcoin-and-blockchain-what-you.html [cited 11 February 2017].
35 The Economist (US). The next big thing: Blockchain. *The Economist*, 2015: p. 16.
36 Kelly, J. *UBS leads team of banks working on blockchain settlement system*, 24 August 2016. Available from: www.reuters.com/article/us-banks-blockchain-ubs-idUSKCN10Z147 [cited 11 February 2017].
37 Arnold, M. *Six global banks join forces to create digital currency*, 31 August 2017. Available from: www.ft.com/content/20c10d58-8d9c-11e7-a352-e46f43c5825d [cited 20 September 2017].
38 Palmer, D. *Australia Post plans blockchain-based e-voting system | Delimiter*, 23 August 2016. Available from: https://delimiter.com.au/2016/08/23/australia-post-plans-blockchain-based-e-voting-system/ [cited 11 February 2017].

39 Forte, P., Romano, D., Schmid, G. *Beyond Bitcoin—Part I: A critical look at blockchain-based systems*. Basel, Switzerland: MDPI, 2015.
40 Yermack, D. *Corporate Governance and Blockchains*. National Bureau of Economic Research, 2015.
41 Norta, A. Creation of smart-contracting collaborations for decentralized autonomous organizations. *International Conference on Business Informatics Research*. New York, Springer, 2015.
42 Lemieux, V.L., Lomas, E. Trusting records: is Blockchain technology the answer? *Records Management Journal* 2016;**26**(2).
43 Umeh, J. Blockchain double bubble or double trouble? *ITNOW* 2016;**58**(1):58–61.
44 Swan, M. *Blockchain: Blueprint for a new economy*. O'Reilly Media, Inc., 2015.
45 Shrier, D., Wu, W., Pentland, A. *Blockchain & Infrastructure (Identity, Data Security)*. Boston, MA: MIT Connection Science: 2016.
46 Cocking, S. The 11 Fintech and banking trends you need to know. 2017. Available from: https://irishtechnews.ie/the-11-fintech-and-banking-trends-you-need-to-follow/ [cited February 24 2017].
47 Kelly, J. Accenture breaks blockchain taboo with editing system. 20 September 2016. Available from: www.reuters.com/article/us-tech-blockchain-accenture-idUSKCN11Q1S2 [cited 2017 February 11].
48 Pilkington, M. Blockchain technology: principles and applications. In: Xavier Olleros, F., Zhegu, M. (eds), *Research Handbook on Digital Transformations*. Cheltenham: Edward Elgar Publishing, 2016.
49 Melone, M. Basics and history of PKI. 2012. Available from: https://blogs.technet.microsoft.com/option_explicit/2012/03/10/basics-and-history-of-pki/ [cited 2017 May 2].
50 Ting, K.K., Yuen, S.C.L., Leong, P.H.W. An FPGA based SHA-256 processor. In: *International Conference on Field Programmable Logic and Applications*. Berlin: Springer, 2002: pp. 577–585.
51 Plassaras, N.A. Regulating digital currencies: bringing Bitcoin within the reach of IMF. *Chicago Journal of International Law* 2013;**14**:377.
52 Johansen, B.E. Dating the Iroquois Confederacy. *Akwesasne Notes* 1995;**1**(4):62–63.
53 Olfati-Saber, R., Fax, J.A., Murray, R.M. Consensus and cooperation in networked multi-agent systems. *Proceedings of the IEEE* 2007;**95**(1):215–233.
54 Seibold, S., Samman, G. *Consensus*. KPMG, 2016: 28. Available from: https://assets.kpmg.com/content/dam/kpmg/pdf/2016/06/kpmg-blockchain-consensus-mechanism.pdf.
55 Davidson, S., De Filippi, P., Potts, J. Economics of blockchain. In: *Proceedings of Public Choice Conference, 2016*. Fort Lauderdale: Public Choice Conference, 2016.
56 Cachin, C., Vukolić, M. *Blockchains Consensus Protocols in the Wild*. arXiv preprint arXiv:1707.01873, 2017.
57 Lamport, L., Shostak, R., Pease, M. The Byzantine generals problem. *ACM Transactions on Programming Languages and Systems (TOPLAS)* 1982;**4**(3):382–401.
58 Castro, M., Liskov, B. Practical Byzantine fault tolerance. In: Proceedings of the third symposium on Operating systems design and implementation, Vol. 1., New Orleans, 1999: 173–186.
59 Pîrjan, A., Petrosanu. D.-M., Huth, M., Negoita, M. Research issues regarding the bitcoin and alternative coins digital currencies. *Journal of Information Systems & Operations Management* 2015:1.

60 Christidis, K., Devetsikiotis, M. Blockchains and smart contracts for the Internet of Things. *IEEE Access* 2016;**4**:2292–2303.
61 Condos, J., Sorrell, W.H., Donegan, S.L. *Blockchain Technology: Opportunities and risks*. Vermont: 2016.
62 Garrod, J. The real world of the decentralized autonomous society. tripleC: Communication, Capitalism & Critique. *Open Access Journal for a Global Sustainable Information Society* 2016;**14**(1):62–77.
63 Zhang, Y., Wen, J. The IoT electric business model: Using blockchain technology for the internet of things. *Peer-to-Peer Networking and Applications* 2016:1–12.
64 O'Dwyer, R. The revolution will (not) be decentralised: Blockchains. *Commons Transition*, 2015. Available from: https://s3.amazonaws.com/academia.edu.documents/37111774/The_revolution_will_not_be_decentralised.pdf?AWSAccessKeyId=AKIAIWOWYYGZ2Y53UL3A&Expires=1525232315&Signature=5JDGkaL%2BroezmtPEHT4OpT6wTEM%3D&response-content-disposition=inline%3B%20filename%3DThe_Revolution_Will_not_be_Decentralised.pdf.
65 Tapscott, D., Tapscott, A. *Blockchain Revolution: How the Technology Behind Bitcoin is Changing Money, Business, and the World*. Penguin, 2016.
66 Polemitis, A. Bitcoin Series 24: The Mega-Master Blockchain list. 2014. Available from: http://ledracapital.com/blog/2014/3/11/bitcoin-series-24-the-mega-master-blockchain-list [cited 11 February 2017].
67 Pash, C. The Commonwealth Bank just used blockchain in a 'world first' global transaction. 24 October 2016. Available from: www.businessinsider.com.au/the-commonwealth-bank-just-used-blockchain-in-a-world-first-global-transaction-2016-10 [cited 2017 February 11].
68 Hoffman, A., Munsterman, R. Dreyfus Teams with banks for first agriculture Blockchain trade. 22 January 2018. Available from: www.bloomberg.com/news/articles/2018-01-22/dreyfus-teams-with-banks-for-first-agriculture-blockchain-trade [cited 2 February 2018].
69 Buterin, V. Ethereum: A next-generation smart contract and decentralized application platform, 2014. Available from: https://github.com/ethereum/wiki/wiki/%5BEnglish%5D-White-Paper.
70 Szabo, N. *Smart Contracts*. 1994. www.fon.hum.uva.nl/rob/Courses/InformationInSpeech/CDROM/Literature/LOTwinterschool2006/szabo.best.vwh.net/smart.contracts.html.
71 Crosby, M., et al. BlockChain technology: beyond Bitcoin. In: *Applied Innovation*, 2016: 6. Available from: http://scet.berkeley.edu/wp-content/uploads/AIR-2016-Blockchain.pdf
72 Morini, M. From 'Blockchain Hype' to a real business case for financial markets, 2016. Available from: https://ssrn.com/abstract=2760184 or http://dx.doi.org/10.2139/ssrn.2760184.
73 Luu, L., et al. *Making smart contracts smarter*, 2016. Cryptology ePrint Archive, Report 2016/633, 201 6. eprint/.iacr.org/2016/633.
74 Finley, K. Someone just stole $50 million from the biggest crowdfunded project ever. (Humans can't be trusted.) 2016. Available from: www.wired.com/2016/06/50-million-hack-just-showed-dao-human/ [cited 2017 February 11].
75 Buterin, V. DAOs are not scary, Part 1: Self-enforcing contracts and factum law—Ethereum blog. 24 February 2014. Available from: https://blog.ethereum.org/2014/02/24/daos-are-not-scary-part-1-self-enforcing-contracts-and-factum-law/ [cited 11 February 2017].

76 Fairfield, J. Smart contracts, Bitcoin bots, and consumer protection. *Washington & Lee Law Review Online* 2014;**71**:35–299.
77 Tsvetkova, M., et al. *Understanding Human–Machine Networks: A Cross-Disciplinary Survey.* arXiv preprint arXiv:1511.05324, 2015.
78 Zyskind, G., Nathan, O. Decentralizing privacy: Using blockchain to protect personal data. In: *Security and Privacy Workshops (SPW).* IEEE, 2015.
79 Wright, A., De Filippi, P. Decentralized blockchain technology and the rise of lex cryptographia. Available at SSRN 2580664, 2015.
80 Norta, A., Othman, A.B., Taveter, K. Conflict-resolution lifecycles for governed decentralized autonomous organization collaboration. In: *Proceedings of the 2015 2nd International Conference on Electronic Governance and Open Society: Challenges in Eurasia.* ACM, 2015.
81 Norta, A. Establishing distributed governance infrastructures for enacting cross-organization collaborations. In: *International Conference on Service-Oriented Computing.* New York, Springer, 2015.
82 Foucault, M. *Discipline and Punishment.* New York: Pantheon, 1977.
83 Kosten, D. *Bitcoin Mission Statement. Or What Does It Mean Sharing Economy and Distributed Trust?* 2015. Available from: https://ssrn.com/abstract=2684256 or http://dx.doi.org/10.2139/ssrn.2684256.
84 Ammous, S.H. Blockchain technology: What is it good for? 8 August 2016. Available from: https://ssrn.com/abstract=2832751 or http://dx.doi.org/10.2139/ssrn.2832751.
85 Buntinx, J. Digix DAO reaches funding target in under 12 hours, 2016 Available from: https://themerkle.com/digix-dao-reaches-funding-target-in-under-12-hours/ [cited 11 February 2017].
86 Rajesh, M. Inside Japan's first robot-staffed hotel, 14 August 2015. Available from: www.theguardian.com/travel/2015/aug/14/japan-henn-na-hotel-staffed-by-robots [cited 11 February 2017].
87 Kalla, S. What is an ICO?—Smith + Crown. 21 June 2016. Available from: www.smithandcrown.com/what-is-an-ico/ [cited 11 February 2017].
88 Scher, T. A Blockchain VC's perspective on ICOs and Appcoins—DCG insights. 27 October 2016. Available from: https://insights.dcg.co/a-blockchain-vcs-perspective-on-icos-and-appcoins-3b2683f30683-.9jgxm8hki [cited 11 February 2017].
89 Chen, C. SEC Sends Inquiry Letters to Hundreds of Bitcoin Companies about Unregistered Securities. 28 October 2014. Available from: www.cryptocoin snews.com/sec-sends-inquiry-letters-hundreds-bitcoin-companies-unregistered-securities/ [cited 11 February 2017].
90 Siegel, D. Understanding the DAO attack—CoinDesk. 25 June 2016. Available from: www.coindesk.com/understanding-dao-hack-journalists/ [cited 11 February 2017].
91 Tayshun, T. Buyer beware! The definitive OneCoin Ponzi exposé. 2016. Available from: www.xbt.money/buyer-beware-the-definitive-onecoin-ponzi-expose/ [cited 11 February 2017].
92 BitScan. *Paycoin scam-master Garza gets pinched—articles—Bitcoin news, analysis, interviews and features.* 2016. Available from: http://bitscan.com/articles/paycoin-scam-master-garza-gets-pinched [cited 11 February 2017].

93 Roberts, J.J. The SEC's Big digital coin ruling: What it means in plain English. 2017. Available from: http://fortune.com/2017/07/26/sec-icos/ [cited 11 February 2017].

94 Russell, J. China has banned ICOs. 1 April 2017. Available from: http://social.techcrunch.com/2017/09/04/chinas-central-bank-has-banned-icos/ [cited 20 September 2017].

95 WeUseCoins. Venture capital investments in Bitcoin and Blockchain companies. 2016. Available from: www.weusecoins.com/en/venture-capital-investments-in-bitcoin-and-blockchain-companies/ [cited 11 February 2017].

96 Buterin, V. I know this may not directly be ethereum related, but . . . • r/ethereum. 2015. Available from: www.reddit.com/r/ethereum/comments/380q61/i_know_this_may_not_directly_be_ethereum_related/crrofl6/ [cited 20 September 2017].

97 McMillan, R. The inside story of Mt. Gox, Bitcoin's $460 million disaster. 2014. Available from: www.wired.com/2014/03/bitcoin-exchange/ [cited 11 February 2017].

98 Higgins, S. The Bitfinex Bitcoin Hack: What we know (and don't know)—CoinDesk. 3 August 2016. Available from: www.coindesk.com/bitfinex-bitcoin-hack-know-dont-know/ [cited 11 February 2017].

99 Malmo, C. Bitcoin is unsustainable. 2017. Available from: https://motherboard.vice.com/en_us/article/ae3p7e/bitcoin-is-unsustainable [cited 20 September 2017].

100 CERN. Powering CERN. 2017 Available from: http://home.cern/about/engineering/powering-cern [cited 2017 September 20].

101 Digiconomist. Bitcoin energy consumption index. 2017 Available from: https://digiconomist.net/bitcoin-energy-consumption [cited 20 September 2017].

102 VISA. *Annual Report VISA 2016*. 2016.

103 Quiggin, J. Bitcoins are a waste of energy—literally. [Opinion] 6 October 2015, T07:28:06+1100. Available from: www.abc.net.au/news/2015-10-06/quiggin-bitcoins-are-a-waste-of-energy/6827940 [cited 20 September 2017].

104 Chapman, J., Garratt, R., McCormack, A., McMahon, W. Project Jasper: Are distributed wholesale payment systems feasible yet? *Financial System* 2017:59.

105 Lansiti, M., Lakhani, K. *The Truth About Blockchain*. 1 January 2017. Available from: https://hbr.org/2017/01/the-truth-about-blockchain [cited 2017 February 13].

106 Medina, M. 4 scary (and real) identity theft stories. 2016. Available from: www.identityforce.com/blog/4-scary-real-identity-theft-stories [cited 2017 April 23].

107 Murray, D. Nick, L. Pregnant Nicole McCabe tell of their terror at being linked to assassination of top Hamas official, 2010. Available from: www.abc.net.au/mediawatch/transcripts/1005_exclusive.pdf [cited 23 April 2017].

108 NewsComAu. Meet Australia's mum-to-be 'assassin'. 2010 Available from: www.news.com.au/national/meet-australian-woman-nicole-mccabe-set-up-in-spy-scandal/news-story/ea29cde4461f6c6882de4d45950f8264 [cited 23 April 2017].

109 Shadel, D. 'She stole my life!': A cautionary true tale about identity theft everyone must read. *Reader's Digest*. 2015 [cited 2017 April 23] Available from: http://www.rd.com/culture/identity-theft/.

110 Levin, A. *I Ate Thanksgiving Dinner With My Identity Thief for 19 Years - ABC News*. 2014 Available from: http://abcnews.go.com/Business/ate-thanksgiving-dinner-identity-thief-19-years/story?id=27194948 [cited 23 April 2017].

111 Wootson, C. Her job was to help victims of identity theft. Instead, she used them to steal from the IRS. 2016. Available from: www.washingtonpost.com/news/post-nation/wp/2016/08/11/her-job-was-to-help-victims-of-identity-theft-instead-she-used-them-to-steal-from-the-irs/ [cited 23 April 2017].

112 Douglas, R. Identity theft statistics, 2017 Available from: www.identitytheft.info/victims.aspx [cited 23 April 2017].

113 Lea, T. *Down the Rabbit Hole. Discover the power of the blockchain*, Vol. 1. Sydney, Australia: Days Pty Ltd, 2017: 54.

114 Whittaker, Z. BBC: Why fans are so 'devoted' to Apple, *ZDNet*. 2011 Available from: www.zdnet.com/article/bbc-why-fans-are-so-devoted-to-apple/ [cited 29 April 2017].

115 Marketing_Minds. Apple's branding strategy. 2016. Available from: www.marketingminds.com.au/apple_branding_strategy.html [cited 29 April 2017].

116 RepTrak. Rolex, Lego, and Disney Top Reputation Institute's 2017 Global RepTrak® 100—The World's Largest Corporate Reputation Study. 2017. Available from: www.prweb.com/releases/2017/03/prweb14104502.htm [cited 29 April 2017].

117 Toyota. How many parts is each car made of? Available from: www.toyota.co.jp/en/kids/faq/d/01/04/index.html [cited 29 April 2017].

118 Cullina, M. 9 alarming statistics about identity theft. 2012. Available from: http://cyberscout.com/education/blog/9-alarming-statistics-about-identity-theft [cited 29 April 2017].

119 Mountain_Alarm. 9 most common types of identity theft—security systems—home security systems—mountain alarm. 2016. Available from: www.mountainalarm.com/blog/9-most-common-types-of-identity-theft/ [cited 29 April 2017].

120 Siciliano, R. The first 3 types of identity theft. 2015. Available from: www.thebalance.com/the-first-3-types-of-identity-theft-1947465 [cited 29 April 2017].

121 McLaughlin, K. Google and Facebook fall for $100 million phishing scam, 28 April 2017. Available from: www.dailymail.co.uk/~/article-4455652/index.html [cited 29 April 2017].

122 Farley, A. Why do European hotels require passports at check-in? Available from: www.travelandleisure.com/blogs/why-do-european-hotels-require-passports-at-check-in [cited 29 April 2017].

123 Grayson, I. *Establishing digital identity causing problems as users giving away too much*. 4 October 2016. Available from: www.afr.com/news/special-reports/digital-identity/establishing-digital-identity-causing-problems-as-users-giving-away-too-much-20161003-grtom7 [cited 1 May 2017].

124 Trulioo. KYCC—Know Your Customer's Customer. 9 March 2017. Available from: www.trulioo.com/blog/kycc-know-customers-customer/ [cited 2017 April 30].

125 US Department of the Treasury. Treasury announces key regulations and legislation to counter money laundering and corruption, combat tax evasion. 2016. Available from: www.treasury.gov/press-center/press-releases/Pages/jl0451.aspx [cited 2017 April 30].

126 Vocativ. Here's how much your stolen passport goes for on the Dark Net, 20 October 2015. Available from: www.vocativ.com/241487/fake-passport-prices-black-market/ [cited 2017 April 30].
127 ID2020, ID 2020 Concept for Public/Private partnership. 2017. Available from: https://id2020.org/.
128 Daijiworld.com. 'Adhaar' most sophisticated ID programme in the world: World Bank—Daijiworld.com. 2017. Available from: www.daijiworld.com/news/newsDisplay.aspx?newsID=442948 [cited 2017 May 1].
129 Law, R. Blockchain: Why the technology powering bitcoin will revolutionise digital identity. 2017. Available from: www.gbgplc.com/uk/blog/blockchain/ [cited 2 May 2017].
130 Rivest, R.L., Shamir, A., Adleman, L. A method for obtaining digital signatures and public-key cryptosystems. *Communications of the ACM* 1978; **21**(2):120–126.
131 Dickson, B. *Blockchain's brilliant approach to cybersecurity*. 22 January 2017. Available from: https://venturebeat.com/2017/01/22/blockchains-brilliant-approach-to-cybersecurity/ [cited 2017 May 2].
132 Lewis, A. A gentle introduction to digital tokens. 28 September 2015. Available from: https://bitsonblocks.net/2015/09/28/a-gentle-introduction-to-digital-tokens/ [cited 2 May 2017].
133 Allen, C. The path to self-sovereign identity—CoinDesk. 27 April 2016. Available from: www.coindesk.com/path-self-sovereign-identity/ [cited 2017 May 3].
134 Accenture. Banking on Blockchain. 2017. Available from: www.accenture.com/t20170120T074124__w__/us-en/_acnmedia/Accenture/Conversion-Assets/DotCom/Documents/Global/PDF/Consulting/Accenture-Banking-on-Blockchain.pdf#zoom=50.
135 Tirrell, M. Unlocking my genome: Was it worth it? 10 December 2015. Available from: www.cnbc.com/2015/12/10/unlocking-my-genome-was-it-worth-it.html [cited 4 May 2017].
136 Harris, D. As genomics data approaches exascale, cloud could save the day. 23 January 2012. Available from: https://gigaom.com/2012/01/23/as-genomics-pushes-big-data-limits-cloud-could-save-the-day/ [cited 4 May 2017].
137 Hern, A. Google's DeepMind plans bitcoin-style health record tracking for hospitals. 9 March 2017. Available from: www.theguardian.com/technology/2017/mar/09/google-deepmind-health-records-tracking-blockchain-nhs-hospitals [cited 2017 May 4].
138 Suleyman, M. Trust, confidence and verifiable data audit. 2017. Available from: https://deepmind.com/blog/trust-confidence-verifiable-data-audit/ [cited 2017 May 4].
139 Metz, C. Google's untrendy play to make the Blockchain actually useful. 2017. Available from: www.wired.com/2017/03/google-deepminds-untrendy-blockchain-play-make-actually-useful/ [cited 2017 May 4].
140 Lohade, N. Dubai aims to be a city built on Blockchain. 2017. Available from: www.wsj.com/articles/dubai-aims-to-be-a-city-built-on-blockchain-1493086080 [cited 3 May 2017].
141 Peters, A. This App helps refugees get bank accounts by giving them a digital identity. 10 April 2017. Available from: www.fastcompany.com/40403583/this-app-helps-refugees-get-bank-accounts-by-giving-them-a-digital-identity [cited 4 May 2017].

142 Library, C. Mexico drug war fast facts—CNN.com. 2016. Available from: www.cnn.com/2013/09/02/world/americas/mexico-drug-war-fast-facts/index.html [cited 20 February 2017].

143 Riley, J.C. Estimates of regional and global life expectancy, 1800–2001. *Population and Development Review* 2005;**31**(3):537–543.

144 Roser, M. Child mortality. 2017 Available from: https://ourworldindata.org/child-mortality/ [cited 20 February 2017].

145 Economist.com. Daily chart: Famine mortality. 2013. Available from: www.economist.com/blogs/graphicdetail/2013/05/daily-chart-10 [cited 20 February 2017].

146 Roser, M. Democracy. 2016. Available from: https://ourworldindata.org/democracy/ [cited 20 February 2017].

147 Roser, M., Ortiz-Ospina, E. Global extreme poverty. 2017. Available from: https://ourworldindata.org/extreme-poverty/ [cited 20 February 2017].

148 ILO. *World Employment and Social Outlook: Trends 2016*. Geneva: International Labour Organization, 2016.

149 Hartogs, J. Poverty increasing in developed countries: ILO. 19 May 2016. Available from: www.cnbc.com/2016/05/19/poverty-increasing-in-developed-countries-ilo.html [cited 20 February 2017].

150 Rosen, A. The other Hurricane Sandy: The storm's impact in Haiti. 2012. Available from: www.theatlantic.com/international/archive/2012/10/the-other-hurricane-sandy-the-storms-impact-in-haiti/264362/ [cited 20 February 2017].

151 wn.com. Mexico announces that 26 percent of GDP comes from the informal economy. 2015. Available from: https://wn.com/Mexico_Announces_That_26_Percent_Of_Gdp_Comes_From_The_Informal_Economy [cited 20 February 2017].

152 Farrell, D. Boost growth by reducing the informal economy. 2014. Available from: www.mckinsey.com/mgi/overview/in-the-news/boost-growth-by-reducing-the-informal-economy [cited 18 February 2017].

153 Ploumen, L. Without rule of law, conflict-affected areas will become poverty ghettoes. *Lilianne Ploumen*. 17 November 2015. Available from: www.theguardian.com/global-development/2015/nov/17/without-rule-of-law-conflict-affected-areas-will-become-poverty-ghettoes [cited 18 February 2017].

154 Banking Technology. Connecting the unbanked key to easing poverty. 2015. Available from: www.bankingtech.com/167242/connecting-the-unbanked-key-to-easing-poverty/ [cited 18 February 2017].

155 World Bank. Global Findex—measuring financial inclusion around the world. 2017. Available from: www.worldbank.org/en/programs/globalfindex [cited 20 September 2017].

155a .Antonopoulos, A. *Internet of Money*. Merkle Bloom, 2016.

156 FarmfromaBox. Farm from a Box—a complete off-grid toolkit for tech-powered farming. *Our Story*, 2016 Available from: www.farmfromabox.com/our-story [cited 20 February 2017].

157 Schiller, B. The 'Farm From A Box' delivers modern agriculture to places that need it. 30 November 2015. Available from: www.fastcoexist.com/3053281/the-farm-from-a-box-delivers-modern-agriculture-to-places-that-need-it [cited 20 February 2017].

158 Hurst, N. A San Francisco startup puts everything you need for a two-acre farm in a shipping container. 2016. Available from: www.smithsonianmag.com/innovation/san-francisco-startup-puts-everything-you-need-two-acre-farm-shipping-container-180961567/ [cited 20 February 2017].

159 Savelli, A. Three technologies that could transform health supply chains. *Chemonics*, 2016 Available from: http://blog.chemonics.com/three-technologies-that-could-transform-health-supply-chains [cited 20 February 2017]

160 AAI. *State of Education in Africa Report 2015*. New York: The Africa–America Institute, 2015.

161 Unesco. *EFA Global Monitoring Report*. Paris: Unesco, 2015.

162 King, K., Prince, K., Swanson, J. *Learning on the Block: Could smart transactional models help power personalized learning?* KnowledgeWorks, 2015.

163 Chwierut, M. Blockchains and the future of learning—Smith + Crown. 4 July 2016. Available from: www.smithandcrown.com/blockchains-future-learning/ [cited 2017 February 21] .

164 Millerat, J. Blockchains for social good/Jean Millerat's bytes for good. 2016. Available from: www.akasig.org/2016/07/28/blockchains-for-social-good/ [cited 21 February 2017].

165 Russell, J. *Sony Plans To Develop An Education And Testing Platform Powered By The Blockchain*. 22 February 2016. Available from: http://techcrunch.com/2016/02/22/sony-is-building-an-education-and-testing-platform-powered-by-the-blockchain/ [cited 21 February 2017].

166 Schmidt, P. Blockcerts—an open infrastructure for academic credentials on the Blockchain. 24 October 2016. Available from: https://medium.com/mit-media-lab/blockcerts-an-open-infrastructure-for-academic-credentials-on-the-blockchain-899a6b880b2f-.marlbqwda [cited 21 February 2017].

167 Weller, C. The largest internet company in 2030? This prediction will probably surprise you. 2017. Available from: www.weforum.org/agenda/2017/01/the-largest-internet-company-in-2030-this-prediction-will-probably-surprise-you [cited 21 February 2017].

168 Rizzo, P. *Sweden's Blockchain Land Registry to Begin Testing in March*. 10 January 2017. Available from: www.coindesk.com/swedens-blockchain-land-registry-begin-testing-march/ [cited 18 February 2017].

169 Chavez-Dreyfuss, G. Honduras to build land title registry using bitcoin technology. 15 May 2015. Available from: http://in.reuters.com/article/usa-honduras-technology-idINKBN0O01V720150515 [cited 18 February 2017].

170 Higgins, S. Republic of Georgia to develop Blockchain land registry. 22 April 2016. Available from: www.coindesk.com/bitfury-working-with-georgian-government-on-blockchain-land-registry/ [cited 18 February 2017].

171 Rizzo, P. Blockchain land title project 'stalls' in Honduras. 26 December 2015. Available from: www.coindesk.com/debate-factom-land-title-honduras/ [cited 18 February 2017].

172 de Soto, H. Dead capital. Available from: www.thepowerofthepoor.com/concepts/c6.php [cited 18 February 2017].

173 Anonymous. The other type of mobile money: airtime is money. 2013 [cited 2017 February 18]; Available from: www.economist.com/news/finance-and-economics/21569744-use-pre-paid-mobile-phone-minutes-currency-airtime-money [cited 18 February 2017].

174 World Bank. Developing countries to receive over $410 billion in remittances in 2013. 2013. Available from: www.worldbank.org/en/news/press-release/2013/10/02/developing-countries-remittances-2013-world-bank [cited 18 February 2017].
175 World Bank. Remittance prices worldwide. 2016. Available from: https://remittanceprices.worldbank.org/sites/default/files/rpw_report_december_2016.pdf [cited 18 February 2017].
176 World Bank. Migration and remittance flows. 2013. Available from: http://siteresources.worldbank.org/INTPROSPECTS/Resources/334934-1288990760745/MigrationandDevelopmentBrief21.pdf [cited 18 February 2017].
177 Breloff, P., Krishnamurthy, N. Bitcoin and the bottom of the pyramid: how cryptocurrency can make good on its promise of financial inclusion. 2014. Available from: http://nextbillion.net/bitcoin-and-the-bottom-of-the-pyramid/ [cited 18 February 2017].
178 The Money Wiki. Rebittance: Bitcoin remittance. Available from: http://themoneywiki.com/wiki/alternative-currency-rebittance-bitcoin-remittance [cited 18 February 2017].
179 Higgins, S. United Nations lab testing Blockchain for remittances. 6 October 2016. Available from: www.coindesk.com/united-nations-blockchain-remittances/ [cited 18 February 2017].
180 Swan, M. *Blockchain: Blueprint for a New Economy*. O'Reilly, 2015.
181 Anonymous. *What is the rule of law?* [cited 2017 February 18]; Available from: www.ruleoflaw.org.au/what-is-the-rule-of-law/ [cited 18 February 2017].
182 CleanGovBiz. *Integrity in Practice*, 2014. Available from: www.oecd.org/cleangovbiz/49693613.pdf.
183 Organisation for Economic Co-operation and Development. *Closing the Tax Gap*. Paris, OECD, 2013.
184 Arruda, M.E., Prinzing, M., Rana, S. Documents, what documents? *Business Law Today* 2003;Jan/Feb:23.
185 Williams, K.S., Carr, I. Crime risk and computers. *Electronic Communication Law Review* 2002;**9**:23.
186 Giddens, A. *The Consequences of Modernity*. Oxford, Polity Press, 1990.
187 Noonan, A.K. Bitcoin or Bust: can one really 'Trust' one's digital assets? *Estate Planning and Community Property Law Journal* 2015: p. 583.
188 Raymond, N. Police found $20 million hidden under a mattress in Boston. 24 January 2017. Available from: www.businessinsider.com/police-found-20-million-hidden-under-a-mattress-in-boston-2017-1?IR=T.
189 Hague, D.R. Expanding the Ponzi Scheme presumption. *DePaul Law Review* 2015;**64**:867.
190 Altman, A. A brief history of Ponzi Schemes. 15 December 2008. Available from: http://content.time.com/time/business/article/0,8599,1866680,00.html.
191 Sands, P. Making it harder for the bad guys: the case for eliminating high denomination notes. *M-RCBG Associate Working Papers* 2016;**52**.
192 Schneider, F. The size of shadow economies in 145 countries from 1999 to 2003. *The Brown Journal of World Affairs* 2005;**XI**:2.
193 Wade, M. Cash-in-hand economy and illegal drugs trade costing Australia billions. 13 September 2013. Available from: www.smh.com.au/national/cashinhand-economy-and-illegal-drugs-trade-costing-australia-billions-20130912-2tnmv.html.

194 Cassella, S.D. Reverse money laundering. *Journal of Money Laundering Control* 2003;**7**(1):92–94.

195 Zabyelina, Y. Reverse money laundering in Russia: Clean cash for dirty ends. *Journal of Money Laundering Control* 2015;**18**(2):202–221.

196 Eurasian Group Secretariat. Money laundering and terrorist financing with use of physical cash and bearer instruments. 17th Plenary Meeting of the Eurasian Group on Combating Money Laundering and Financing of Terrorism, 28 December 2012, New Delhi.

197 Interpol Staff Writer. Trafficking in illicit goods and counterfeiting. Available from: www.interpol.int/Crime-areas/Trafficking-in-illicit-goods-and-counterfeiting/Trafficking-in-illicit-goods-and-counterfeiting.

198 Belot, H. Federal Government taskforce to crack down on cash economy, assess future of $100 note. 14 December 2016. Available from: www.abc.net.au/news/2016-12-14/federal-government-to-crackdown-on-cash-economy/8118844.

199 CleanGovBiz. *Integrity in Practice*. Organisation for Economic Co-operation and Development: 2014.

200 Tax Justice Network. Cost of tax abuse: A briefing paper on the cost of tax evasion worldwide. 2011. Available from: www.taxjustice.net/wp-content/uploads/2014/04/Cost-of-Tax-Abuse-TJN-2011.pdf.

201 White, A. Australian Taxation Office turns to Facebook to catch cheats. 14 November 2016. Available from: www.theaustralian.com.au/national-affairs/treasury/australian-taxation-office-turns-to-facebook-to-catch-cheats/news-story/6d4bca2d0223dcb3924c061fa28bc3f9.

202 Kaouris, D. Is Delaware still a tax haven for incorporation. *Delaware Journal of Corporate Law* 1995;**20.3**:965.

203 Neate, R. Trump and Clinton share Delaware tax 'loophole' address with 285,000 firms. 25 April 2016. Available from: www.theguardian.com/business/2016/apr/25/delaware-tax-loophole-1209-north-orange-trump-clinton.

204 Phillips, R., et al. International securities law enforcement: recent advances in assistance and cooperation. *Vanderbilt Journal of Transnational Law* 1994;**27**:635.

205 Suisse Security Bank & Trust Ltd v Francis (in the Capacity of Governor of the Central Bank of The Bahamas), in *Weekly Law Reporter*. 2006, UKPC, p. 1660.

206 Metaxetos, E. Thunder in paradise: the interplay of broadening United States anti-money laundering legislation and jurisprudence with the Caribbean law governing offshore asset preservation trusts. *Miami Inter-American Law Review* 2008–2009;**40**:169.

207 Trautman, L. Following the money: Lessons from the Panama Papers: Part 1: Tip of the iceberg. *Penn State Law Review* 2017;**121.3**:807.

208 McMahon, A., Thomson, J., Williams, C, *Understanding the Australian welfare state: key documents and themes*, 2nd edn. Croydon, Victoria, Tertiary Press, 2000.

209 Reeve, G. Human services administration: A more intelligent approach to reducing benefit fraud. Public Administration Today 2006;Jan/Mar:37–45.

210 Prenzler, T. Welfare fraud in Australia: Dimensions and issues. *Trends & Issues in Crime and Criminal Justice* 2011(**421**).

211 Bradbury, B. *Welfare Fraud, Work Incentives and Income Support for the Unemployed*. Sydney: Social Welfare Research Centre, University of New South Wales, 1988.

212 Kuhlhorn, E. Housing allowances in a welfare society: Reducing the temptation to cheat. In: Clarke, R. (ed.), *Situational Crime Prevention: Successful case studies*. Monsey, NY: Criminal Justice Press, 1997.

213 Canberra: Centrelink. *Data-matching Program: Report on progress 2005–2006.* Centrelink & The Data-matching Agency, 2006.
214 Internal Revenue Service. *The Tax Gap: Tax Gap Estimates for Tax Years 2008–2010.* 4 April 2017. IRS.
215 Saint-Amans, P., Russo, R. *What the BEPS are we talking about? Organisation for Economic Co-operation and Development*, 2013.
216 Why big banknotes may be on the way out. *The Economist*, 7 May 2016.
217 Reuters. Wealthy are hoarding cash out of fear of what the election will bring. *Fortune*, 13 July 2016. Available from: http://fortune.com/2016/07/13/wealthy-cash-investors/.
218 Kumar, S.V., Kumar, T.S.. Demonetisation and complete financial inclusion. *International Journal of Management Research and Review* 2016;**6**(12):1703–1707.
219 Anand G.K.H. Narendra Modi bans India's largest currency bills in bid to cut corruption. *The New York Times*, 8 November 2016. Available from: www.nytimes.com/2016/11/09/business/india-bans-largest-currency-bills-for-now-n-bid-to-cut-corruption.html.
220 Davies, R. Dirty money? Mystery over shredded €500 notes in Swiss sewers. *The Guardian*, 2017.
221 Sharman, C. Havens in a storm: the struggle for global tax regulation. In: *Cornell Studies in Political Economy*. Cornell University Press, 2006.
222 Ring, D.M. Prospects for a multilateral tax treaty. *Brooklyn Journal of International Law* 2001;**XXVI**:1699–1709.
223 Thuronyi, V. Principal paper: international tax cooperation and a multilateral treaty. *Brooklyn Journal of International Law* 2001;**26**.
224 Reid, F., Harrigan, M., eds. An analysis of anonymity in the Bitcoin system. In: *Security and Privacy in Social Networks*. New York: Springer, 2013 .
225 Small, S., *Bitcoin*: The Napster of currency. *Houston Journal of International Law* 2015;**37**(2):581–641.
226 Bulkin, A. *Explaining Blockchain—how proof of work enables trustless consensus.* Hackernoon, 2016. Available from: https://keepingstock.net/explaining-blockchain-how-proof-of-work-enables-trustless-consensus-2abed27f0845.
227 Hannam, P. Red hot: NSW smashes February statewide heat records two days in a row. 12 February 2017. Available from: www.smh.com.au/environment/weather/red-hot-nsw-smashes-february-statewide-heat-records-two-days-in-a-row-20170212-gub14c.html [cited 17 February 2017].
228 Freedman, A. North Pole to warm to near melting point this week: 50 degrees above normal. 21 December 2016. Available from: http://mashable.com/2016/12/20/north-pole-to-warm-to-near-melting-point-this-week/ [cited 17 February 2017].
229 Harvey, C. Temperatures in the Arctic are skyrocketing—for the third time this winter. 2017. Available from: www.washingtonpost.com/news/energy-environment/wp/2017/02/10/temperatures-in-the-arctic-are-skyrocketing-for-the-third-time-this-winter/ [cited 17 February 2017].
230 Belles, J. All-time February heat in the Southern Plains. 2017. Available from: https://weather.com/forecast/regional/news/four-corners-texas-record-heat-snow-cold-mid-february?_escaped_fragment_ [cited 17 February 2017].
231 Kreft, S., Eckstein, D., Melchior, I. Global climate risk index 2017. 2017 Available from: https://germanwatch.org/de/download/16411.pdf [cited 17 February 2017].

232 Rosenzweig, C., Parry, M.L. *Potential impact of climate change on world food supply. Nature* 1994;**367**(6459):133–138.
233 Patz, J.A., et al. Impact of regional climate change on human health. *Nature* 2005;**438**(7066):310–317.
234 Hoegh-Guldberg, O., Bruno, J.F. *The impact of climate change on the world's marine ecosystems. Science* 2010;**328**(5985):1523–1528.
235 Thomas, C.D., et al. Extinction risk from climate change. *Nature* 2004;**427**(6970):145–148.
236 Mendelsohn, R., Neumann, J.E. *The Impact of Climate Change on the United States Economy*. Cambridge: Cambridge University Press, 2004.
237 UNFCCC. Paris Agreement, FCCC/CP/2015/L.9/Rev.1. 2015 Available from: http://unfccc.int/resource/docs/2015/cop21/eng/l09r01.pdf [cited 17 February 2017].
238 Churchman, C.W. Wicked Problems. *Management Science* 1967;**14**(4):B-141–B-146.
239 Agrawal, A., Gans, J., Goldfarb, A. *The Simple Economics of Machine Intelligence*. 17 November 2016 Available from: https://hbr.org/2016/11/the-simple-economics-of-machine-intelligence [cited 17 February 2017].
240 Bleich, K.G., Dantas, R. *Renewable Infrastructure Investment Handbook: A Guide for Institutional Investors*. 2016. Available from: www3.weforum.org/docs/WEF_Renewable_Infrastructure_Investment_Handbook.pdf [cited 17 February 2017].
241 Vanham, P. A convenient truth—fighting climate change turned into a profitable business. 2016. Available from: www.weforum.org/press/2016/12/a-convenient-truth-fighting-climate-change-turned-into-a-profitable-business/ [cited 17 February 2017].
242 CBS. Obama signs emergency declaration for states of New York, New Jersey. 2012. Available from: http://newyork.cbslocal.com/2012/10/28/obama-signs-emergency-declaration-for-state-of-new-york/ [cited 18 February 2017].
243 Gibson, K. NYC shutting down transit, evacuating 375,000. 2012. Available from: www.marketwatch.com/story/cuomo-orders-nyc-transit-system-to-shut-down-2012-10-28 [cited 18 February 2017].
244 Staff, W. Decaffeinated storm: Sandy shutters NYC's Starbucks stores. 2012. Available from: http://blogs.wsj.com/metropolis/2012/10/28/decaffeinated-storm-sandy-shutters-nycs-starbucks-stores/ [cited 18 February 2017].
245 Gutner, T. Hurricane Sandy grows to largest Atlantic tropical storm ever. 2012. Available from: http://boston.cbslocal.com/2012/10/28/hurricane-sandy-grows-to-largest-atlantic-tropical-storm-ever/ [cited 18 February 2017.
246 Library of Congress. Hurricane Sandy Fast Facts—CNN.com. 2012. Available from: www.cnn.com/2013/07/13/world/americas/hurricane-sandy-fast-facts/index.html [cited 18 February 2017].
247 Siemens. Siemens and U.S. startup LO3 Energy collaborate on blockchain microgrids. 2016. 28 May 2015. Available from: http://www.siemens.com/press/en/pressrelease/?press=/en/pressrelease/2016/energymanagement/pr2016110080emen.htm&content[]=EM [cited 18 February 2017].
248 Liess, S. Brooklyn microgrid world's first peer-to-peer, Blockchain energy transaction. 10 April 2016. Available from: www.theepochtimes.com/n3/2027695-worlds-first-peer-to-peer-energy-transaction-on-the-blockchain-has-arrived/ [cited 18 February 2017].

249 Rutkin, A. Blockchain-based microgrid gives power to consumers in New York. 2016. Available from: www.newscientist.com/article/2079334-blockchain-based-microgrid-gives-power-to-consumers-in-new-york/ [cited 18 February 2017].

250 Lacey, S. The energy Blockchain: How Bitcoin could be a catalyst for the distributed grid. 2016. Available from: www.greentechmedia.com/articles/read/the-energy-blockchain-could-bitcoin-be-a-catalyst-for-the-distributed-grid [cited 18 February 2017].

251 Bates Ramirez, V. The 6 Ds of tech disruption—SingularityU—Medium. 2016 24 November 2016. Available from: https://medium.com/singularityu/the-6-ds-of-tech-disruption-b38c14ff0147 - .g5fwqj481 [cited 18 February 2017].

252 Reuters. Tesla boss Elon Musk unveils solar roof tiles. 29 October 2016. [cited Available from: www.theguardian.com/environment/2016/oct/29/tesla-boss-elon-musk-unveils-solar-roof-tiles [cited 18 February 2017].

253 Blasing, T., Jon, S. *Current greenhouse gas concentrations*. Updated February, 2005.

254 Mora, C., et al. The projected timing of climate departure from recent variability. *Nature* 2013;**502**(7470):183–187.

255 Mann, M.E. Earth will cross the climate danger threshold by 2036. *Scientific American* 2014;**18**.

256 Doig, A. Re: Adoption of a Block Chain [Open Ledger] method for carbon credit transactions. 2016. Available from: www.asbg.net.au/attachments/article/353/ASBG - Blockchain for Carbon credits.pdf [cited 19 February 2017].

257 Reuters. Carbon market monitor. 2016. Available from: http://trmcs-documents.s3.amazonaws.com/3501ec8eae589bfbef9cc1729a7312f0_20160111104949_Carbon Market Review 2016_1.5.pdf [cited 18 February 2017].

258 Hamrick, K. Goldstein, A. *Raising Ambition: State of the Voluntary Carbon Markets 2016*. Forest Trends' Ecosystem Marketplace, 2016.

259 Korizky, R. AiraLab and Microsoft Russia to start blockchain platform for carbon credit trading, *Coinfox*. 2017. Available from: www.coinfox.info/news/6812-airalab-and-microsoft-russia-to-start-blockchain-platform-for-carbon-credit-trading [cited 18 February 2017].

260 Shen, X. Building a 'frictionless' network of exchange in China using IBM Blockchain. 2016. 23 September 2015. Available from: www.ibm.com/blogs/research/2016/12/building-a-frictionless-network-of-exchange-in-china-using-ibm-blockchain/ [cited 18 February 2017].

261 Gifford, J. Power Ledger expands trials of blockchain electricity trading. 28 October 2016. Available from: http://reneweconomy.com.au/power-ledger-expands-trials-blockchain-electricity-trading-38771/ [cited 18 February 2017].

262 Parkinson, G. NSW Coalition supports peer-to-peer trading for solar households. 31 October 2016. Available from: http://reneweconomy.com.au/nsw-coalition-supports-peer-to-peer-trading-for-solar-households-42663/ [cited 18 February 2017].

263 Gartner. Gartner says a typical family home could contain more than 500 smart devices by 2022. 2014. Available from: www.gartner.com/newsroom/id/2839717 [cited 18 February 2017].

264 Kar, S. IDC: The Market of the Internet of Things in More Concrete Than Other Technologies. *CloudTimes*, 2014. Available from: http://cloudtimes.org/2014/11/14/idc-the-market-of-the-internet-of-things-in-more-concrete-than-other-technologies/ [cited 18 February 2017].

265 Cisco. *The Internet of Everything—A $19 Trillion Opportunity. Cisco*, 2014.
266 BI Intelligence. Here's how the Internet of Things will explode by 2020. 2016 31 August 2016. Available from: www.businessinsider.com/iot-ecosystem-internet-of-things-forecasts-and-business-opportunities-2016-2 [cited 18 February 2017].
267 BREEAM. BREEAM: The Edge, Amsterdam. 2016. Available from: www.breeam.com/index.jsp?id=804 [cited 18 February 2017].
268 Randall, T. The world's smartest office building knows how you like your coffee. 2015 Available from: www.bloomberg.com/features/2015-the-edge-the-worlds-greenest-building/ [cited 18 February 2017].
269 Van Rijmenam, M. *Think Bigger: Developing a Successful Big Data Strategy for Your Business*. AMACOM Division of American Management Association, 2014.
270 Hirtenstein, A., Zha, W. Bitcoin technology harnessed to push electricity revolution. 2016 Available from: www.bloomberg.com/news/articles/2016-09-12/bitcoin-technology-harnessed-to-push-electricity-revolution [cited 18 February 2017].
271 De Meijer, C. Blockchain may fuel the energy industry. 22 November 2016. Available from: www.finextra.com/blogposting/13394/blockchain-may-fuel-the-energy-industry [cited 18 February 2017].
272 Johnson, N. *Blockchain Smart Meters: Solution to Africa's Utility Crisis and Struggling Schools?* 2015 2015-09-21 [cited 2017 February 18]; Available from: http://bitcoinist.com/blockchain-smart-meters-solution-africas-utility-crisis-struggling-schools/ [cited 18 February 2017].
273 Clancy, H. How the blockchain will disrupt energy markets, *GreenBiz*, 3 October 2016. Available from: www.greenbiz.com/article/how-blockchain-will-disrupt-energy-markets [cited 18 February 2017].
274 Ruggie, J. Report of the Special Representative of the Secretary-General on the issue of human rights and transnational corporations and other business enterprises. *Netherlands Quarterly of Human Rights*, 2017;**29**(2):224–253.
275 Sylla, N.S. Fairtrade is an unjust movement that serves the rich. *The Guardian* 5 September 2014.
276 Novak, J. It's not just the rich who benefit from free markets. ABCNews Australia, 24 Jan 2014.
277 Elliott, L. Rising inequality threatens world economy, says WEF. *The Guardian*, 2017.
278 Mullaney, G. World's 8 richest have as much wealth as bottom half, Oxfam says. *The New York Times*, 2017.
279 Kochhar, R. *A Global Middle Class is More Promise than Reality*. Pwe Research Centre, 13 August 2015.
280 Stenzel, P.L. The pursuit of equilibrium as the eagle meets the condor: supporting sustainable development through fair trade. *American Business Law Journal* 2012;**49**(3):557–642.
281 Barsh, R.L. Indigenous people and the global trade regime. *American Society of International Law Proceedings* 2002;**96**.
282 Fair Trade USA (formally TransFair USA). *Almanac: 2009*. Available from: www.fairtradeusa.org/sites/default/files/Almanac_2009.pdf.
283 Amnesty International. *Oil, Gas and Mining Industries*. Amnesty International, 2017.
284 Stenzel, P. Mainstreaming Fair Trade and resulting turmoil: where should the movement go from here? *William and Mary Environmental Law and Policy Review* 2012–2013;**37**:617.

285 De Pelsmacker, P., Driesen, L., Rayp, G. Do consumers care about ethics? Willingness to pay for Fair-Trade coffee. *Journal of Consumer Affairs* 2006;**39**(2):363.
286 Doane, D. *Taking Flight: The Rapid Growth of Ethical Consumerism*. London: New Economics Foundation, 2001.
287 Campbell, C. Consuming the goods and the goods of consuming. In: Cracker, D.A., Linden, T. (eds), *Ethics of Consumption: The good life, justice and global stewardship*. London: Rowman & Littlefield, 1998: pp. 139–154.
288 FairTrade International. *Minimum Price and Premium Information*. FairTrade International, 2018.
289 Baggini, J. Why are foodies turning their backs on Fairtrade? *The Guardian*, 24 Feb 2015.
290 TMS RUGE, T. Fairtrade and neo-imperialism. *TMS Ruge*, 25 Feb 2015.
291 Hainmueller, J., Hiscox, M.J., Sequeira, S. Consumer demand for the Fair Trade label: evidence from a multi-store field experiment. 2011. Available from: www.hbs.edu/faculty/conferences/2014-launching-the-star-lab/Documents/FT_final_2_20.pdf.
292 Knoblock, C.A., Szekely, P. Exploiting semantics for big data integration. *AI Magazine* 2015;**36**(1):25–38.
293 Kaye, M., Spataro, N. Redefining democracy. 2017. Available from: https://vote-flux.org/pdf/Redefining%20Democracy%20-%20Kaye%20&%20Spataro%20 1.0.2.pdf.
294 Meola, A. Western Union is investing in one of the hottest trends in fintech. *Business Insider*, 3 May 2016.
295 Lessig, L. Déjà vu all over again: Thinking through law & code, again. Speech delivered at the Sydney Blockchain Workshop, Sydney, 11 December 2015.
296 Fischer, E.F., Victor, B. High-end coffee and small holding growers in Guatemala. *Latin American Research Review* 2014;**49**(1):155.
297 Valimised. Statistics—internet voting—voting methods in Estonia—Estonian National Electoral Committee, 2017 Available from: www.vvk.ee/voting-methods-in-estonia/engindex/statistics [cited 10 May 2017].
298 Raaflaub, K.A., Ober, J., Wallace, R. *Origins of Democracy in Ancient Greece*. Berkeley, CA: University of California Press, 2007.
299 Golay, V., Mix and Remix. *Swiss Political Institutions,* Éditions LEP Loisirs et pédagogie. Le Mont-sur-Lausanne, 2008.
300 Schiener, D. Liquid democracy: True democracy for the 21st century. 23 November 2015 Available from: https://medium.com/organizer-sandbox/liquid-democracy-true-democracy-for-the-21st-century-7c66f5e53b6f [cited 12 May 2017].
301 Halperin, M., Siegle, J., Weinstein, M. *The Democracy Advantage: How democracies promote prosperity and peace*. London: Routledge, 2009.
302 Langworth, R. *Churchill by Himself: The definitive collection of quotations*. New York City: PublicAffairs, 2011.
303 Wingfield, R. APAC Blockchain Conference, Sydney, Australia, 2017.
304 Blum, C., Zuber, C.I. Liquid democracy: potentials, problems, and perspectives. *Journal of Political Philosophy* 2016;**24**(2):162–182.
305 Ford, B. Delegative democracy. 2002. Available from: www/brynosaurus.com/deleg/deleg.pdf.

306 Aru, L. Blockchain voting may lead to liquid democracy globally in 20 years. 201 Available from: https://cointelegraph.com/news/blockchain-voting-may-lead-to-liquid-democracy-globally-in-20-years [cited 18 May 2017].
307 Hardt, S., Lopes, L.C. Google votes: a liquid democracy experiment on a corporate social network. 2015. Available from: www.tdcommons.org/cgi/viewcontent.cgi?article=1092&context=dpubs_series.
308 Daniel, L. Democratizing policymaking online: liquid feedback—the Governance Lab @ NYU. 10 June 2013. Available from: http://thegovlab.org/democratizing-policymaking-online-liquid-feedback/ [cited 18 May 2017].
309 Interactive_Demokratie. LiquidFeedback—The democracy software. 2017. Available from: www.interaktive-demokratie.org/files/downloads/LF-Information-Kit-EN.pdf.
310 Peters, A. Democracy is getting a reboot on the blockchain. 10 August 2016. Available from: www.fastcompany.com/3062386/democracy-is-getting-a-reboot-on-the-blockchain [cited 18 May 2017].
311 Wile, R. A Venture capital firm just named an algorithm to its board of directors—here's what it actually does. 14 May 2014. Available from: www.businessinsider.com.au/vital-named-to-board-2014-5 [cited 18 May 2017].
312 NSD. National Settlement Depository tested a Blockchain-based e-proxy voting prototype. 2016 Available from: www.nsd.ru/en/press/ndcnews/index.php?id36=628973 [cited 18 May 2017].
313 David, E. Broadridge, Banco Santander, and Partners complete proxy voting Blockchain pilot—WatersTechnology.com. 11 April 2017. Available from: www.waterstechnology.com/node/3320806 [cited 18 May 2017].
314 Higgins, S. Nasdaq declares Blockchain voting trial a 'success'—CoinDesk. 23 January 2017. Available from: www.coindesk.com/nasdaq-declares-blockchain-voting-trial-a-success/ [cited 18 May 2017].
315 DeMarinis, R., Uustalu, H. , Voss, F. Is Blockchain the answer to e-voting? Nasdaq believes so, *Nasdaq MarketInsite*. 2017 Available from: http://business.nasdaq.com/marketinsite/2017/Is-Blockchain-the-Answer-to-E-voting-Nasdaq-Believes-So.html [cited 18 May 2017].
315a Antonopoulos, A.M. *The Internet of Money*, Volume 1. Merkle Bloom, 2016: p. 5.
316 Edwards, L. Pornography, censorship and the internet. In: Edwards, L., Waelde, C. (eds), *Law and the Internet*. Oxford: Hart, 2009.
317 Fish, E.S. Is Internet censorship compatible with democracy?: Legal restrictions of online speech in South Korea. *Asia–Pacific Journal on Human Rights and the Law* 2009;**10**(2):43–96.
318 Bennett, P., Naim, M. 21st-century censorship: Governments around the world are using stealthy strategies to manipulate the media. *Columbia Journalism Review* Jan/Feb 2015.
319 Neuborne, B. Editorial: Pushing free speech too far, in Supreme Court Preview. *The New York Times*, 1996.
320 Hauptman, R. The irony of free speech/dilemmas in free speech. *Journal of Information Ethics*, suppl. Special Issue: *First Amendment Rights* 1997;**2**:91–93.
321 Bowcott, O., Halliday, J. Twitter users and the courts go to war over footballer's injunction. 21 May 2011. Available from: www.theguardian.com/technology/2011/may/20/twitter-users-courts-footballer-injunction.

322 Dershowitz, A., Mier, M. Should free expression be limited to preclude hate speech? *The Jerusalem Report* 1999.

323 Orttung, R., Walker, C. Authoritarian regimes retool their media-control strategy. 10 January 2014. Available from: www.washingtonpost.com/opinions/authoritarian-regimes-retool-their-media-control-strategy/2014/01/10/5c5bfa6e-7886-11e3-af7f-13bf0e9965f6_story.html?utm_term=.96f6a195763a.

324 Xu, B., Albert, E. Media censorship in China. 17 February 2017. Available from: www.cfr.org/backgrounder/media-censorship-china.

325 Al-Saqaf, W. Internet censorship circumvention tools: escaping the control of the Syrian regime. *Media and Communication* 2016;**4**(1):39–50.

326 NewsDay Zimbabwe Staff Reporter. Mugabe's daughter joins Censorship Board. 24 May 2017. Available from: www.newsday.co.zw/2017/05/24/mugabes-daughter-joins-censorship-board/?

327 Quentson, A. Endemic censorship raises urgency for Blockchain based social networks. 23 October 2016. Available from: www.cryptocoinsnews.com/endemic-censorship-raises-urgency-blockchain-based-social-networks/.

328 Rexaline, S. Where in the world are Julian Assange and Edward Snowden? *Benzinga* 18 May 2017.

329 Pazzanese, C. Pursuing veritas in a 'post-truth' era. 1 February 2017. Available from: http://news.harvard.edu/gazette/story/2017/02/pursuing-veritas-in-a-post-truth-era/.

330 Barcelo-rico, F., Diez, J.-l. Geometrical codification for clustering mixed categorical and numerical databases. *Journal of Intelligent Information Systems* 2012;**39**(1):167–185.

331 Buntinx, J.-P. Not even Wikipedia is safe from Bitcoin & Blockchain censorship. 12 April 2016. Available from: https://news.bitcoin.com/wikipedia-bitcoin-censorship/.

332 Price, R. A free speech advocate's dream—the next Reddit could be based on bitcoin and impossible to censor. 7 July 2015. Available from: www.businessinsider.com.au/fred-wilson-blockchain-reddit-openbazaar-uncensorable-2015-7.

333 Deprez, E.E., Chen, C. Medical journals have a fake news problem. 29 August 2017. Available from: www.bloomberg.com/news/features/2017-08-29/medical-journals-have-a-fake-news-problem [cited 18 December 2017].

334 Committee to Protect Journalists. Sustainable Development Goals Backgrounder: Press Freedom for Development. 2015. Available from: https://cpj.org/campaigns/press-freedom-for-development/sustainable-development-goals-backgrounder-mdgs.php.

335 Latouche, M.A. Venezuela has a fake news problem too. *The Conversation*, 18 May 2017.

336 Cawthorne, A., Chinea, E. Venezuela hunts for rogue helicopter attackers. *Huffpost*, 28 June 2017.

337 Central, R. Maduro huye de Venezuela y se refugia en Nicaragua. *Hoy*, 28 December 2015.

338 Ossa, K. ¡TENSIÓN! Rumor de levantamiento en Fuerte Tiuna terminó con chavistas en la calle. *NotiExpressColor*, 21 April 2017.

339 Viana, N. Fake news is threatening democracy In Venezuela. *Huffpost*, 30 June 2017.

340 FocusEconomics. *Venezuela Economic Outlook*, 13 July 2017.

341 Singh, J., Rana, A. Exploring the big data spectrum. *International Journal of Emerging Technology and Advanced Engineering*, 2013;**73**.

342 Brown, T. Design thinking. *Harvard Business Review* 2008;**86**(6):84–92.

343 George, G., Haas, M.R., Pentland, A. Big data and management. *Academy of Management Journal* 2014:321–326.

344 Barton, D., Court, D. Making advanced analytics work for you. *Harvard Business Review* 2012;**90**(10):78–83.

345 Goodwin, T. The battle is for the customer interface. 3 March 2015. Available from: http://social.techcrunch.com/2015/03/03/in-the-age-of-disintermediation-the-battle-is-all-for-the-customer-interface/ [cited 18 February 2017].

345a van Rijmenam, M., Erekhinskaya, T., Schweitzer, J., Williams, M.A. Avoid being the turkey: How big data analytics changes the game of strategy in times of ambiguity and uncertainty. *Long Range Planning*, 2019.

346 LaValle, S., et al. Big data, analytics and the path from insights to value. *MIT Sloan Management Review* 2011;**52**(2):21–32.

347 Gandomi, A., Haider, M. Beyond the hype: Big data concepts, methods, and analytics. *International Journal of Information Management* 2015;**35**(2):137–144.

348 Koch, R., CMA, PMP. From business intelligence to predictive analytics. *Strategic Finance* 2015;**96**(7):56.

349 Marr, B. How big data is helping to tackle climate change. 17 November 2015. Available from: http://data-informed.com/how-big-data-is-helping-to-tackle-climate-change/ [cited 26 May 2017].

350 Gupta, S. Could these big data projects fix climate change? 2015 Available from: http://fortune.com/2015/02/14/big-data-climate-change/[cited 26 May 2017].

351 Newton, A. Big data for development: Beyond transparency, *Private Sector Development*. 23 July 2012. Available from: http://blogs.worldbank.org/psd/big-data-for-development-beyond-transparency [cited 26 May 2017].

352 *The Guardian*. SMS for Life: saving lives through improving access to malaria treatments. 22 June 2012. Available from: www.theguardian.com/sustainable-business/sms-life-saving-lives-malaria [cited 26 May 2017].

353 Banerjee, A., Duflo, E. *Poor Economics: A radical rethinking of the way to fight global poverty*. New York City: PublicAffairs, 2012.

354 Griffin, R. Using big data to combat enterprise fraud. *Financial Executive* 2012;**28**(10):44–47.

355 Pemberton Levy, H. The arrival of algorithmic business—smarter with Gartner. 5 October 2015. Available from: http://blogs.gartner.com/smarterwithgartner/the-arrival-of-algorithmic-business/ [cited 26 May 2017].

356 Van Rijmenam, M. 7 reasons why the algorithmic business will change society. 2015. Available from: https://datafloq.com/read/7-Reasons-Algorithmic-Business-Change-Society/1676 [cited 26 May 2017].

357 Van Rijmenam, M. Big data at Walmart is all about big numbers: 40 petabytes a day! 2015 Available from: https://datafloq.com/read/big-data-walmart-big-numbers-40-petabytes/1175 [cited 26 May 2017].

358 Stylianou, N., et al. Will a robot take your job? BBC News. 2015. Available from: www.bbc.com/news/technology-34066941 [cited 26 May 2017].

359 Abadi, M., Andersen, D.G. Learning to protect communications with adversarial neural cryptography. 2016. Available from: https://arxiv.org/pdf/1610.06918.pdf.

360 Knight, W. Tech companies want AI to solve global warming. 2016. Available from: www.technologyreview.com/s/545416/could-ai-solve-the-worlds-biggest-problems/ [cited 26 May 2017].
361 King, R. Cisco CEO: Internet of Things poised to be $19 trillion market, *ZDNet.* 2014. Available from: www.zdnet.com/article/cisco-ceo-internet-of-things-poised-to-be-19-trillion-market/ [cited 26 May 2017].
362 Higgins, S. UK Government trials Blockchain welfare payments system–CoinDesk. 7 July 2016. Available from: www.coindesk.com/uk-government-trials-blockchain-welfare-payments-system/ [cited 26 May 2017].
363 Naumoff, A. Blockchain to run welfare show, Finland may set example. 2017. Available from: https://cointelegraph.com/news/blockchain-to-run-welfare-show-finland-may-set-example [cited 26 May 2017].
364 Taplin, J. *Move Fast and Break Things: How Facebook, Google, and Amazon Cornered Culture and Undermined Democracy*. London: Hachette, 2017.

Index

For Product Safety Concerns and Information please contact our EU representative GPSR@taylorandfrancis.com
Taylor & Francis Verlag GmbH, Kaufingerstraße 24, 80331 München, Germany

www.ingramcontent.com/pod-product-compliance
Ingram Content Group UK Ltd.
Pitfield, Milton Keynes, MK11 3LW, UK
UKHW020140200926
475702UK00005B/834
* 9 7 8 1 1 3 8 3 1 3 2 2 4 *